STANLEY COMPLETE
WIRING

Meredith® Books
Des Moines, Iowa

Stanley® Books
An imprint of Meredith® Books

Stanley Complete Wiring
Editor: Ken Sidey
Senior Associate Design Director: Tom Wegner
Assistant Editor: Harijs Priekulis
Copy Chief: Terri Fredrickson
Copy and Production Editor: Victoria Forlini
Editorial Operations Manager: Karen Schirm
Managers, Book Production: Pam Kvitne,
    Marjorie J. Schenkelberg, Rick von Holdt
Technical Editor, The Stanley Works: Mike Maznio
Contributing Copy Editor: Steve Hallam
Technical Proofreader: George Granseth
Contributing Proofreaders: Stacey Schildroth, Julie Cahalan,
    Sara Henderson
Indexer: Donald Glassman
Contributing Photographer: Jay Wilde
Electronic Production Coordinator: Paula Forest
Editorial and Design Assistants: Renee E. McAtee,
    Karen McFadden

Additional Editorial Contributions from
Greenleaf Publishing
Publishing Director: Dave Toht
Writers: Steve Cory, Dave Toht
Art Directors: Jean DeVaty, Rebecca Anderson
Editorial Assistant: Betony Toht
Photography: Dan Stultz, Stultz Photography
Illustrators: Dave Brandon, Art Rep Services; Tony Davis
Technical Consultant: Joe Hansa
Indexer: Nan Badgett

Meredith® Books
Editor in Chief: Linda Raglan Cunningham
Design Director: Matt Strelecki
Executive Editor, Gardening and Home Improvement:
    Benjamin W. Allen
Executive Editor, Home Improvement: Larry Erickson

Publisher: James D. Blume
Executive Director, Marketing: Jeffrey Myers
Executive Director, New Business Development: Todd M. Davis
Executive Director, Sales: Ken Zagor
Director, Operations: George A. Susral
Director, Production: Douglas M. Johnston
Business Director: Jim Leonard

Vice President and General Manager: Douglas J. Guendel

Meredith Publishing Group
President, Publishing Group: Stephen M. Lacy
Vice President-Publishing Director: Bob Mate

Meredith Corporation
Chairman and Chief Executive Officer: William T. Kerr

In Memoriam: E.T. Meredith III (1933-2003)

With thanks to:
Leviton Voice and Data Division; Suntouch, a division of
    Watts Heatway
Advanced Lighting Co., Inc., Des Moines

All of us at Stanley® Books are dedicated to providing you with
the information and ideas you need to enhance your home and
garden. We welcome your comments and suggestions about
this book. Write to us at:
    Meredith Corporation
    Stanley Books
    1716 Locust St.
    Des Moines, IA 50309–3023

If you would like more information on other Stanley products,
call 1-800-STANLEY or visit us at: www.stanleyworks.com
Stanley® and the notched rectangle around the Stanley name
are registered trademarks of The Stanley Works and
subsidiaries.

If you would like to purchase any of our home improvement,
cooking, crafts, gardening, or home decorating and design
books, check wherever quality books are sold. Or visit us at:
meredithbooks.com

Note to the Readers: Due to differing conditions, tools,
and individual skills, Meredith Corporation assumes no
responsibility for any damages, injuries suffered, or losses
incurred as a result of following the information published
in this book. Before beginning any project, review the
instructions carefully, and if any doubts or questions remain,
consult local experts or authorities. Because codes and
regulations vary greatly, you always should check with
authorities to ensure that your project complies with all
applicable local codes and regulations. Always read and
observe all of the safety precautions provided by
manufacturers of any tools, equipment, or supplies,
and follow all accepted safety procedures.

CONTENTS

CONTENTS

WORKING SAFELY

Approach household electricity with caution and respect. Professional electricians take steps to ensure themselves double and even triple protection against shocks. You need to be just as careful to stay safe while doing the work.

Be insulated

The effect of a shock varies according to how much power is present, your physical constitution, and how well insulated you are. Of these three variables, you have control over the latter. Wear rubber-soled shoes. Remove jewelry. Keep yourself dry. If the floor of your work area is damp or wet, put down some dry boards and stand on them. Use rubber-gripped tools.

If you are wearing dry clothes and rubber-soled shoes, receiving a 120-volt shock will grab your attention, but it probably will not harm you. However, if you have a heart condition or are particularly sensitive to shock, the effects could be more serious. If you haven't taken proper precautions, chances are greater that a shock could cause injury.

If you are working with 240-volt current, the danger is much greater.

Maintain a healthy respect for electrical power. Even if you have survived one shock, the next one could be more serious.

Shut off the power

Before starting any electrical project, always shut off power to the circuit. Then test to make sure there is no power present in the electrical box or wires *(page 46–47)*.

You may be tempted to skip this step and save a trip to the service panel. Or you may think you can change a receptacle or light without touching any wires. Don't take that risk. It takes only a few minutes to provide yourself with the necessary protection against shock.

How circuits work:

For more information see *pages 24–25*. To learn how to check overloaded circuits, see *pages 35, 57*.

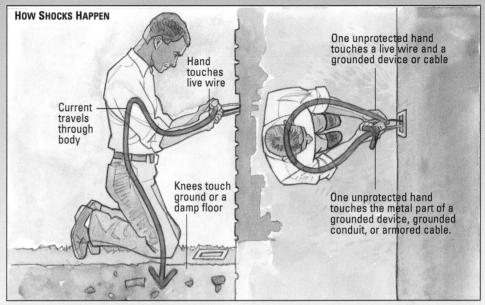

HOW SHOCKS HAPPEN

Hand touches live wire

Current travels through body

Knees touch ground or a damp floor

One unprotected hand touches a live wire and a grounded device or cable

One unprotected hand touches the metal part of a grounded device, grounded conduit, or armored cable.

Shocks occur because your body is conductive and can become a path for electricity. Here's how shocks happen:

You become the pathway to ground. If you touch only a hot wire (usually black or colored), current passes through you and toward the ground. To greatly reduce or eliminate a shock, wear rubber-soled shoes and/or stand on a thick, nonconducting surface (such as a dry wood floor).

You become part of the circuit. If you touch both a hot (black or colored) wire and a neutral (white) wire or a ground (green or bare copper) wire at the same time, your body completes the circuit and current passes through you. If this happens, you can receive a painful shock even when standing on a nonconductive surface. Avoid touching any bare wire; use rubber-gripped tools and hold them only by the handle.

SAFETY ALERT
Safety glasses and rubber-gripped tools

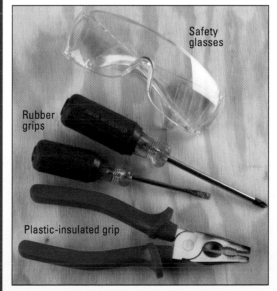

Safety glasses

Rubber grips

Plastic-insulated grip

Electrician's tools have heavy-duty rubber grips to protect hands from wayward power. Use these special tools *(pages 12–13)* rather than regular carpentry tools. Always grasp them by the rubber grips—never touch the metal parts of the tools.

Safety glasses are a good idea when you're doing any construction work. They protect your eyes from irritants such as drywall or plaster dust, which flies up whenever holes are being cut in walls or ceilings. More importantly safety glasses guard your eyes against dangerous bits of metal that can fly when you saw metal or snip wires. Porcelain and glass fixtures also can chip and pose hazards.

DEVELOPING SAFE HABITS

Most electrical work is not difficult. If you shut off the power and test to be sure it is off, you will be safe. It doesn't take a lot of time or effort to avoid a shock—just a little care and a few simple steps. Learn these steps, then make them habits.

Pretend it's live
Professional electricians have this simple rule: **Even after shutting off power, always act as if the wires are live.** That way if someone accidentally turns on the power, or a tester gives the wrong reading, you're still protected.

Pretending each wire is live means you should never touch two wires at once. Nor should you touch a wire and a ground at the same time. In fact it is good practice to only touch the bare end of a wire with an insulated tool, not your fingers. As an added precaution, lightly twist a wire nut on the bare end of any wire that you are not working on—good assurance that it will cause no harm.

Redundant protection
Get into the habit of taking the time and trouble to provide yourself with double—even triple—protection. In addition to shutting off power and testing to make sure power is off, wear rubber-soled shoes and use tools with rubber grips specifically designed for electrical work. Use safety glasses when dust or debris is a hazard. And wear ear protection when working with power tools.

Maintain concentration
It takes only one little lapse of concentration to create a dangerous situation. Eliminate all possible distractions. Keep nonworkers (especially children) away from the work site. Don't even play the radio while you work. Check and recheck your connections before restoring power.

Give yourself plenty of time to finish a job. If you need to leave a job and pick it up again the next day, start at square one: **Make sure the circuit is shut off and test for power** before proceeding.

Go the extra mile to be safe

1 Make sure that no one will turn on the power while you are working. Tape a note to the service panel door. You may even want to lock the panel.

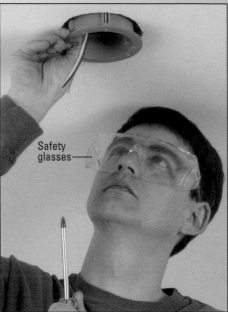

Safety glasses

2 Dress for success by avoiding loose garments that may get tangled on wires. Wear safety glasses anytime you might get dust, metal pieces, or other material in your eyes. Wear protective clothing and rubber-soled shoes. Remove all jewelry, including a wristwatch.

STANLEY PRO TIP

Cut with care

Use caution any time you cut into a wall or ceiling; an electrical cable may lie behind the surface. Use a voltage detector to **check if live wires are present** *(page 13)*. Another way to check is to drill a hole in the wall or ceiling and insert a bent wire to feel for a cable. Still, you may miss a cable. To be safe, cut with a handsaw, not a power tool. Stop if you feel any resistance; it might be a cable.

Test all the wires

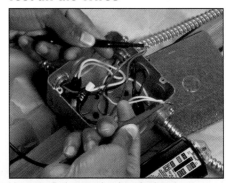

You may find several pairs of wires in an electrical box. This indicates that more than one electrical circuit may be present. In that case, even when you shut off one circuit, some of the wires in the box may still be hot. Extra care is needed. Shut off the circuit you plan to work on at the service panel. Open the box, then carefully remove the wire nuts and **test all the wires in the box for power.**

Checking that power is off

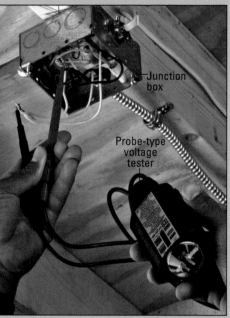

Circuit index shows which outlets each breaker or fuse controls

MAIN

Voltage tester

Junction box

Probe-type voltage tester

1 At the service panel, flip off the breaker or unscrew the fuse controlling the electrical box or device you will work on.

2 Test for the presence of power using a voltage tester *(page 46–47)*. If you are working on a receptacle, test both plugs. **Test the tester**, too. Touch the probes to a live circuit to make sure the indicator bulb lights.

3 It's possible that a single box has more than one circuit running through it. Carefully remove the device or fixture, unscrew the wire nuts, and test all the wires for power.

Testing tools

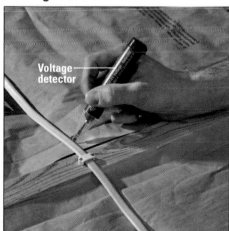

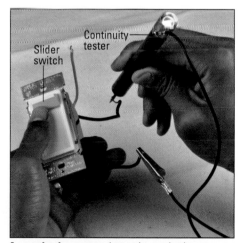

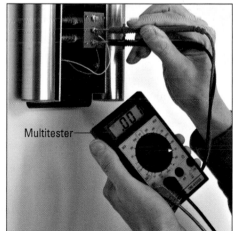

Voltage detector

Slider switch

Continuity tester

Multitester

A voltage detector senses the presence of power inside cables and, in some cases, even inside walls. Before using it, test this battery-powered tool on a line you know to be live. If the end glows, the tester is working.

A continuity tester determines whether a break in wiring or electrical contacts exists. Use it to test a fuse, a switch, or the wiring in a lamp or light fixture. Use it only when the power is off.

A multitester does the work of both a voltage tester and a continuity tester. Use it also to test low-voltage wiring, such as in a door chime or appliance. A digital model is easier to use than one with a needle.

GETTING READY

Though many homeowners fear working with electricity, wiring is an amateur-friendly trade. A handy person carefully following instructions can produce safe and reliable electrical installations. Attention to detail is the key.

Wiring help for the whole house
Before you begin a project in this book, read the safety information found on *pages 5–7* and understand how to shut off power and know how to test that power is off *(pages 10–11)*. This first chapter describes the tools and supplies needed for electrical projects. The second chapter, Checking Your Electrical System, helps you understand your electrical

system—and spot problems that may need attention. Basic Techniques shows how to strip wires, splice wires together, and join wires to terminals—essential skills for safe, secure, and reliable electrical connections. The Repairs, Switches & Receptacles, and Lights & Fans chapters guide you through basic repairs and upgrades. Planning New Electrical Service introduces you to the important preliminary steps for more demanding wiring projects. It also explains how to work with a local building department to ensure your project meets electrical safety code.

Help extending or adding circuits begins with Installing Cable & Boxes.

The balance of the book gets into specific projects: Installing New Receptacles & Lights, and Installing Fans & Heaters. The final chapters deal with household communication and security, outdoor wiring, and how to connect appliances and new circuits.

How to use this book
Each project includes a Prestart Checklist, which outlines the time, skills, tools, materials, and preparations needed. In addition to the project steps, you'll find Stanley Pro Tips and other extra information. Since no two houses are exactly alike, "What If..." boxes provide help for unusual situations.

Proper tools and quality materials save time and help ensure a safe and reliable installation.

CHAPTER PREVIEW

Turning off power
page 10

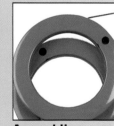
Assembling a tool kit
page 12

Special-duty tools
page 14

Cable and wire
page 15

You don't need an elaborate computer design program or a drafting table to work out plans for an electrical project. A pad of graph paper, a ruler, and some colored pencils will do the job. In addition to this book, you will need information on safety code requirements from your local building department.

Check the instructions or packaging of the fixtures you plan to install for wattage and any special installation requirements.

Your local building department has guidelines that describe what permits and inspections are required for electrical projects.

To learn how to draw up a plan suitable for applying for a permit, see pages 124–125.

Electrical boxes
page 16

Fasteners and clamps
page 18

Wire nuts
page 19

Receptacles
page 20

Switches
page 21

TURNING OFF POWER

Every electrical project must start with an extremely important safety measure—the wires and devices you work on must be de-energized. Follow the steps on these pages to make sure the power to your home circuits has been turned off.

The information here will also let you know what to do when some receptacles or lights suddenly go dead, indicating that a circuit has overloaded. The place to begin is the electrical service panel.

Accessing the service panel
A home's main service panel, which contains circuit breakers or fuses, is usually located in a utility area, easily reached but away from daily traffic flow in the house. It may be in a garage, in a basement, or (in warm climates) on the outside of the house. Unless it has been painted, the service panel will probably be a gray metal box. If you live in an apartment or condo, it may be recessed into the wall of a closet or laundry area.

You may find more than one service panel in your home. Especially in older homes, subpanels sometimes contain fuses or breakers that control power to part of the house. De-energize these just as you would a fuse or breaker in a main service panel.

You may need to get at the panel in the dark or in a hurry during an emergency. Keep the path to the panel clear; don't lean things against it, and make sure all adults in your home know where to find it.

To access the fuses or breakers inside, you probably need only to open the panel door. **If the panel appears damaged or if bare wires are visible, call a professional electrician** to repair or replace it.

Need more help? If you have trouble locating the service panel, **check** *pages 28–29*. If you still can't locate it, or if you are confused about how to shut it off, call an electrician.

Breaker box

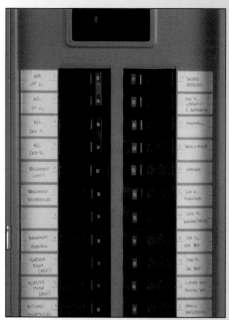

1 After opening the service panel door, you will find rows of individual circuit breaks, which look like toggle switches, and a main breaker on top. An index indicates which parts of the house each breaker controls. (If your panel does not have an index, see *pages 52–53*.)

2 The index should identify which breaker controls the receptacle or fixture you want to de-energize. To shut off an individual breaker, flip the switch to the OFF position. **Test the device to make sure power is off** before working on it. See *page 46* to learn how to test devices.

CIRCUIT BREAKERS
Two other types of breakers

Toggle switch

Push-in switch

Breakers vary in the way they shut off when they sense an overload. One toggle type (left) has a red button that pops up when the breaker has tripped. Reactivate it by turning the switch back on. Some toggles turn partway off when they blow. To restore power, flip the switch all the way off, then on. To reset a breaker with a push-in switch (right), push on the switch to turn off power or to restore power.

3 To turn off power to the entire house, flip off the main breaker, usually a double-wide switch located at the top of the service panel. You may want to have a flashlight handy when you turn off power.

Fuse box

1 If you have a fuse box, shut off power by unscrewing and removing a fuse. If there is no index telling which fuse you need to remove, see *pages 52–53*. **Test the device to make sure the power is off** *(page 46)* before doing any work. If a fuse has blown, replace it with a new one.

Main fuse block

2 To turn off power to the entire house, pull the main fuse block, which looks like a rectangular block with a handle. It is usually located at the top of the panel. Tug hard and straight out on the handle. **Use caution.** If you have just removed the block, its **metal parts may be hot.**

SAFETY FIRST
Hands off live wires!

When turning off or restoring power in a service panel, take care not to touch any wires. Open only the door: Do not remove the inner cover that hides the wires. (See *pages 34–35* if you need to open the cover.) Touch only the breaker. For added safety, wear rubber-soled shoes. If the floor near the box is wet, lay down a dry board and stand on it.

   Never touch the thick wires that enter the service panel from outside the home. They are always energized, even if the main breaker is turned off.

WHAT IF ...
A fuse blows often?

When a fuse blows often, it's tempting to replace it with one of a greater amperage. This is a dangerous mistake—house wires could burn up before the fuse blows. Check the wire gauge used in the circuit to make sure the fuse rating is correct *(pages 34–35)*. A 15-amp circuit should have 14-gauge or larger wire; a 20-amp circuit, 12-gauge or larger; and a 30-amp circuit, 10-gauge or larger.

   Checking the wire gauge is easy if you have nonmetallic cable running into the box. Examine the sheathing for a stamped or printed identification which will include the gauge *(page 39)*. With armored sheathing or conduit, open a receptacle on the circuit *(pages 36–37)*. Check the insulation on the wires for a gauge listing or compare with a wire of known gauge.

MAIN FUSE BLOCK
Check the fuses inside

Cartridge fuses are found inside a fuse block, which is used as a main block or as a 240-volt circuit. Remove an individual cartridge fuse by pulling its blades out from holders. Test the fuse *(page 47)* and, if necessary, replace it.

ASSEMBLING A TOOL KIT

Don't skimp when buying tools for electrical work; your safety and the quality of the installation are at stake. Assembling a complete kit of professional-quality electrician's tools will cost far less than hiring a professional to do even a simple installation.

Wiring tools
These tools enable you to cut, strip, and join wires tightly. A pair of **side cutters** (also called diagonal cutters) makes working inside a crowded electrical box or snipping off sheathing from nonmetallic cable easier.

Cutting pliers help with general chores such as snipping armored cable. Use **long-nose pliers** to bend wires into loops before attaching them to terminals. The **combination strippers** shown below—with holes for the wires near the tip—are easier to use than strippers with holes back near the handle. Use **lineman's pliers** to twist wires together after stripping them; no other tool works as well. You can also use lineman's pliers to cut wire.

Use **screwdrivers** designed especially for electrical use. They have thick rubber grips, which shield a hand from shock. You'll most

often use screwdrivers with 6- to 7-inch shanks; buy two sizes of **slot screwdrivers** and two sizes of **phillips screwdrivers**. Occasionally you may need a short "stubby." A **wire-bending screwdriver** quickly forms a perfect loop in a stripped wire end. A **rotary screwdriver** drives screws quickly; use it when you have several coverplates to install.

Testers
For most work you will need a **voltage tester** to test for the presence of power and a **continuity tester** to see whether a device or

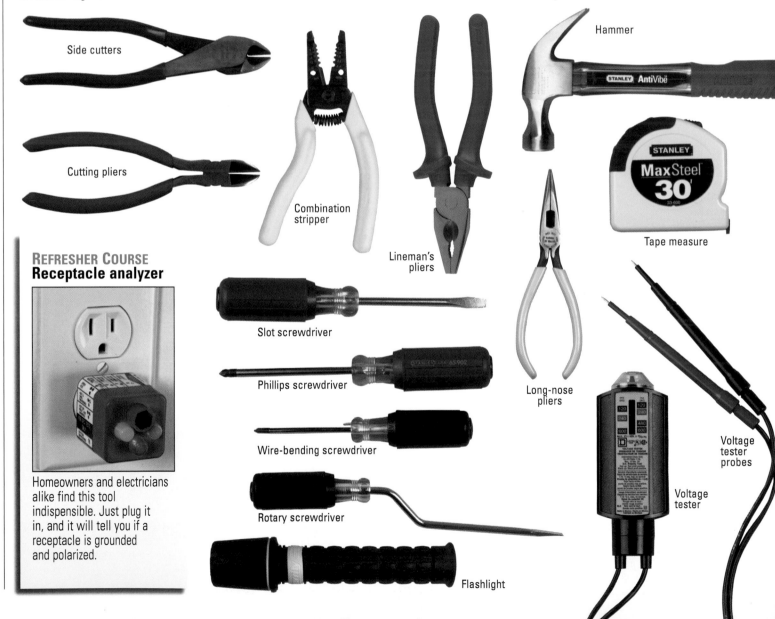

Side cutters

Cutting pliers

Combination stripper

Lineman's pliers

Hammer

Tape measure

Long-nose pliers

Slot screwdriver

Phillips screwdriver

Wire-bending screwdriver

Rotary screwdriver

Flashlight

Voltage tester probes

Voltage tester

REFRESHER COURSE
Receptacle analyzer

Homeowners and electricians alike find this tool indispensible. Just plug it in, and it will tell you if a receptacle is grounded and polarized.

fixture is damaged inside. A **multitester** does the job of both but is a bit more complicated to use. Professional-quality testers have probes and clips with thick rubber grips and lights or readouts that are clearly visible.

In addition, you may want a **voltage detector,** which senses power through cable sheathing, a box cover, or even a wall or ceiling. (Testers are shown in use on *page 7.*) Also buy a **receptacle analyzer** *(page 12).*

General tools

For jobs that involve running cable, assemble a tool bucket's worth of carpentry hand tools. Keep a reliable **flashlight** within easy reach, in case you have to work with the lights off. A **hammer** and a pair of **groove-joint pliers** come in handy for just about any wiring job. To remove moldings with minimal damage, use a **pry bar.** Make initial cuts in walls and ceilings with a **utility knife.** Complete the cuts in plaster walls with a **saber saw;** use a **drywall saw** to cut through drywall. Use a **hacksaw** to cut rigid conduit and to cut through screws holding boxes.

Fishing tools

These tools help minimize damage to walls and ceilings when running cable. A ⅜-inch **drill** is powerful enough for most household projects; rent or buy a ½-inch model for extensive work. In addition to a standard **¾-inch spade bit,** buy a **fishing bit,** which can reach across two studs or joists and pull cable back through the holes it has made *(page 147).*

You can use a straightened coat hanger wire to fish cable through short runs, but a **fish tape** is easier to use *(pages 146–147).* Occasionally you may need to run one tape from each direction so buy two. Also use a fish tape when pulling wires through conduit *(page 135).*

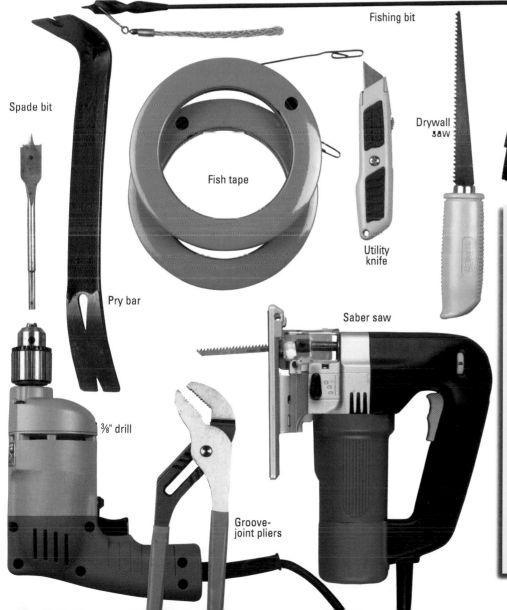

Fishing bit

Spade bit

Fish tape

Drywall saw

Hacksaw

Utility knife

Pry bar

Saber saw

⅜" drill

Groove-joint pliers

STANLEY PRO TIP

Electrician's tool belt

An electrician's tool belt holds all the tools you need and it will help you keep electrician's tools separate from general tools.

SPECIAL-DUTY TOOLS

The tools shown on *pages 12–13* are needed for almost any wiring project. They're essential for any wiring project that involves running new lines. The tools on this page are specialized. Buy or rent them only as the need arises.

Cutting tools

If you have old plaster walls, cutting into them to run cable is difficult and messy. There's no simple solution, but many people find that it helps to use a **rotary-cutting tool.** It slices through both the lath and plaster without vibrating. It does, however, kick up a good deal of dust.

A **reciprocating saw** cuts notches in walls quickly and is ideal for reaching into tight spots. Use this tool carefully if you suspect electrical cable may lie behind the wall or ceiling surface; if in doubt, use a hand saw.

When running outdoor electrical lines *(pages 220–221)*, a simple **spade** is usually all you need. Rent a trencher for projects requiring a lot of digging. Use a **clamshell digger** to dig postholes.

Tools for drilling holes

A ⅜-inch drill is powerful enough to drill six or seven holes in an hour, but it will overheat and even break if you use it continuously. If you have a lot of drilling to do, rent or buy a heavy-duty **½-inch drill.** The right-angle model shown below makes it possible to drill straight holes in studs and joists. For leveling and plumbing boxes, use a **torpedo level.** To make sure your holes are level with each other, use a 4-foot or 8-foot **carpenter's level.**

Other useful tools

Most electrical components are fastened with screws, but some use nuts. For these, use a **nut driver** or a socket and ratchet. A **conduit reamer** slips onto a square-shanked screwdriver to clean out pieces of metal conduit cut by a hacksaw. A **cordless screwdriver** saves time if you are installing many devices. Often framing will need notching and trimming—have a ¾-inch **wood chisel** on hand.

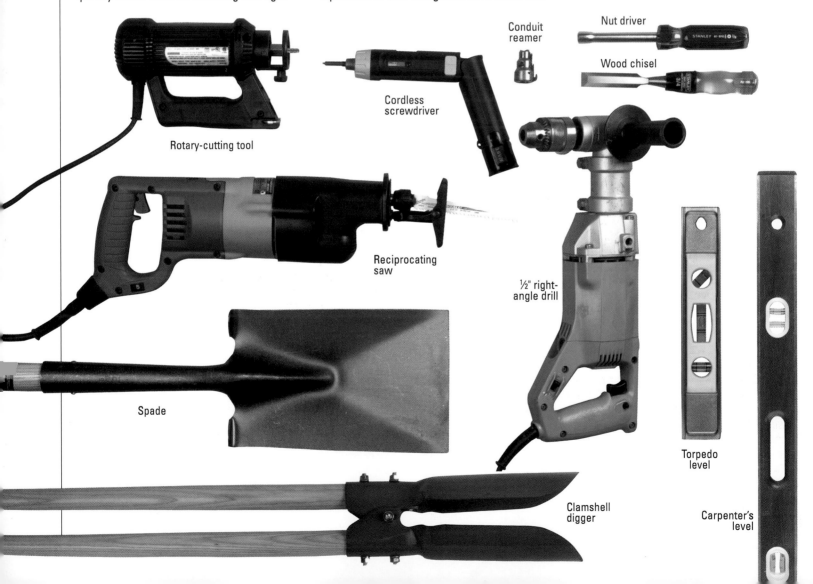

Rotary-cutting tool

Cordless screwdriver

Conduit reamer

Nut driver

Wood chisel

Reciprocating saw

½" right-angle drill

Spade

Torpedo level

Clamshell digger

Carpenter's level

CABLE AND WIRE

Most house wires—the wires that run from the service panel through walls and to electrical boxes—are solid-core, meaning they are made of a single, solid strand. Light fixtures and some switches have leads—wires made of many strands of thin wire, which are more flexible. The thicker a wire, the lower its number; for instance, #12 wire is thicker than #14.

Cable refers to two or more wires encased in a protective sheathing. Cable packaging indicates the gauge and number of wires. For example, "12/2" means two (black and white) 12-gauge wires, plus a ground wire.

Nonmetallic (NM) cable, sometimes called Romex, has two or three insulated wires, plus a bare ground wire, wrapped in plastic sheathing *(pages 128–129)*. Many local codes permit NM cable inside walls or ceilings, and some codes allow it to be exposed in basements and garages. **Underground feed (UF) cable** has wires wrapped in solid plastic for watertight protection. Use it for outdoor projects *(pages 220–221)*.

Armored cable encases insulated wires in metal sheathing for added protection. **Metal-clad (MC)** has a green-insulated ground wire. **BX (also called AC)** has no ground wire, only a thin aluminum wire unsuitable as a ground; the metal sheathing provides the path for grounding. Some local codes require armored cable or conduit (see below) wherever wiring is exposed.

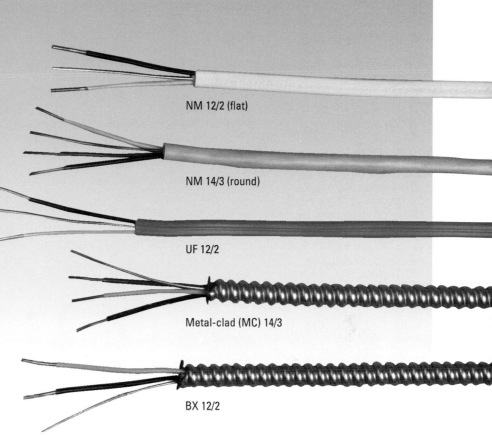

NM 12/2 (flat)

NM 14/3 (round)

UF 12/2

Metal-clad (MC) 14/3

BX 12/2

Conduit types

EMT rigid metal conduit

PVC ½" conduit

Greenfield

EMT ½"

Conduit—pipe that wires run through—offers the best protection against damage to wires. It also makes it easy to change or install new wires in the future: Pull the wires through the conduit, rather than cutting into walls to run new cable. **Metal conduit** *(pages 132–133)* once was used as a path for grounding; recent codes require a green-insulated ground wire. **PVC (plastic) conduit** is cheaper but not quite as strong *(page 134)*. Metal **Greenfield** and plastic **EMT tubing** are flexible types of conduit. They are expensive but useful when working in tight spots.

Wire colors and sizes

The thicker a wire, the more amperage (amps) it can carry without overheating. A #14 wire carries up to 15 amps; a #12 wire, up to 20 amps; and a #10 wire, up to 30 amps. Never overload a wire—for instance, never place a #14 wire on a 20-amp circuit.

Wires coated with insulation that is black, red, or another color are hot wires, carrying power from the service panel to the electrical user. (White wires are neutral, meaning they carry power back to the service panel.) Green or bare wires are ground wires. **Be aware, however, that not all electrical work has been done correctly, so the wires in your house could be the wrong color.**

HOT WIRES

#14 red

#12 blue

#10 brown

#12 black

GROUND WIRES

#12 green

#12 copper

ELECTRICAL BOXES

Wiring installations usually begin by adding a box. All connections—whether splices or connections to terminals—must be made inside a code-approved electrical box. (Some fixtures, such as fluorescent and recessed lights, have self-contained electrical boxes approved by most building departments.)

Plastic or metal?
Check with your building department to see whether plastic boxes are acceptable. Some municipalities require metal boxes, which are more expensive but usually no more trouble to install. Use special boxes for outdoor work *(page 218)*.

In older systems that use conduit or the sheathing of armored cable as a grounding path, the boxes must be metal because they are part of the grounding system *(page 118)*. Homes with NM or MC cable use green-insulated or bare copper wires for grounding and don't require metal boxes. However, some local codes call for metal boxes, which provide a stronger bond for the grounding wire *(page 118)*.

Remodel and new-work boxes
A remodel box has fittings that secure it to a finished wall. Plastic boxes have "wings" *(page 17, far right)*; metal boxes have expandable clips or bendable ears that hold them in the wall *(page 143)*. See pages *142–143* for various types and how to install them. Remodel boxes all have internal clamps that clasp the cable to the box.

New-work boxes install quickly in framing that has not been covered with drywall or plaster *(page 138)*. To install most models, hold the box in place (allowing the box to

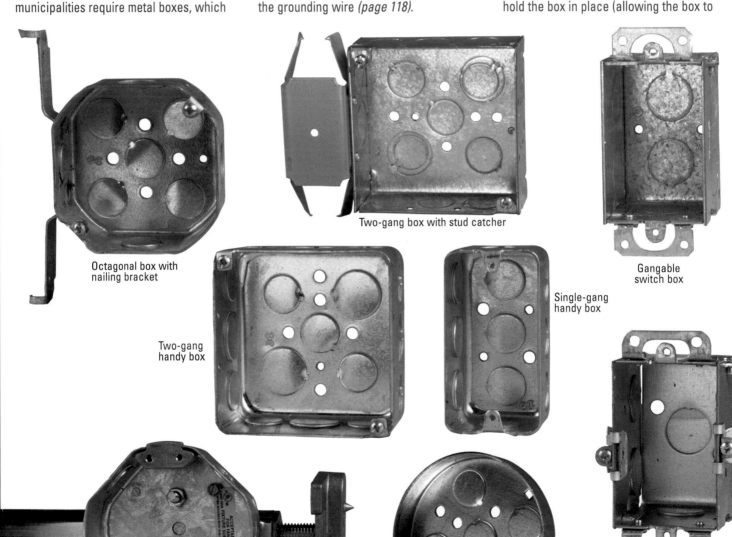

Octagonal box with
nailing bracket

Two-gang box with stud catcher

Gangable
switch box

Two-gang
handy box

Single-gang
handy box

Remodel ceiling
fan box with brace

Pancake
box

Remodel
switch box

protrude beyond the framing far enough to allow for the thickness of the wall material) and drive two nails.

Number of gangs

A "single-gang" box has room and screw holes for one switch or receptacle; a "two-gang" box has room for two, and so on. "Gangable" metal boxes can be partly dismantled and joined together to form a box of as many gangs as are needed.

Adapter rings

A box may be installed with its front edge flush with the wall or ceiling. Or the box may be installed ½ inch behind the wall, in which case an adapter ring, also called a "mud ring," is installed onto the front edge of the box. Use a 4×4-inch box and a single-gang mud ring when installing a 240-volt receptacle (*pages 154–155*) so there will be room for the wiring.

Two-device adapter ring

Ceiling remodel box

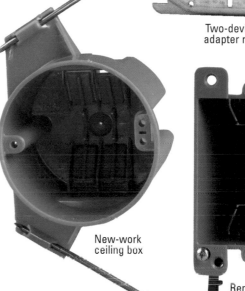
New-work ceiling box

Remodel box with wings

Single-gang box

Two-gang box

STANLEY PRO TIP: **Buy boxes that are big enough**

Capacity label

To make sure a box will not be overcrowded, always buy as big a box as will fit the space available. The cubic-inch capacity of electrical boxes should be listed by the store selling them. To calculate whether a box will be crowded, use these figures: A #14 wire takes up 2 cubic inches; a #12 wire takes up 2.25 cubic inches. Count the fixture or device as one wire. For instance, this box contains eight #12 "wires"—two blacks, two whites, three grounds, and one receptacle—for a total of 18 cubic inches.

FASTENERS AND CLAMPS

In addition to cable and boxes, electrical jobs call for a few other supplies: tape, staples, or straps to secure cable to framing members, and clamps that hold cable to boxes.

Light fixtures usually come with all the necessary hardware for fastening to the ceiling box. If you have old boxes, you may need to buy extra hardware.

Cable fasteners

Codes require that all exposed cable be tightly stapled to the wall, ceiling, or a framing member. Also use staples when running cable in unfinished framing. For NM cable, buy plastic-insulated staples that are the right size for the cable.

To anchor metal conduit, hammer in drive straps every few feet. For PVC conduit or armored cable, use one- or two-hole straps; make sure they fit snugly around the cable or conduit.

Avoid the black drywall (or all-purpose) screws because they break easily. Wood screws cost more but are more reliable.

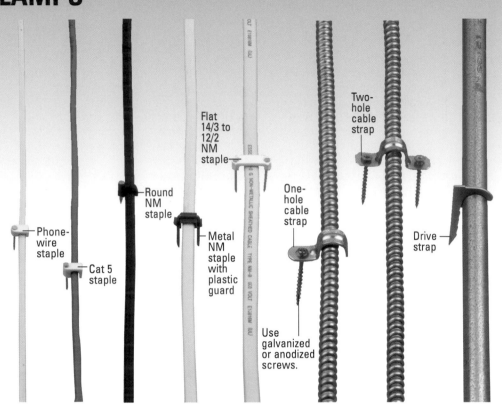

Phone-wire staple

Cat 5 staple

Round NM staple

Metal NM staple with plastic guard

Flat 14/3 to 12/2 NM staple

One-hole cable strap

Two-hole cable strap

Drive strap

Use galvanized or anodized screws.

Clamp types

Built-in clamp

Armored cable clamp

NM cable clamp

New-work plastic boxes have holes with plastic flaps that lightly grab NM cable. With that type of box, you must staple the cable to a framing member near the box *(page 129)*. Use these only in unfinished framing. When installing a remodel box or when installing a box that will be exposed, the cable or conduit must be firmly clamped directly to the box.

A cable clamp comes in two parts: the clamp and the locknut. An NM clamp holds the cable using a strap with two screws; an armored-cable clamp holds the cable using a single setscrew.

For instructions on how to clamp cable to a box, see *page 129.*

WIRE NUTS

In old installations, wire splices often were covered with thick electrician's tape. That is not only a slow way to cover a splice, but it is also a code violation. Cover every splice with an approved wire nut.

Assemble a collection of various size nuts so you will be ready for any splice. Wire nuts are color-coded according to size. The colors and sizes may vary according to manufacturer. Read the containers to make sure the nuts you buy will fit over your splices. The most common arrangement is like this:

■ The smallest wire nuts—which usually come with a light fixture—are often white, ivory, or blue. If these have plastic rather than metal threads inside, throw them away and get orange connectors with metal threads for a secure connection.
■ Orange nuts are the next size up and can handle splices of up to two #14 wires.
■ Midsize yellow wire nuts are the most common. Use them for splices as small as two #14s or as large as three #12s.
■ Red connectors are usually the largest

wire nuts and can handle a splice of up to four #12s.
■ Green wire nuts are used for ground wires. They have a hole in the top, which allows one ground wire to poke through and run directly to a device or box.
■ Gray "twister" wire nuts are designed to be all-purpose—they can handle the smallest to the largest splices. However, they are bulky and expensive.
■ "B-cap" wire nuts are slim, which makes them useful if a box is crowded with wires.

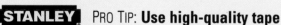

Two #16 stranded wires

Two #14 solid wires

Two #14 solid grounding wires

Three #12 wires

Four #12 wires

All-purpose "twister" wire nuts

Space-saving B-cap wire nuts

STANLEY PRO TIP: **Use high-quality tape**

Professional-quality electrician's tape costs more than bargain-bin tape, but it sticks better and is easier to work with.

You should cut pieces of tape rather than ripping them off the roll; ripped pieces have rippled ends that do not stick. Cutting with a utility knife is often awkward and time-consuming, so buy tape in a dispenser—just pull out and down to make a clean cut.

Grounding pigtail

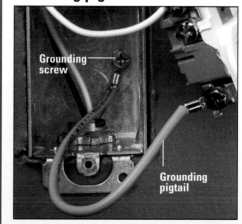

Grounding screw

Grounding pigtail

If codes require you to attach grounds to metal boxes, save time and work by buying grounding pigtails. If your boxes do not already have them, buy green-tinted grounding screws that fit into threaded holes in the boxes.

RECEPTACLES

The 120-volt duplex receptacle (a receptacle with two outlets) is the workhorse of any residential electrical system. Because household wiring has remained standardized almost from the time it was first introduced, the duplex receptacle accepts even the oldest tools and appliances.

Receptacles are easy to replace, so install new ones if your old receptacles are damaged, paint-encrusted, or simply ugly. (See *page 85* for more on how to install them.) However, do not replace an older, ungrounded receptacle with a three-hole receptacle unless you can be sure it will be grounded. (See *page 46* to test grounding.)

If the wires connecting to a receptacle are 12-gauge or thicker, and it is protected by a 20-amp circuit breaker or fuse, you can safely install a 20-amp receptacle. Otherwise, install a standard 15-amp receptacle. Amp ratings are printed or stamped on the side of the receptacle.

Some people prefer to mount the receptacle in the box with the ground hole on top; others prefer it on the bottom. In terms of safety, it does not matter. For appearance, be consistent.

Bargain-bin receptacles are fine for most purposes. But if a receptacle will receive a lot of use or is in a high-traffic area—a busy hallway, for example—purchase a "spec-rated" or "commercial" receptacle, which is stronger and more resistant to damage.

The most common electrical device in your home is probably a **grounded 15-amp, 120-volt receptacle.** It supplies adequate power for all but the most power-hungry appliances and tools.

If a receptacle's neutral slot (the longer one) has a horizontal leg, it is rated at 20 amps. Codes often call for **20-amp receptacles** in kitchens or workshops, where power use is heavy.

A **GFCI** (ground fault circuit interrupter) receptacle provides extra protection against shocks and is required by code in damp areas. (See *page 86* for more on GFCIs.)

An **ungrounded receptacle** has two slots and no grounding hole. If one slot is longer than the other, it is polarized *(page 26).*

240-volt receptacles

Appliances that use 240 volts are all rated for certain levels of amperage and have plugs configured to fit only one type of receptacle. Here are the common types:

A **dryer receptacle** supplies the heating element with 240 volts and the timer and buzzer with 120 volts. The receptacle shown requires four wires; older models use only three wires. (See *page 71* for how to replace a dryer cord.)

An **electric range receptacle** provides 240 volts for the heating elements and 120 volts for the clock, timer, and light.

This single-outlet **air-conditioner receptacle** provides 240 volts only. Check your air-conditioner to make sure its amperage and plug configuration match the receptacle.

SWITCHES

Turn a switch on and it completes the circuit, letting electricity flow through it. Turn it off, and the circuit is broken; the switch creates a gap that stops the flow.

Essential switches
The most common household switch, a single-pole, has two terminals and simply turns power on or off.

A three-way switch has three terminals; a four-way has four. These are used to control a light from two or three locations, such as in a stairwell, at either end of a hallway, or in a large room with more than one entrance.

A dimmer switch (or rheostat) controls a light's intensity. Usually you can replace any single-pole switch with a dimmer. However, buy a special fan or fluorescent dimmer switch to control a fan or a fluorescent light—a standard dimmer will overheat and can burn out a fan motor or a fluorescent tube.

Special switches
In addition to the familiar toggle and rotary switches, specialty switches can do everything from turning on when you walk into a room to varying the speed of whole-house fans. You'll also find special-duty switches that can be time-programmed or that let you know if a remote light is on or off. Decorative switches include styles that rock back and forth or slide up and down rather than toggling. (See *pages 82–83* for other switch options.)

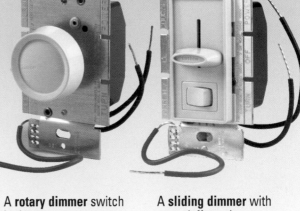
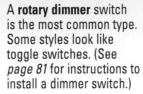

A **single-pole** switch has two terminals and a toggle labeled ON and OFF. Always connect two hot wires to it, not two neutrals.

A **three-way** switch has three terminals, and its toggle is not marked for on or off. (See *page 80* for wiring instructions.)

A **rotary dimmer** switch is the most common type. Some styles look like toggle switches. (See *page 81* for instructions to install a dimmer switch.)

A **sliding dimmer** with an on/off toggle "remembers" how bright you left the light the last time it was on.

Two ways to wire a switch

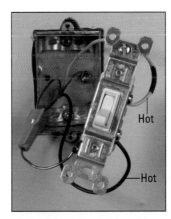
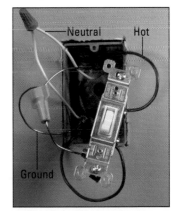

End-line switch wiring: If power goes to the fixture first and then to the switch, you have "end-line" wiring. Only one cable enters the box, coming from the fixture. Here, the white wire is taped or painted black to indicate that it is hot.

Hot
Hot

Power through switch: With "through wiring," power enters the switch box. The feed wire (the hot wire coming from the service panel) runs to the switch before it goes to the fixture. Two cables enter the box—one coming from power and one going to the fixture. The neutrals are spliced, and a hot wire connects to each terminal.

Neutral Hot
Ground

To ground or not to ground?
Your switches may not have a grounding screw terminal—the ground wire may travel past the switch to the light fixture. This is not unsafe, but recent building codes call for switches to be grounded.

CHECKING YOUR ELECTRICAL SYSTEM

You should never feel that you are exploring uncharted territory when doing electrical work. Take time to become familiar with your electrical system first, before you begin any project. If you are in doubt about what to do, don't start until you are sure.

This chapter will help you understand your home's wiring, and you won't need to handle a single tool. Beginning with an overview of residential wiring, it guides you through the elements of the electrical system you'll find in your own home.

The knowledge you need
In this chapter, you'll learn:
■ How to test for power and make sure power is off
■ How circuits work, and which parts of your house are protected by each fuse or circuit breaker in the service panel
■ How switches and receptacles work
■ How your total system is grounded
■ How each electrical box is grounded
■ How a ground fault circuit interrupter (GFCI) receptacle works, and how to make sure it is protecting you
■ How to determine the purpose and function of any wire you may encounter.

A surface inspection
Most electrical problems are easy to spot once you know what to look for. You'll be able to see many problems without removing a cover plate or fixture. The inspection described in this chapter will help you find and correct the dangerous situations and electrical code violations commonly found around a home.

Getting more information
This book covers the common situations encountered in home wiring. If your house has some unusual installations, seek additional advice. You might find help at a home center or hardware store. Or call your local building department and ask for an appointment with an electrical inspector. Or you could hire an electrician to look things over and do whatever work is needed to correct the problems.

Take time to evaluate the overall safety of your household electrical system.

CHAPTER PREVIEW

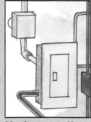
Understanding circuits
page 24

How circuits are grounded and polarized
page 26

The house ground
page 27

Service entrance and meter
page 28

Surface inspection
page 30

Knob-and-tube wiring:
This older system uses two separate wires, rather than a cable, and passes them through porcelain knobs and tubes. It is not unsafe as long as the wires are undisturbed. However, it is ungrounded.

Armored cable:
Two or more insulated wires, and perhaps a ground wire, are encased in flexible metal sheathing.

NM cable:
Nonmetallic (NM) cable contains two or more insulated wires, plus a bare ground wire, wrapped in plastic sheathing.

If an older home has been remodeled several times, various types of cable may exist in one electrical system. As shown above, vintage knob-and-tube wiring, NM cable, and armored cable enter the same electrical box.

Service panels
page 34

Opening boxes
page 36

Junction boxes and subpanels
page 38

Cable and conduit
page 39

Inspecting boxes
page 40

Grounding
page 42

Difficult wiring configurations
page 43

UNDERSTANDING CIRCUITS

Electricity moves efficiently when it is flowing through a metal conductor, such as a wire or the metal insides of a switch or receptacle. Electrical current must move in a loop, or circuit. If the circuit is broken at any point, the flow of power stops.

From power grid to service panel
Power comes to a home through the power company's thick wires, passes through a meter, and enters a service panel. The service panel parcels the power out to individual circuits, called branch circuits.

Each circuit supplies power to a number of outlets. An outlet is any place where power leaves the wires to provide service. Devices (receptacles and switches), ceiling lights and fans, and appliances (such as a water heater or a dishwasher) are the most common outlets.

Circuit wiring
Power leaves the service panel via a "hot" (energized) wire—usually coated with insulation that is black, red, or a color other than green—and returns to the panel via a neutral wire—usually a wire with white insulation.

Another wire, typically bare or with green insulation, provides the ground. (For more about grounding, see *page 26*.)

The thicker the wire, the more electrical power it can safely carry. If too much power passes through a wire, the wire will overheat, the insulation will melt, and a fire or shock could result. The service panel (often called the fuse box or breaker box) provides protection against this possibility.

Power lines enter the service panel and energize two strips of metal called bus bars. Circuit breakers or fuses attach to the hot bus bars. Power must pass through a breaker or fuse before it leaves the service

panel and goes into the house through a branch circuit.

Breakers and fuses
A breaker or fuse is a safety device. When it senses that its circuit is using too much power, it automatically shuts off. A breaker "trips" and can be reset; a fuse "blows" and must be replaced. Both devices keep wires from overheating.

Volts
Voltage, measured in volts, is the amount of force exerted by the power source. Wires from the power company, as well as wires in a house, carry 120 volts. (Actually, voltage varies constantly but stays within an acceptable range, from 115 to 125 volts.)

Most outlets use 120 volts, which is provided by one hot wire bringing the power to the outlet, with one neutral wire carrying it back to the service panel. Some heavy-duty appliances, such as large air conditioners, electric ranges, and electric water heaters, use 240 volts. This power is

supplied by two 120-volt hot wires connected to the outlet or appliance, with one neutral wire.

Amps and watts
Though the force running through all wires is the same—120 volts—different fixtures and appliances use varying amounts of power. Amperes (commonly called amps) refer to the carrying capacity of the wire. Wattage refers to the amount of power an electrical device consumes. The thicker the wire in a circuit, the more amps it can handle; the thicker the wire in a fixture or appliance, the more watts it uses. For example, a 100-watt bulb contains slightly thicker wires and uses more power than a 75-watt bulb.

The thinner a wire is, the fewer amps it can handle before it starts to overheat. That is why, for example, a circuit will overload (causing a breaker to trip or a fuse to blow) when you plug a toaster, microwave, and radio into its receptacles and use them all at the same time.

Terms you may hear inspectors and electricians use:

Device refers to any electrical receptacle or switch.

Feeder refers to an incoming hot wire. On a ground fault circuit interrupter (GFCI) receptacle, the word "line" refers to the incoming feeder and neutral wires.

Conductor is basically another word for a wire.

Outlet is any place where electricity leaves the wiring to be used, including fixtures, receptacles, and appliances.

Receptacle is a device with holes, into which you can insert a plug to deliver power to an appliance, power tool, or lamp.

Service panels:
Panels have varying styles of covers and different styles of breakers. See *pages 34–35* for more information.

Bus bars:
For more about bus bars and the inner workings of service panels, see *page 35*.

Avoid overloads:
For more about how to avoid overloading household circuits, see *page 57*.

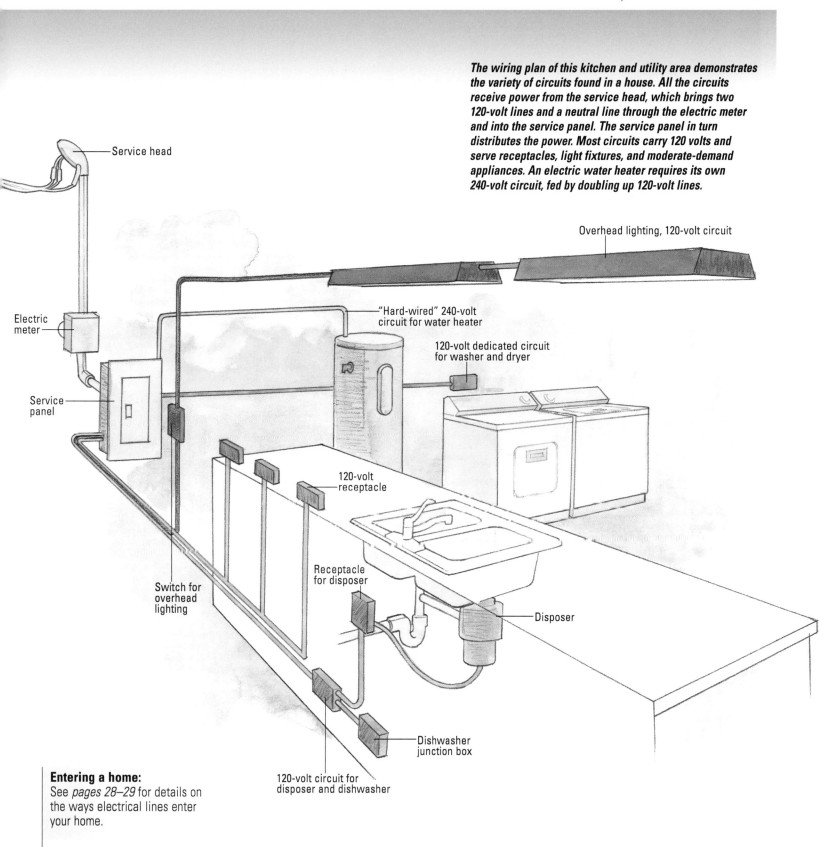

The wiring plan of this kitchen and utility area demonstrates the variety of circuits found in a house. All the circuits receive power from the service head, which brings two 120-volt lines and a neutral line through the electric meter and into the service panel. The service panel in turn distributes the power. Most circuits carry 120 volts and serve receptacles, light fixtures, and moderate-demand appliances. An electric water heater requires its own 240-volt circuit, fed by doubling up 120-volt lines.

Service head

Electric meter

Service panel

Overhead lighting, 120-volt circuit

"Hard-wired" 240-volt circuit for water heater

120-volt dedicated circuit for washer and dryer

120-volt receptacle

Switch for overhead lighting

Receptacle for disposer

Disposer

Dishwasher junction box

120-volt circuit for disposer and dishwasher

Entering a home:
See *pages 28–29* for details on the ways electrical lines enter your home.

HOW CIRCUITS ARE GROUNDED AND POLARIZED

If an electrical system works correctly, power travels safely through insulated wires, fixtures, and appliances. However if a receptacle suffers damage or a wire comes loose, power may flow to unwanted places, such as a metal electrical box or the metal housing of an appliance. Because the human body is a fairly good conductor of electricity, a person touching these objects will receive a painful shock. Grounding and polarization reduce this danger.

You can quickly find out whether a receptacle is grounded and polarized by using a receptacle analyzer *(page 30).*

Grounding
Electricity always travels the path of least resistance, either in a circuit back to its place of origin or toward the earth. A grounded electrical system provides an alternate path for the power to follow in case something goes wrong.

Many homes built prior to World War II have 120-volt circuits with only two wires and 240-volt circuits with only three wires, and no metal sheathing or conduit to act as a ground. These homes are not grounded, and receptacles in them should have only two slot-shaped holes.

Most modern homes are grounded. They have a third (or fourth) wire, usually bare copper or green insulated, called a ground wire; or their wires may run through metal conduit or flexible metal sheathing that can be used as a path for ground. A ground wire or metal sheathing carries misguided electricity harmlessly to the earth. Receptacles in these homes should have a third, rounded hole, which connects to the ground wire or sheathing.

Polarization
Most receptacles—grounded or ungrounded—have one slot that is longer than the other, so that a plug that has one prong wider than the other can be inserted only one way. These receptacles and plugs are polarized.

If a polarized receptacle is wired correctly, the narrow slot connects to the hot wire (delivering power to the receptacle) and the wide slot connects to the neutral wire (carrying power back to the service panel). When you plug a light or appliance into the receptacle, its switch controls the hot wire. If the receptacle or plug is not polarized, or if a receptacle is wired incorrectly, the switch will control the neutral wire. This means that power will still be present in the wires inside the light or appliance when you turn it off, posing a safety hazard.

120-Volt Light Circuit

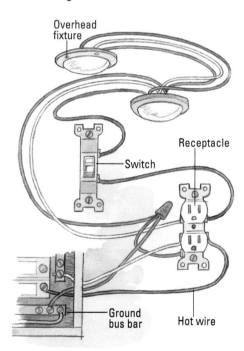

Any circuit that includes lights should be protected by a 15-amp breaker or fuse. (A light fixture's wires are thin and may burn up before they trip a 20-amp breaker.)

120-Volt Receptacle Circuit

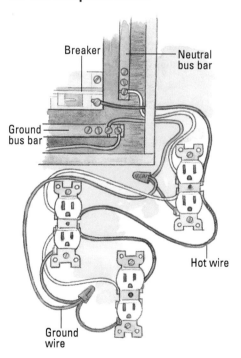

A receptacle circuit may be 15- or 20-amp. Black wires carry power to the receptacles, and white wires lead back to the service panel.

Armored cable: Some codes do not allow use of armored cable as a ground. Check before you install.

240-Volt Circuit

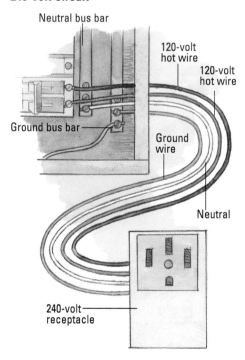

A 120/240-volt circuit supplies power to a heavy user of power, such as an electric range or dryer. Two hot wires bring power, and one neutral wire leads back to the service panel. Recent codes call for a fourth ground wire.

THE HOUSE GROUND

Ground wires for individual branch circuits (or metal sheathing that acts as a ground) lead back to the neutral or ground buss bar of the service panel. The service panel itself must be connected to the earth, so that the entire electrical system is safely grounded.

Usually, a service panel is grounded by a thick wire—bare copper or green insulated—leading to a ground rod or to a cold-water pipe. Follow the ground wire from the service panel to find how it is attached to the earth.

Ground rod

A ground rod, made of thick copper, is driven at least 8 feet into the ground. Its top may be visible, or it may be sunk beneath the ground. It is important that the house ground wire be firmly attached to the ground rod. The connection may be a weld, or a special toothed clamp may attach the wire to the rod. Recent building codes often call for two or more ground rods, for added security.

Cold-water pipe

The house ground wire may lead to a cold-water pipe, which is connected to supply pipes that lead deep underground. The connection must be firmly clamped.

Other methods

In rocky areas, where it is difficult to drive a ground rod 8 feet down, a grounding plate may be used. This is a thick piece of metal that is buried underneath a footing or foundation. Or a ground wire may connect to a metal reinforcing rod embedded in a house's concrete foundation.

If you have any doubts about your home's grounding—and especially if a receptacle analyzer shows that the receptacles are not grounded—consult with a professional electrician.

Ground rod: Many ground lines are clamped to an 8-foot-long copper rod pounded into the ground. Often the connection is above ground (above), but it may be a few inches beneath.

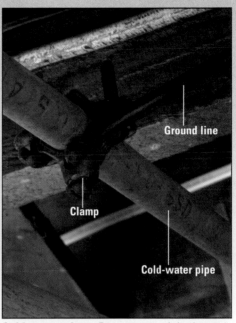

Cold-water pipes: Because municipal water pipes lead far underground, a firm cold-water-pipe connection forms an effective ground.

WHAT IF...
Your house is ungrounded?

If your home's receptacles have only two holes, or if a receptacle analyzer indicates that they are ungrounded, don't panic—people have lived with ungrounded homes for decades. However, grounding considerably improves a home's safety and is well worth adding.

If you want to ground an entire system, you'll have to call in a pro to rewire the entire home—an expensive job. If you want to ground only one receptacle, ask an electrician to run an individual ground wire from the receptacle to a cold-water pipe.

Here's a simpler solution: Install ground fault circuit interrupter (GFCI) receptacles. These offer protection similar to grounding. Installed correctly, a single GFCI can protect all the receptacles on a circuit. (For more on GFCIs, see *page 86*.)

STANLEY PRO TIP

Add a meter jumper

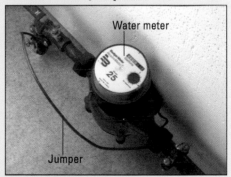

If your house ground connects to a cold-water pipe, the pipe must connect directly to municipal pipes underground. A newer water meter or a water filter may have nonmetal parts and break the connection. Clamp a copper jumper cable to either side of any such obstruction to complete the connection.

SERVICE ENTRANCE AND METER

A power company generates electrical power and sends it to your neighborhood through overhead or underground wires. Transformers, located on utility poles or on the ground, reduce the voltage before electricity enters a home.

Power arrives at most homes via two insulated hot wires, each carrying 120 volts, plus a bare neutral wire. A pre-World War II-era home may have only one hot wire, which will provide limited service possibilities. It should be upgraded; contact your local power company.

A service entrance consists of several parts: the wires leading from the transformer to the house (overhead wires are sometimes referred to as a service drop), the point of attachment for those wires to the house (the service head), the meter, and the wires leading from the meter to the service panel (commonly called the breaker box or fuse box).

The power company is usually responsible for the wires up to the utility splices or to the service head. A professional electrician installs the wires after the service head, as well as the meter and service panel.

With an underground service entrance, the power company brings power all the way to the meter base (see opposite page).

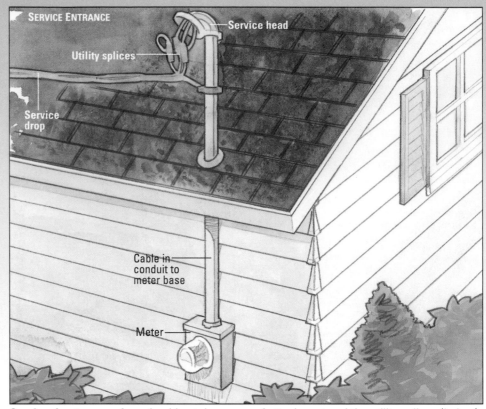

Overhead entrance wires should not droop lower than 12 feet from the ground at any point, and should be clear of branches, which can damage the insulation. The point of attachment and the utility splices (below) must be firm. The wires leading to the meter base should be protected by conduit.

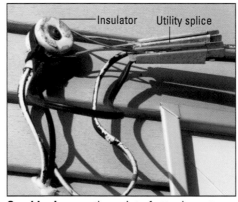

On older homes, the point of attachment may be a porcelain insulator, securely screwed into a framing member within the wall. Call the power company if the insulator is cracked or loose.

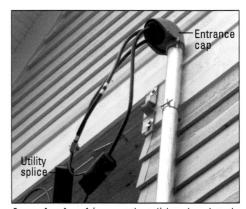

A service head (or masthead) has insulated openings with an entrance cap to keep the wires dry. Older variations have a gooseneck pipe with an opening that points downward so rainwater will not enter. On either, check that the insulation is not frayed near the opening and that the pipes are firmly anchored.

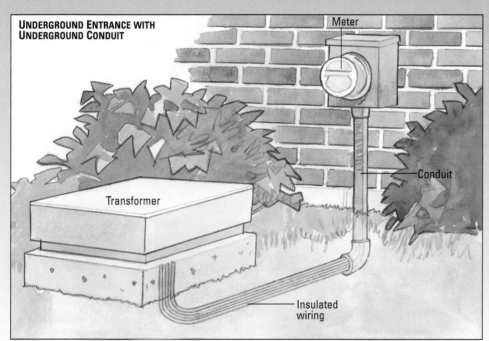

UNDERGROUND ENTRANCE WITH UNDERGROUND CONDUIT

Meter

Conduit

Transformer

Insulated wiring

An underground entrance begins with a transformer, usually sitting on a concrete pad. Three insulated wires, buried 3 or 4 feet underground, run to the house. These wires may be encased in conduit. When they reach the house, they extend up, through metal or PVC conduit, to reach the meter.

In some locales the meter may be placed away from the house, near the transformer. Find out where the underground wires are located to avoid accidentally nicking them with a shovel. Call your local utility company to mark the locations before you start digging.

Read your meter: Even if the power company doesn't require you to read your meter, you may want to compare numbers at the beginning and end of each billing cycle to make sure the utility is charging you correctly. To read a dial meter, write down the digit that each dial is pointing to, working from left to right.

From the meter back to the service panel

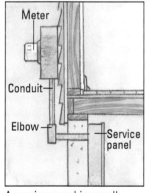

Meter

Conduit

Elbow

Service panel

A service panel is usually located as near as possible to the meter, linked in one of the ways pictured above.

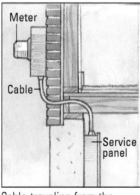

Meter

Cable

Service panel

Cable traveling from the meter to the panel may be exposed, or it may be encased in conduit.

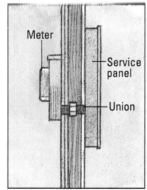

Meter

Service panel

Union

In warm climates, the service panel may be on the outside of the house.

SAFETY FIRST
Check watertight connections

Check here

Wherever rainwater might seep into a conduit connection, check to see that the connection is watertight. Call an electrician or the power company if any connection appears damaged.

SURFACE INSPECTION

Even if your electrical system has been trouble-free for decades, it may not be completely safe. On the next four pages, you'll learn how to spot some obvious shortcomings often found in household electrical systems.

To perform this inspection, the only tools you'll need are a receptacle analyzer and a flashlight. You won't have to remove any cover plates or open any boxes, but be prepared to move furniture to uncover every outlet and device.

In addition to living areas, check in out-of-the-way places, such as garages, basements, attics, utility rooms, or crawl spaces. There you may find exposed cables and electrical boxes, which will help you better understand your wiring.

SAFETY FIRST
Three-prong adapters are for grounded circuits only

If your home has ungrounded receptacles that lack a third hole for grounding, you may be tempted to use a three-hole adapter like this one. Be aware, however, that since the box is not grounded, the appliance or tool plugged into it will not be grounded.

Testing receptacles

Receptacle analyzer

Grounded and polarized: Begin an inspection by plugging a receptacle analyzer into each outlet of every 120-volt receptacle in your home. It quickly tells whether receptacles are grounded and polarized. If only one or two receptacles lack grounding or polarizing, examine the wiring in each more closely. (See *pages 40–42* for more in-depth inspections. To wire them correctly, see *page 85*.) If all or most of the receptacles test as ungrounded, check that the house ground wire is firmly attached *(page 27)*. If you cannot solve the problem, call a professional electrician.

Test button

GFCI: A GFCI receptacle offers effective protection against shock, but it can wear out and lose its ability to work properly. Test the device once a month by pushing the test button. Doing so should shut off power. If it doesn't, replace the GFCI *(page 86)*.

Mounting screw

Short slot

Two-hole receptacles: The box still may be grounded, even if the receptacle lacks a grounding hole. Poke one probe of a voltage tester into the short slot and touch the other to the mounting screw (scrape off any paint first). If the tester glows, you can install a grounded receptacle *(page 85)*.

Checking receptacles for damage

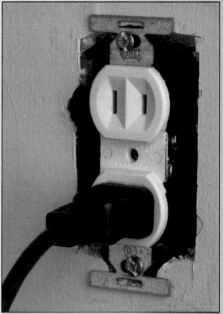

Cracks: A cracked receptacle may work just fine, but don't take a chance. The contacts on the inside could be damaged, creating sparking and shorts. Replace the receptacle (page 85).

Missing plate: A cover plate is not just for show; it protects you from the live wires that lie just an inch or so behind the wall's surface. Install cover plates wherever they are missing.

SAFETY FIRST
Protecting kids from shocks

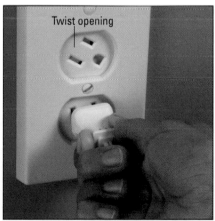

Receptacles are located at a tempting height for babies and toddlers. Protect them by pushing plastic inserts into each outlet.

For more secure protection, purchase a special cover plate with outlet covers that must be twisted before a plug can be inserted or buy a receptacle with sliding protective covers.

Problems with switches

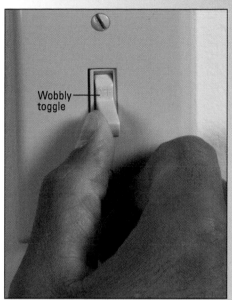

Loose switch: If a toggle feels loose or wobbly, **shut off power to the circuit**, remove the cover plate, and tighten its mounting screws. If it still wobbles, replace the switch (page 79).

Missing knob: A dimmer switch missing its knob or lever is more than just an eyesore and an inconvenience; it is easily damaged. Replace the knob or install a new dimmer.

Dangerous cords and plugs

Overload: This tangle of cords plugged into one receptacle places it and its circuit at risk of overloading. The cords also create a tripping hazard. A safer alternative: Install an additional receptacle or two, using surface-mounted raceway components (*pages 88–89*).

Cracked plug body

Cracked plug: A cord plug protects your fingers from dangerous amounts of electricity. If a plug is damaged in any way, replace it (*page 58*).

Taped cord: A repair like this is not only unsightly; it's dangerous. Tape, even if wound tightly and neatly, can come loose, tempting youngsters to unwrap it. Replace the cord (*page 59*).

Risky wires and cables

Loose cable: All exposed cable should be securely anchored to minimize the risk of accidentally snagging it. Anchor the cable using staples or straps (*page 18*). Never hang anything on exposed electrical cable.

Exposed splices: Safety codes strictly forbid any wire splices outside of approved electrical boxes. Exposed splices like this may come loose if bumped, causing shock or fire. Have an electrician install a junction box.

Light fixture problems

No cable clamp: Anytime cable enters a metal box, it must be held firmly in place with an approved clamp. Cable that is loose like this is easily damaged by the metal box's edges. Install a clamp like the one shown on *page 41*.

Bare bulb: An illuminated lightbulb is hot enough to ignite nearby clothing or cardboard, and it is easily broken. Install a protective globe fixture *(pages 94 95)*.

Loose fixtures: Sometimes a ceiling fan or a heavy chandelier will come loose and fall from the ceiling. Check that your fan is securely mounted to a fan-rated box *(pages 102–103)*.

Old wiring: If you find old knob-and-tube wiring like this, don't panic. If it was properly installed and is not damaged, it can be safe. Check that the insulation is not cracked and take steps to ensure that the wiring will not get bumped.

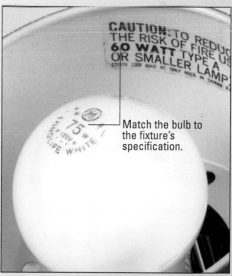

Overheating: When you remove a light fixture's cover to change a bulb, check for evidence of overheating. If you see a brown spot, or if the wire insulation has become brittle, replace the fixture *(pages 94–95)*.

Match the bulb to the fixture's specification.

Wrong wattage: Heed the sticker telling you how much wattage a light fixture can handle. If you use bulbs of higher wattage, the fixture will overheat.

SERVICE PANELS

If your home has undergone remodeling through the years, new circuits probably have been added to the service panel. Even if the panel was properly installed, mistakes may have been made later. Here's how to safely remove the cover of a service panel and inspect for damage or incorrect wiring.

Shut off power

Before removing a cover, **shut off the main breaker or pull the main fuse** *(pages 10–11)*. This will de-energize everything in the panel except the thick wires that come from the outside and attach to the main shutoff. Those are still live, so stay away from them. Wear rubber-soled shoes and stand on a dry surface, just in case you accidentally touch a live wire.

Check the obvious

A service panel must be kept dry, clean, and undisturbed. If you see dampness or signs of rust, find out how water is getting in and seal off any cracks or holes. If the panel is badly dented or if rust is extensive, have an electrician inspect it.

Clean away any dust, dirt, and construction debris inside the service panel. They pose a fire hazard.

Wire problems

The wires in a service panel should run in an orderly fashion around the perimeter of the panel. They should be clear of bus bars and breakers.

Carefully inspect for any nicked or cracked wire insulation. If the damage is minor to just a few wires, you may be able to fix it yourself. See *pages 69–70* to learn how to repair damaged wires. Call in a pro if the damage is extensive.

One wire should connect to each circuit breaker or fuse, although sometimes two wires are allowed. If you see more than two wires on any connection, call in a professional.

Shut off power: See *pages 10–11* for how to access and shut off power in a service panel.

Opening the panel

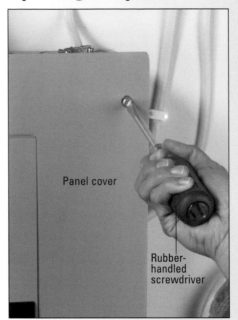

Panel cover

Rubber-
handled
screwdriver

1 **Shut off the main breaker.** Locate the cover screws; placement varies according to manufacturer. Unscrew each and set them where they won't get lost.

2 Grasp the cover at the bottom and gently pull the bottom outward. Lift up to unhook the cover at the top and remove the cover.

REMOVE THE COVER
Opening panels with two covers

Some panels have two covers. Remove the outer cover to access all the breakers and the inner cover to access the wires.

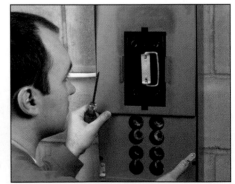

1 Remove the mounting screws. You may have to remove a mounting screw below the cover. Lift the outer cover up and out.

2 The inner cover has mounting screws attached to tabs. Unscrew them, then pull the inner cover off.

Inspecting the panel

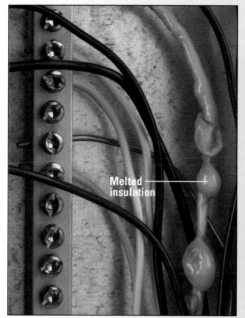

Overheated wires: Look for signs of overheating. If you spot a wire with melted insulation, check to see if the circuit breaker or fuse that protects it is the correct amperage. If you find obvious signs of fire, such as a charred bus bar or housing, call a professional electrician for evaluation.

Wires too close: If any wire comes close to an electrical connection, move the wire to the side, if possible. Don't push too hard or you may disconnect it. If things seem hopelessly tangled, call in a pro.

Wrong amperage: Check the wire gauge. If it is not printed on the wire's insulation, compare the wire with a known gauge—a #14 wire is thinner and belongs on a 15-amp circuit; a #12 wire is thicker for a 20-amp circuit *(page 15)*. If a breaker's amperage is too high for its circuit's wire, call a pro.

SAFETY FIRST
Correct amperage of fuses

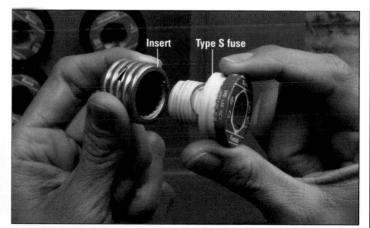

Likely overload: If you find a 30-amp fuse on a typical household circuit, it likely was installed by someone who got tired of changing 20- or 15-amp fuses on an overloaded circuit. This is very unsafe. Only circuits using #10 or thicker wire should be on a 30-amp circuit; smaller wires may burn up before the fuse blows.

Inserts for safety: To make sure no one can install an incorrectly sized fuse, use Type S fuses, which come with inserts. Once the insert is screwed into the panel, it is impossible to install a fuse of a higher amperage.

OPENING BOXES

Some homeowners fear the power that lurks behind a receptacle cover plate or light fixture. Others dive in with reckless abandon. These pages chart a middle course, preparing you to work with both confidence and caution.

Shut off power to the circuit first *(page 10)*. Do an initial test for power *(pages 46–47)*. Test a receptacle by inserting the prongs of a voltage tester into the slots of one outlet, then the other. Test a switch or light fixture by flipping on the switch. Even if the initial test indicates no power, there still might be power in the box. Use a voltage tester to double-check inside the box *(Step 2)*.

Removal tips

Grasp a rubber-grip screwdriver only by the rubber handle when removing screws. Stand on a fiberglass or wood ladder (not aluminum) when removing an overhead light fixture.

Cover plates are cheap, so don't hesitate to replace one that is ugly or slightly damaged.

If your light fixture installation has hardware different from what is shown here, see *pages 94–97* for mounting options.

PRESTART CHECKLIST

☐ **TIME**
A minute to open a switch or receptacle; several minutes to remove a fixture

☐ **TOOLS**
Rubber-grip #1 slot and phillips screwdrivers, voltage tester

☐ **PREP**
Spread an old dish towel or small drop cloth to catch debris when you remove receptacle cover plates. Use a sturdy fiberglass ladder for reaching ceiling fixtures.

Receptacle and switch boxes

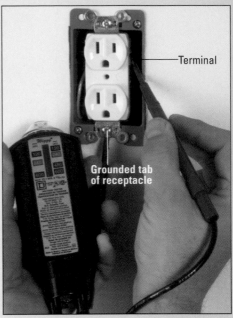

— Terminal

Grounded tab of receptacle

1 **Shut off power and test for power.** Use a small-tipped (#1) slot screwdriver to remove cover plate mounting screws. If the cover plate does not come off easily, pry it gently from the wall. If it has been painted over, cut lightly around its perimeter with a utility knife.

2 **Test again for power**—there may be live wires in the electrical box that do not connect to the device or fixture. Touch voltage tester probes to all possible wire combinations. If you have a metal box, also test by touching one probe to the box and the other probe to each wire.

STANLEY PRO TIP: **What the wire colors mean**

Wire insulation colors have straightforward meanings: A black wire is hot, bringing power from the service panel to the box; a white wire is neutral, carrying power back to the panel; and a bare or green-insulated wire is the ground. Other colored wires—red is the most common—also carry power. (See *pages 24–26* for more on circuits.) However, it is not unusual to find amateur wiring with the colors mixed up. If you suspect this is true in your house, call in a pro.

If you have old wires that all look black or gray, it may not be obvious which is hot and which is neutral. If your metal boxes are grounded, remove wire nuts and touch one probe of a voltage tester to the box. Touch the other probe to each wire in turn. The tester will glow when you touch the hot wire. If the wiring is in a receptacle box, plug in a receptacle analyzer. It will indicate a fault if the hot wire has been improperly connected to the silver terminal of the receptacle.

Stay safe: A voltage tester is an essential tool for electrical work. Buy one and use it.

Opening a fixture

3 Unscrew the screws holding the device to the box; they will come out of the holes in the box but may remain attached to the device by little pieces of plastic or cardboard. Carefully grab the device by its plastic parts only and gently pull it out. Inspect the wiring and the box.

👆

1 **Shut off power.** Position the ladder so you can reach and see all around the light fixture. With your fingers, loosen but do not remove at least two of the setscrews that hold the globe. If a screw is rusted, you may need a screwdriver or pliers to turn it. Remove the globe.

2 Find the screws that hold the fixture to the ceiling box (usually there are two). Unscrew them, supporting the fixture with your other hand. Gently pull the fixture down. If the fixture is heavy, support it with a coat hanger or stiff wire attached to the box while you inspect the box and wiring.

👆

WHAT IF...
Your house has aluminum wiring?

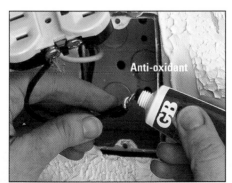

Anti-oxidant

Some houses built in the early 1970s have aluminum wiring. It is dull silver in color, thicker than copper wiring, and often has "AL" printed on its insulation.

Aluminum wiring expands and contracts with changing temperatures. Over time it often works loose from terminals. Wherever aluminum contacts a copper terminal or wire, it will eventually oxidize, creating a bad connection. For these reasons, aluminum was banned from electrical systems a few years after builders started using it.

Don't panic if you find aluminum wiring in your house. Rewiring a house with copper is probably not necessary. Instead make sure that all the switches and receptacles are labeled CO/ALR, meaning it is safe to wire them with aluminum. Wherever you must splice an aluminum wire with a copper lead (for example, when you install a light fixture), squirt a bit of anti-oxidant on the connection before you put on the wire nut. Anti-oxidant and CO/ALR devices are available at home centers or electrical suppliers.

CEILING BOX
Center-mount ceiling fixture

Some light fixtures mount via a nut and a single-threaded nipple (small pipe). Support the fixture with one hand and unscrew the nut. Then slide the fixture down and out.

JUNCTION BOXES AND SUBPANELS

In addition to a service panel, switches, receptacles, and light fixtures, most houses have junction boxes. These are metal or plastic electrical boxes that enclose spliced wires. No electrical splice or connection should exist outside of an approved electrical box.

Where to find junction boxes
You'll find junction boxes in utility areas, such as a garage or basement. Less commonly, they are located in living areas. A junction box is covered with a blank cover plate, usually held in place with screws, which can be removed in order to inspect the box. Most junction boxes are about 4 inches square; some are larger.

Subpanels expand service
A subpanel holds not only wires but also circuit breakers or fuses. It is used to expand service—for instance, when an addition is built and new circuits are added. Open and inspect a subpanel the same way you would a service panel (pages 34–35).

A subpanel connects to the main service panel by a feeder cable with thick wires. A double-pole circuit breaker or a large fuse in the main service panel controls power to the subpanel. To de-energize it, shut off the "feeder breaker" or fuse in the main panel.

Double-pole breaker:
This circuit breaker has two connected toggle switches. It attaches to both hot bus bars to provide 240 volts of power. It usually provides power to a 240-volt appliance; sometimes, it supplies two 120-volt circuits.

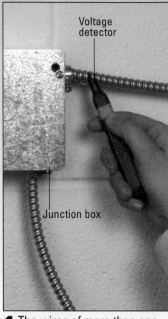

1 The wires of more than one circuit are often in the same junction box. **Shut off power at the service panel** (page 10), then use a voltage detector (page 46) to test each cable in the box, as well as the box itself.

2 In a utility area, the blank cover will probably be metal; in a living area, you may find a plastic cover. Loosen or remove the screws and remove the cover.

3 Double-check for power using a voltage tester (page 46) on all the wires.

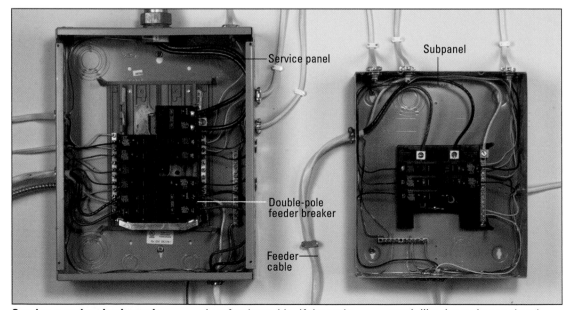

Service panel and subpanel:
In a typical setup, a 30-amp or more double-pole feeder breaker in the service panel controls the power that goes to the subpanel via a feeder cable. If the main service panel is a fuse box, a fuse block containing cartridge fuses supplies power to the subpanel. The subpanel is wired much like the main panel and protects individual circuits in the same way (see pages 34–35 to remove covers).

CABLE AND CONDUIT

Make sure any new cable being installed will handle the electrical load safely and satisfy local building code requirements *(page 118)*. Cable packaging indicates the gauge and number of wires *(page 15)*. For instance, "14/2" means the cable contains two #14 wires, plus a bare ground wire; "12/3" indicates three #12 wires plus a ground.

Nonmetallic (NM) cable has a plastic sheathing and is available in a flat profile or a round profile. Printing on NM sheathing indicates the number and size of its wires. The forerunner to NM was **fabric-sheathed cable,** no longer sold but found in older homes.

Armored cable has a flexible metal sheathing. There are two types: **MC,** which carries two or three wires plus a ground wire, and older **BX,** which has no ground wire but has a thin, brittle aluminum wire running through it. **Metal conduit** is pipe through which wires are run. (Because they are made of metal, BX and metal conduit can be used for ground, taking the place of a ground wire.)

Underground feed (UF) cable has sheathing that is molded to the wires to protect against moisture in outdoor installations. Telephone cable with four

thin wires is increasingly being replaced by **Category 5** cable, which can carry lines for telephone, modem, and computer networking. **Coaxial** cable, used for cable TV and radio antennas, contains a single solid wire encased in sheathing that includes metal mesh.

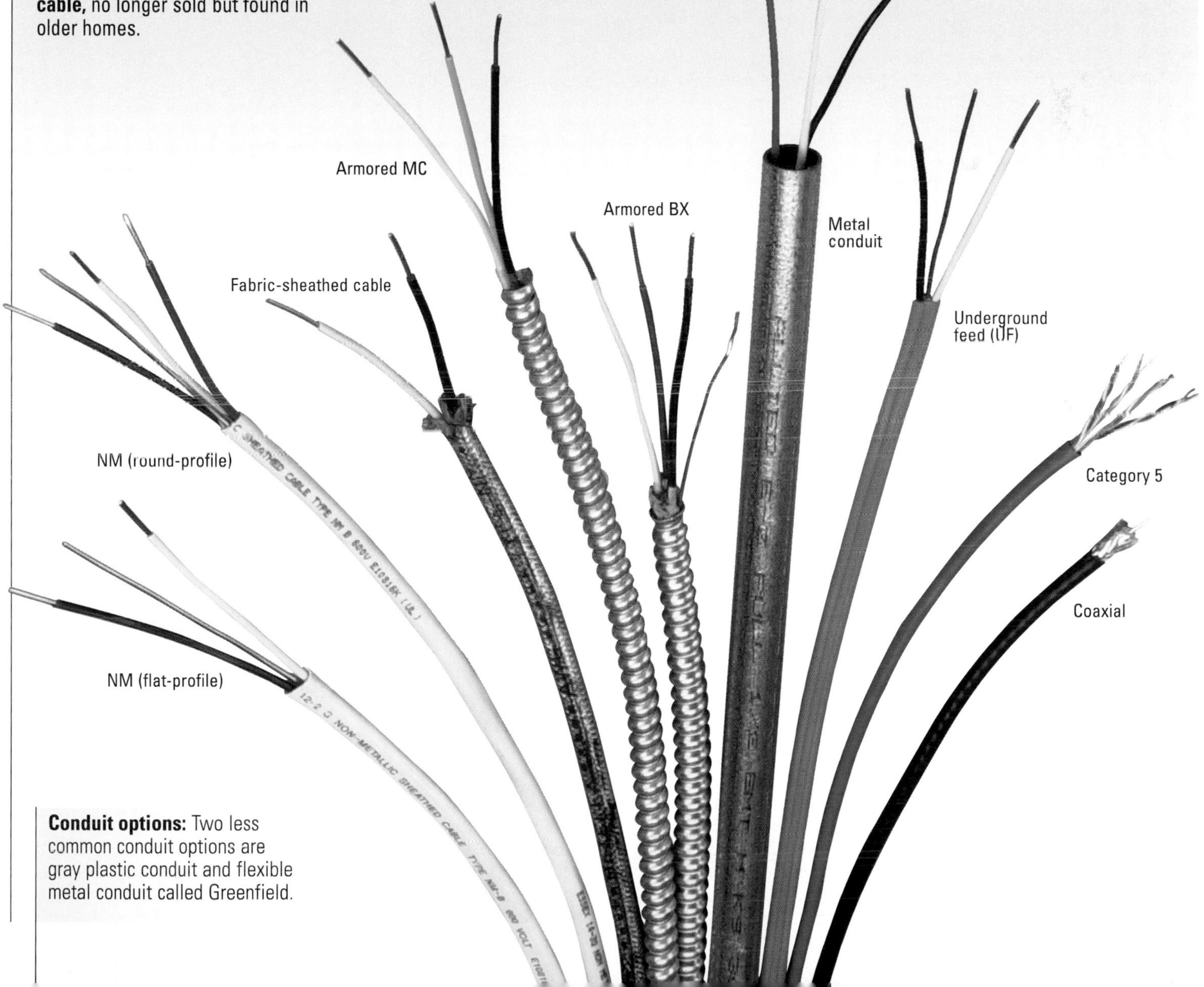

Armored MC

Fabric-sheathed cable

Armored BX

Metal conduit

Underground feed (UF)

NM (round-profile)

Category 5

Coaxial

NM (flat-profile)

Conduit options: Two less common conduit options are gray plastic conduit and flexible metal conduit called Greenfield.

INSPECTING BOXES

Once you've removed a cover plate or light fixture, it takes only a few seconds to check the wiring inside for damage or unsafe connections.

Shut off power and test to see that power is off before you touch any wires. Use rubber-gripped tools. Often you'll need to gently pull the device out of the box to inspect it.

Always assume that the wires are hot, even though you have de-energized the circuit. Touch only wire nuts or wire insulation—never bare wires—with your fingers.

Before you replace the devices into their boxes, wrap the terminal connections with electrical tape. The added protection helps hold wires in place and keeps terminal screws from touching the sides of a metal box.

STANLEY PRO TIP

Check the GFCI wiring

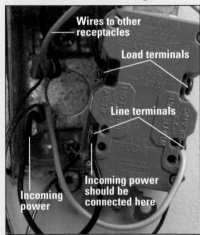

A ground fault circuit interrupter (GFCI) protects you from shock, but only if it is wired correctly. The wires coming from the power source must connect to the terminals labeled LINE. These wires will test "hot" when disconnected from the device when the circuit is live. Remember it this way—L"in"E. The wires leading out to other receptacles must connect to the LOAD terminals *(page 86)*.

Check for incorrect wiring

Reversed connections: The black or colored wire (hot) must be connected to a brass-colored terminal; the white wire (neutral) to the silver terminal. If the wires are reversed, the receptacle will supply power but will not be polarized *(page 26)*. Connect the wires to the correct terminals.

Too many wires: It is against building safety code to connect two or more wires to a single terminal because they can easily come loose. Splice the two wires into a pigtail, and connect the pigtail to the terminal *(page 51)*.

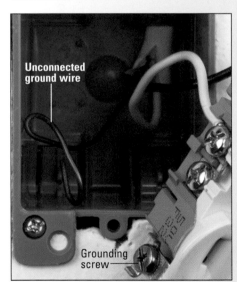

No ground: A receptacle that is not grounded delivers power but lacks an important safety feature. Connect the ground wire to the receptacle's ground screw and test with a receptacle analyzer. For other grounding methods, see *page 42*.

Not enough insulation: A good electrician covers as much bare wire as possible. The bottom wire has too much insulation stripped, making it unsafe. Cover it with tape. Better yet, cut, restrip, and reconnect the wire *(page 69)*.

Check for damaged wire

Exposed bare wire: Even new wiring may have nicks and cuts in the insulation, leaving bare wire dangerously exposed. Wrap a small nick tightly with electrician's tape.

Cracked insulation: Older insulation or insulation behind an inadequately shielded fixture may become brittle and easily cracked. Seal it with heat-shrink tubing *(page 69)*.

NICKS AND CUTS
Protecting wires in armored cable

If your wiring system uses armored cable, check to see that plastic bushings were installed wherever wires enter a box. Armored cable's sheathing has sharp edges, which can gouge insulation. If you don't see bushings, buy a packet of them and install them. Do this whether you see damaged insulation or not, to protect the wires from any sharp edges. Slip a bushing around the wires, then slide it down into the sheathing.

Box problems

Loose box: A loose box can lead to damaged wires and a faulty connection. If the box is next to a stud, remove the cover and pull out the device. Drill a hole in the side of the box and secure it with a screw into the stud. Or replace with an "old-work" box that fastens to drywall.

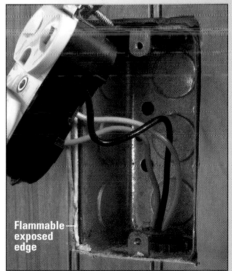

Recessed box: Codes call for all boxes to be nearly flush with the surrounding wall surface so wires are safely enclosed. If you have wood paneling, an improperly recessed box poses a fire danger. Install a box extender *(page 69)*.

GROUNDING

Building codes have changed over the years, and they differ from region to region. As a result, grounding methods can vary widely. You may find any of the configurations shown here in your home.

No matter the method used, it's important that the ground circuit provides an unbroken path to the earth *(pages 26–27)*. Ground wires must be firmly connected at all points. If conduit or sheathing is used, all the connections must be tight. A receptacle analyzer *(page 30)* will tell you right away whether your receptacles are grounded.

METAL BOXES
Other grounding methods

Grounding clip

Armored cable connector

In a system with metal boxes, the pigtail method shown at right is considered by many to be the most secure. However, other methods also work well if installed correctly. For instance, some systems use a grounding clip to clamp the ground wire to the side of the box.

If a house is wired with armored cable or conduit *(page 39)*, often there is no ground wire. The cable connector joins the metal sheathing or conduit to the box to provide the path for ground.

In boxes

Ground to box

Grounding wire nut

Metal boxes: In this secure arrangement, both the receptacle and metal box are grounded. Ground wires are spliced together and attached via pigtails to the box and receptacle. A grounding wire nut has been used. It has a hole in its top that makes installing a pigtail easier.

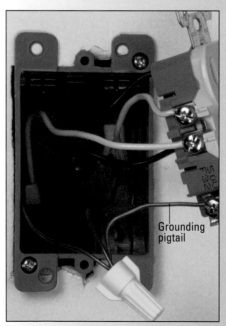

Grounding pigtail

Plastic boxes: Where plastic boxes are used, a ground wire typically connects to the receptacle only. Here, where wiring runs through this box to another box, a grounding pigtail is used to connect to the device.

In fixtures and switches

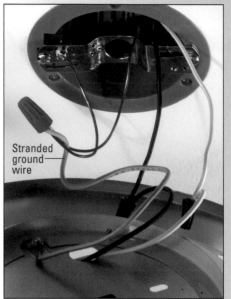

Stranded ground wire

Old fixtures: Many older ceiling fixtures are not grounded. Recent codes, however, call for grounding. Connect the fixture's ground lead (usually a stranded wire) to the strap on a metal box or to a ground wire.

Ground screw

Old switches: Like ceiling fixtures, most older switches are not grounded—in fact, many switches do not even have a grounding screw. Recent codes call for switches to be grounded. Replace an older switch with a newer one that has a ground screw and connect to a ground wire.

DIFFICULT WIRING CONFIGURATIONS

Usually wiring is easy to figure out: A hot wire, a neutral wire, and a ground wire attach to a device or fixture. Sometimes, however, you may find configurations that aren't as clear.

■ **Two cables in a switch box:** Switch wiring may involve two cables entering the box or only one *(page 21)*.

■ **Through wires:** If wires travel through a box but are not connected to a device or fixture, they may belong to another circuit.

■ **Three-way switch:** A switch with three terminals (and three wires connected to it) is a three-way switch *(page 80)*.

■ **Unusual colors:** Some homes have color-coded circuits. For instance, one circuit may have a brown hot wire, while another circuit has a purple hot wire. You will find this only in houses with conduit.

■ **Aluminum wire:** Silver-color wires with "AL" printed on the insulation are aluminum wiring *(page 37)*.

■ **Three-wire cable:** Electricians sometimes save work and materials by using three-wire cable (with a black, red, white, and ground) to carry power from two different circuits. The black wire is attached to one circuit; the red wire to another.

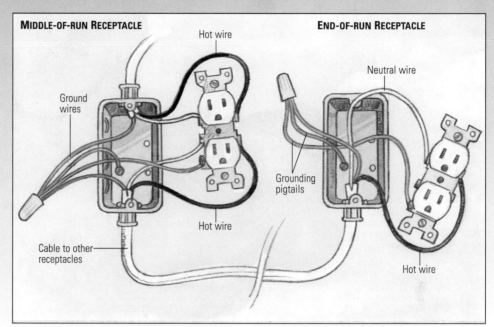

MIDDLE-OF-RUN RECEPTACLE — END-OF-RUN RECEPTACLE

Hot wire · Ground wires · Cable to other receptacles · Hot wire · Neutral wire · Grounding pigtails · Hot wire

If a receptacle is in the **middle of the run,** wires continue through it, delivering power to other receptacles or fixtures. Two cables enter the box. Usually the two blacks connect to the two brass terminals and the two whites connect to the two silver terminals. Sometimes pigtails are used instead. If only one cable enters a receptacle box, the receptacle is at the **end of the run,** meaning that it is the last receptacle on the circuit. Wiring is simple: black to the brass (gold) terminal and white to the silver terminal.

WHAT IF...
Two switches share a box?

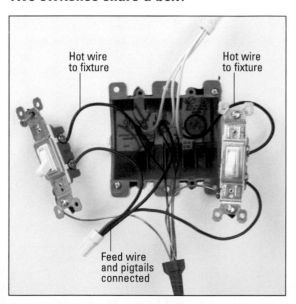

Hot wire to fixture · Hot wire to fixture · Feed wire and pigtails connected

When two switches share a box and are on the same circuit, they may share a single hot wire. The feed wire (the wire bringing power into the box) connects to two pigtails, each of which attaches to a switch. Each switch has another hot wire, leading to its light fixture.

How a split receptacle works

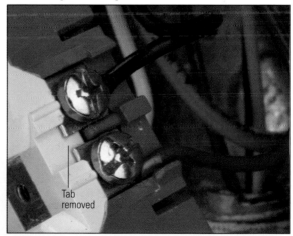

Tab removed

If the tab that joins the two brass terminals has been broken off and two hot wires connect to the brass terminals, the receptacle is "split." Either each outlet is on a separate circuit, or one of the outlets is controlled by a wall switch while the other is always hot.

BASIC TECHNIQUES

A clear understanding of how an electrical system works is an important part of basic wiring. Equally important are the techniques that produce safe and secure electrical connections. The skills you need to do your own projects—cutting and stripping wire and making solid connections—are the same ones that professional electricians use every day. You don't need to be as fast as a pro, but your work can and should be as safe and accurate.

Why good technique matters

If wires are spliced or connected haphazardly, the repair or installation may function—at first. But there is a good chance a wire will work its way loose, creating a dangerous condition.

Wiring the right way is not difficult. It takes only an hour or two to learn how to make splices and connections just as solid as those made by professionals. In fact, using the right technique often proves faster than doing it the wrong way. For example, looping a wire around a terminal screw clockwise *(page 50)* keeps it from sliding away from the screw shaft as you tighten the screw.

Use the right tools

Before beginning electrical work, gather the basic set of tools described on *pages 12–13*. These tools are designed for wiring; don't scrimp by using general-purpose tools. For example, if you try to strip wires using a knife, you will probably nick the copper and weaken the wire. Twisting wires together using a pair of household pliers is difficult and produces connections that might come apart. With wire strippers and lineman's pliers, making professional-quality connections will be a snap rather than a struggle.

Safety while working

The most important safety measure is to shut off power and test to make sure power is off *(page 46)*. Review the safety tips on *pages 5–7* before beginning a project.

Proper splices and connections are the key to safe and durable electrical installations.

CHAPTER PREVIEW

Testing
page 46

Stripping and splicing wire
page 48

Joining wire to a terminal
page 50

Mapping and indexing circuits
page 52

Lay a small drop cloth (an old towel works well) on the floor or countertop beneath the electrical box you are working on. It will catch all the debris and protect surfaces from scratches. Complete a repair by wrapping all bare wires and wire nuts with electrician's tape for an extra measure of protection.

Screwdriver

Wire strippers

Long-nose pliers

TESTING

Electricians keep their testers handy at all times—a practice worth imitating. Make it a habit to test thoroughly for the presence of power before beginning work.

In addition to a receptacle analyzer *(page 30),* a home do-it-yourselfer needs a voltage tester to see if the power is on and a continuity tester to check for broken connections or disconnected wires.

Good testing habits

You need no special knowledge to operate a tester. However, work methodically to gain reliable results from your tests.

■ Be sure to make contact with the metal parts you are testing. Pressing hard isn't necessary, but the probe must make direct contact with metal, not plastic insulation or electrician's tape.

■ Insert the voltage tester probes at least an inch into the receptacle being tested.

■ If a wire or screw is painted, use a rubber-grip screwdriver to scrape some paint off before testing it.

Test for power

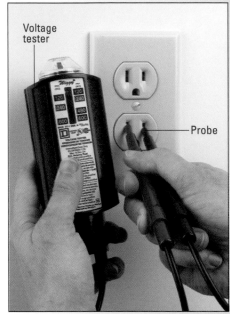

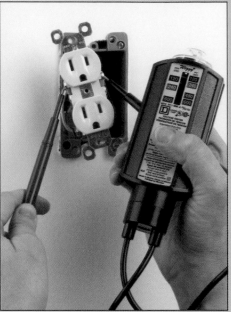

1 Insert the probes of a voltage tester into the two slots of a receptacle to test for the presence of power. The light will glow or the needle will move if electrical current is present.

2 Once you have opened a box, test again to be sure there is no current. Hold one probe to each screw terminal on either side of the receptacle, where wires are connected. Also touch each wire.

Voltage detector

A voltage detector senses power through insulation, wallboard, or plastic boxes. Just hold it on or near a cable, wire, or electrical box and press the detector's button; it will light or buzz to signal the presence of current.

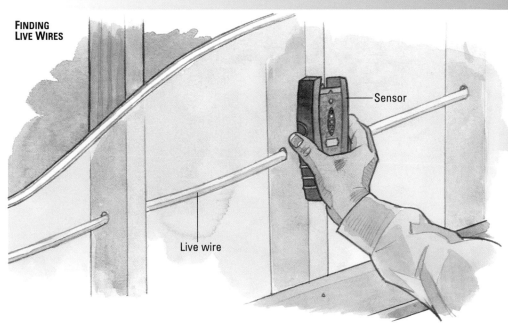

FINDING
LIVE WIRES

Some stud sensors not only detect the presence of joists and studs behind the wall surface, but also indicate the presence of any live wires. Follow the instructions carefully to *tune the tool to the thickness of the wall. Use a sensor before cutting into a wall or ceiling. It still pays to be safe and probe carefully (page 6) to make sure there are no hidden risks.*

Test for continuity

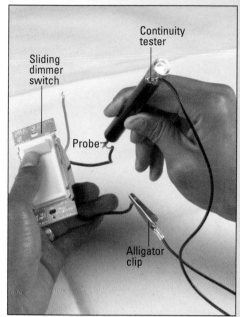

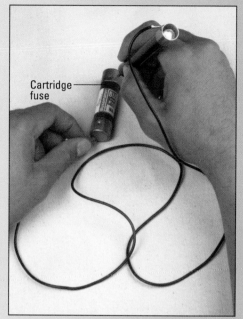

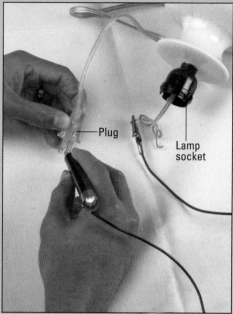

Switch: Use a continuity tester only when the wiring is disconnected from power. To test a switch, attach the alligator clip to one terminal and hold the probe against the other terminal. If the tester glows when the switch is on and does not glow when it is off, the switch is OK.

Fuse: To test a cartridge fuse, hold the alligator clip against one end and the probe against the other. If the tester does not glow, the fuse should be replaced.

Lamp wiring: To test lamp wiring, attach the alligator clip to one end of a wire and touch the probe to the other end. If the tester does not glow, the wire is broken at some point along its length.

STANLEY PRO TIP

Test the tester

Testers can malfunction. To make sure it is working properly, always test the tester. Each time you get a reading of no power when using a voltage tester, insert the probes into a receptacle you know is hot. The tester should glow, confirming that it is working properly.

Consider a digital multitester

A multitester does the work of a voltage tester *and* a continuity tester. In addition, it is invaluable for appliance repairs because it tells you exactly how much power is present. However, it is a bit complicated to figure out and somewhat expensive. A digital multitester is easier to use than one with a dial.

Avoid cheap testers
You may be tempted to buy an inexpensive tester with a neon bulb. These bulbs are notorious for failing, and they are easily damaged. A reliable tester is well worth a little extra money.

STRIPPING AND SPLICING WIRE

Before an electrical connection can be made, a wire end must be stripped of its insulation. This is a simple process, but it's important to do it right so the copper wire won't be damaged. Use a good pair of strippers like those shown below.

It will take a bit of practice—say, 15 minutes' worth—to learn how to make firm splices. The right tool is essential: Nothing does the job like a pair of lineman's pliers.

Always take a few moments to check your work. Check the bare wire you have just stripped to make sure it is not gouged. After splicing wires and adding the correct size wire nut, tug on the wires to make sure they are securely joined.

Both of these tools will do a good job stripping wire, but the long-nose strippers get into tight places more easily.

Standard combination strippers

Long-nose combination strippers

Stripping wire

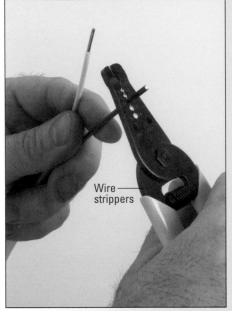

Wire strippers

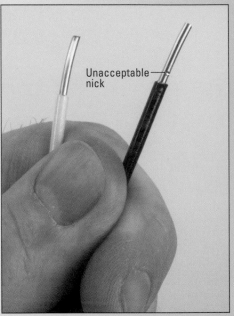

Unacceptable nick

1 Determine the size of the wire you will strip *(page 15)*. Open the strippers, place the wire in the correct hole, and squeeze them shut. Give a slight twist, then slide the insulation off.

2 The insulation should slide off easily with no more than a slight mark on the wire. If you have to pull hard or the stripper leaves a nick, check that you are using the right hole. If the problem persists, buy a new pair of strippers.

Working with cord

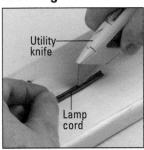

Utility knife

Lamp cord

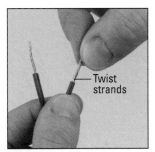

Twist strands

Hand-splice

1 Separate lamp cord (also known as zip cord) before stripping. Poke the tip of a utility knife between the two wires. Pull the cord to split it.

2 Strip the wire ends. With your fingers, twist the exposed strands clockwise until tight.

3 Do not attempt to splice cord wire using lineman's pliers; it's too easy to break strands. Instead, twist the wires together clockwise by hand and add a wire nut.

How much insulation should be stripped?
If you will be joining the wire to a terminal, remove about ¾ inch. If you will be splicing a wire to another wire, remove about 1 inch.

Splicing wire

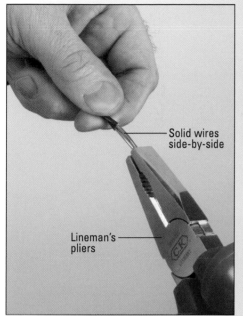

Solid wires side-by-side

Lineman's pliers

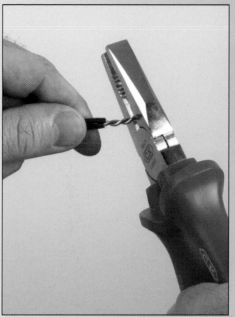

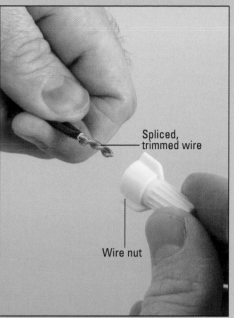

Spliced, trimmed wire

Wire nut

1 Hold the stripped wire ends tightly next to each other. Grip both with lineman's pliers. Twist clockwise until you feel a slightly stronger resistance, then stop. If you twist too hard, you could break a wire. Practice on some scrap wire before you start a project.

2 Using diagonal cutters or lineman's pliers, cut the tails off the tip of the splice. This makes it easy to push the splice into a wire nut and ensures that both wires will be held firmly together. Trim so that about ¾ inch of spliced wire remains.

3 Choose a wire nut to fit the size and number of wires you have spliced *(page 19)*. Push the spliced wires in, then twist the nut clockwise to tighten. Tug on the wires to make sure the connection is tight, then wrap the bottom of the nut with electrician's tape.

WHAT IF...
Solid wire joins to stranded wire?

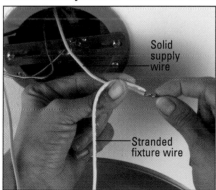

Solid supply wire

Stranded fixture wire

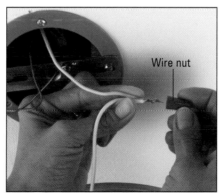

Wire nut

1 Light fixtures typically have stranded wires that connect to solid feed wires. Strip 1¼ inches of insulation from the stranded wire. Using your fingers, twist the stranded wire tightly around the solid wire, leaving about ⅛ inch of stranded wire sticking beyond the end of the solid wire.

2 Carefully poke the wires into a wire nut so that the protruding tip of the stranded wire goes as far as possible into the nut. Twist the nut until tight. Tug on the stranded wire to check the connection. Wrap the bottom of the nut with electrician's tape.

STANLEY PRO TIP

Twist three or more wires all at once

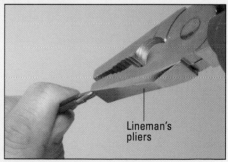

Lineman's pliers

When splicing more than two wires, it's tempting to splice two and then twist the third to the splice. Don't—the wires might break. Instead grab all three (or four) wires at the same time with your lineman's pliers and twist. It may take you a few attempts to master this technique.

JOINING WIRE TO A TERMINAL

Joining a wire to a terminal screw seems like a simple procedure. But it's worth a few minutes of time and a little practice to learn how to make a secure connection. Terminal connections come under a lot of stress when devices such as switches or receptacles are pushed into boxes, and one poor connection can create a nasty short.

Wrap the wire almost all the way around the screw before tightening it. Make sure the wire is wrapped clockwise around the terminal screw so that as the screw tightens the loop is pulled in, not out.

In an ideal connection, all the wire under the screw head is stripped and no more. (*Page 40* shows how stripping too much insulation leads to an unsafe situation.)

Most homeowners use long-nose pliers to bend a loop in the wire (see steps at right), but if you plan to install a number of devices, consider purchasing a wire-bending screwdriver.

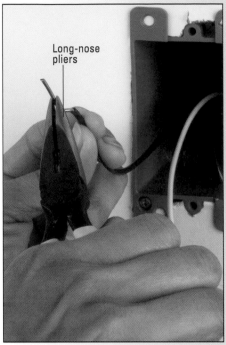

1 With the tip of a pair of long-nose pliers, grab the bare wire just past the insulation. Twist to the left. Slide the pliers up a little, and bend to the right.

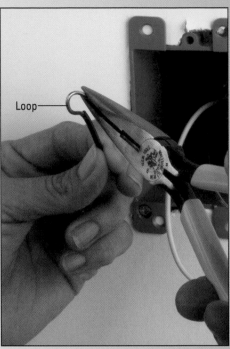

2 Move the pliers again and bend again to the right. This should complete a partial circle with an opening just wide enough to fit over the threads of a terminal screw.

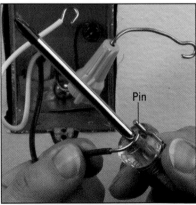

WIRE-BENDING SCREWDRIVER
A perfect loop every time

This handy tool makes it easy to form perfect loops in wire ends. Just slip the wire between the screwdriver shaft and the pin and twist.

SAFETY FIRST
Avoid push-in connections

In the back of a switch or receptacle, you'll find connection holes designed to accept stripped wire ends. Using them saves a little time, but the resulting connection is not as secure as one made to a terminal screw.

STANLEY PRO TIP

Save time by bending with long-nose strippers

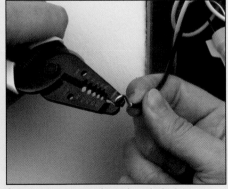

Some strippers are shaped so their tips act much like long-nose pliers. This allows you to strip and bend without changing tools. You can also use them to squeeze the wire around the terminal *(Step 3)*.

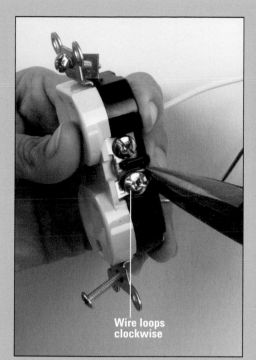

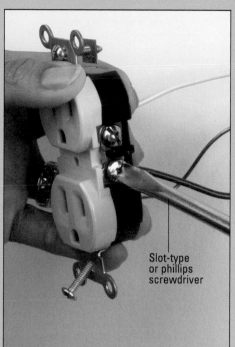

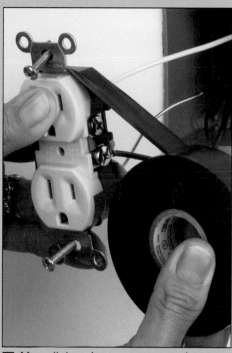

Wire loops clockwise

Slot-type or phillips screwdriver

3 Unscrew the terminal screw until it becomes hard to turn. Slip the looped wire end over the screw threads. Grab the wire on either side of the screw with long-nose pliers and tighten around the screw.

4 Check that the loop is on the terminal screw clockwise. Tug to make sure the wire cannot come loose. Tighten the terminal screw until the wire is snug between the screw head and the terminal surface.

5 After all the wires are connected, wrap electrician's tape tightly around the device to cover the terminal screws.

WHAT IF...
The job calls for an unusual connection?

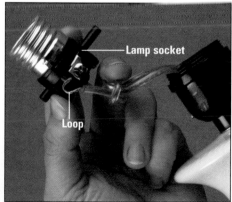

Lamp socket

Loop

Pigtail

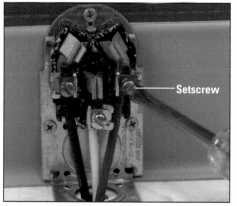

Setscrew

Stranded wire: To join a stranded wire to a terminal, strip the wire end and twist the strands together *(page 48)*. Use your fingers to form a loop. Wrap the bare wire clockwise around the terminal screw. You may need to push the wire into place as you tighten the screw to make sure no strands slip out.

Two wires, one terminal: Never attach two wires to a single terminal. Instead make a pigtail. Cut a piece of wire about 6 inches long and strip both ends. Splice one end to the two wires you need to connect and attach the other end to the terminal.

Setscrew terminals: In service panels, 240-volt receptacles, and other high-voltage connections, you will find setscrew terminals. Loosen the setscrew, poke the stripped wire end into the terminal hole, and tighten the setscrew.

MAPPING AND INDEXING CIRCUITS

Somewhere inside the service panel—usually stuck on the door—there should be an index that shows which areas of the house are covered by each circuit breaker or fuse. The index will help you shut off power to the correct circuit before working on it.

Codes require service panels to be indexed, but sometimes installers don't bother to trace down each circuit. If there is no index, make one. To complete the index, work systematically to identify the circuit for every electrical outlet in the house. Be prepared to find some odd combinations. In older homes, a single circuit may travel through several floors. Or you may find an entire circuit serving only a couple of receptacles. Avoid attaching family members' names to the index; they might change rooms. Use more permanent directional designations like "east bedroom" or "front hall."

Indexing is easiest working with a helper who can turn circuits on and off while you test the lights, receptacles, and appliances.

WORKING WITH A HELPER
Communication methods

If two people are working, the one stationed at the service panel must let the other know which circuit is off. Once the roamer has finished testing outlets, he or she needs to tell the other person to flip the breaker back on and a new one off.

If the house is small, just shouting back and forth can work. In a larger home, use cell phones or walkie-talkies.

If you are working alone, follow this process: Go into every room and flip on all the light switches and lamps. Then shut off all the circuits except one and look for the lights that are on. To tell from a distance whether a receptacle is on or off, plug in a radio and turn it up loud. Once you know the general area covered by a circuit, test all the receptacles systematically.

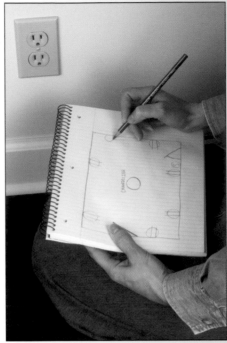

1 Make a rough sketch of each room in the house, showing the location of all electrical outlets—lights, receptacles, and hard-wired appliances. Don't forget the basement, hallways, attic, garage, and outdoor electrical service.

2 Flip on all the lights in the house. Assign a circuit number to each fuse or breaker in the service panel. Shut off one breaker or unscrew one fuse.

USING A CIRCUIT FINDER

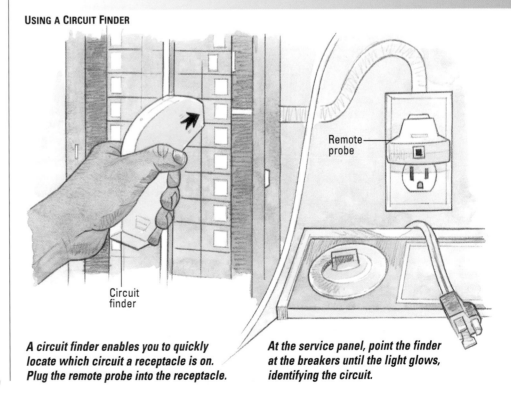

Remote probe

Circuit finder

A circuit finder enables you to quickly locate which circuit a receptacle is on. Plug the remote probe into the receptacle.

At the service panel, point the finder at the breakers until the light glows, identifying the circuit.

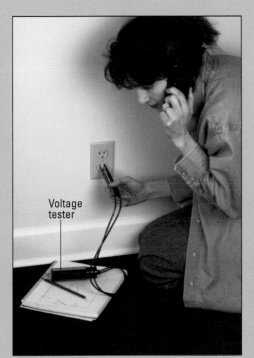

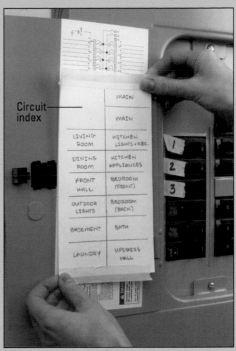

3 Test outlets throughout the house. Note lights that have turned off. Open the refrigerator door so you can see whether the interior light is on, turn on appliances, and test each outlet in each receptacle.

4 When you encounter an outlet that has been turned off, mark the circuit number on that room's sketch. After you have tested all outlets, restore power to the circuit you just tested and shut off the next circuit. Work systematically.

5 Transfer your findings in chart form to a piece of paper that fits the panel door. For clarity, position the circuit numbers near the actual fuses or breakers.

Situations to watch out for

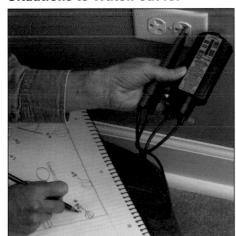

Same receptacle, different circuits: The two outlets of a receptacle may be connected to different circuits *(page 43)*. Always check both outlets and mark the drawing accordingly.

Low-voltage circuits: Don't forget low-voltage power devices, such as a doorbell. The thermostat is especially important. Crank it all the way up or down so that the heat or air-conditioning stays on during the test.

Appliances: Test all appliances, such as the garbage disposal, by turning them on. If you have an electric range, air-conditioner, or water heater, it should be controlled by a separate 240-volt circuit.

REPAIRS

It may not be worth your while to repair an inexpensive lamp or a small appliance. But if the piece is valuable—for economic or sentimental reasons— you can give it new life with just a little work. The basic tools and techniques presented in the preceding chapters will equip you to make most of the repairs needed around a home.

Finding and solving problems
Any electrical repair project begins with safety. **Before dismantling a lamp or appliance, unplug it. Shut off power to the circuit before working on a light fixture.**

To diagnose a problem, you'll often use a continuity tester *(page 47)*. It tells you if there is a break (i.e., a lack of continuity) along the length of a wire, or if the contacts of an electrical device have broken. It can help you isolate and identify the problem: a bad plug, cord, socket, or switch.

Lamps, which plug in, and light fixtures, which are permanently connected to household circuits, are wired in much the same way. Most parts, such as sockets and cords, are widely available and cost little. Repair techniques are largely a matter of common sense: Pull the new cord through the lamp to replace the old

cord, or replace a faulty socket with a new one of the same type and wire it the same way as the old one.

For best results, work away from distraction. Try to finish a repair in one sitting, so you can remember where all the parts should go.

Chronic problems
This chapter also demonstrates easy and safe solutions for a circuit that chronically overloads. It shows how to repair damaged wire inside an electrical box. In addition you'll learn how to solve problems with door chimes and thermostats.

Most problems can be traced with a continuity tester and solved using simple wiring techniques.

CHAPTER PREVIEW

 **Changing lightbulbs** *page 56*

 **When a circuit overloads** *page 57*

 **Plugs and cord switches** *page 58*

 **Lamp sockets and switches** *page 60*

 **Rewiring a lamp** *page 62*

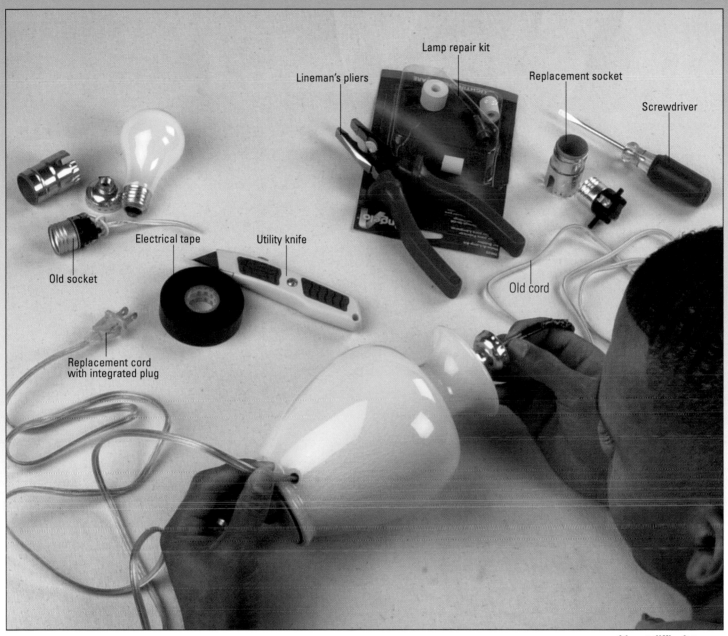

Lamp repair kit

Lineman's pliers

Replacement socket

Screwdriver

Electrical tape

Utility knife

Old socket

Old cord

Replacement cord
with integrated plug

*It's not difficult to
completely replace
the electrical innards
of a lamp. When you
finish, the lamp will
be as good as new.*

Fluorescents
page 64

**Chandelier
repairs**
page 66

**Repairing
wiring in
boxes**
page 68

**New dryer
cord**
page 71

**Repairing a
door chime**
page 72

Thermostats
page 75

CHANGING LIGHTBULBS

It takes only one homeowner to change a lightbulb, but you may want to consult with family members before choosing which bulb to use. For instance, if you have to change the bulb in a fixture more than once every few months, buying a long-life bulb will save you both hassle and money. If a light fixture or lamp is brighter than needed, install bulbs of lower wattage or replace the switch with a dimmer *(page 81)*.

If a light stops glowing altogether, chances are you simply need to replace the bulb. If a bulb won't glow unless you screw it in hard, or if the bulb flickers, the problem may be the socket or wiring, not the bulb; see *pages 60–63* for the remedy.

Get the wattage right

Don't ignore the warning sticker that tells how much wattage a fixture can handle. Installing a bulb of too-high wattage overheats the fixture, causing bulbs to burn out quickly, damaging the fixture and the ceiling material, and creating a potential fire hazard. If you need more light than the fixture can deliver, replace the fixture.

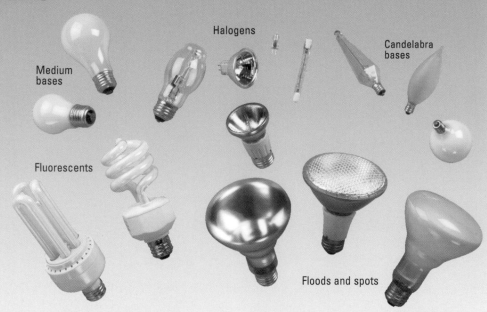

Halogens

Candelabra bases

Medium bases

Fluorescents

Floods and spots

Make sure the bulb will fit the fixture's socket; several sizes exist. To improve energy efficiency in standard incandescent fixtures, buy a screw-in fluorescent; several shapes and sizes are available. Halogen fixtures deliver more light for the power; see page 63. For recessed canister lights, use a flood bulb for general illumination, and a reflector bulb (also called a directional flood) for a spotlight effect.

Low-voltage halogen fixtures (pages 107–110) and lamps call for single- or double-ended bulbs. For information on fluorescent tubes, see page 64.

SAFETY FIRST
Handling halogens

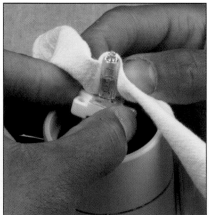

Halogen bulbs get very hot, and they're sensitive to oils—just touching one with fingers can greatly shorten a bulb's life. So let a bulb cool, then handle it with a clean cloth or light gloves.

STANLEY PRO TIP: **When the bulb breaks**

Changing a lightbulb is no joking matter if the glass has broken. **Make sure the power is off.** Rather than handling it with fingers, gently push a raw potato onto the shards and twist.

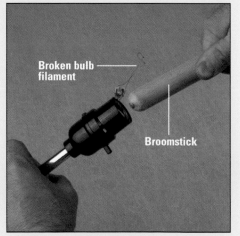

Broken bulb filament

Broomstick

If most of the glass is gone from a broken bulb, insert a broomstick into the bulb's socket and twist it out.

WHEN A CIRCUIT OVERLOADS

Many homes have a similar problem: When you run the toaster and the microwave at the same time, or use a blow dryer while the bathroom fan is on, a circuit overloads, causing a fuse to blow or a breaker to trip.

One solution is to install a new circuit with new receptacles—a messy, expensive job. But there is a simpler solution: Plug that toaster or blow dryer into a receptacle powered by another circuit.

If you have a detailed index of your circuits (pages 52–53), it will be easy to find alternative receptacles. If none is nearby, use an extension cord option, shown below, or hire a pro to install a new circuit.

1 List the items on the problem circuit. Using your circuit index, find out which items can be moved to another circuit to relieve overloading. In this example, moving any of the three items will work. Make sure the change won't overload the other circuit.

2 Make sure you have the correct size breaker or fuse for the circuit. A circuit using #12 wire can be on a 20-amp circuit; a circuit using #14 wire must be on a 15-amp circuit (page 35).

#12 wire

#14 wire

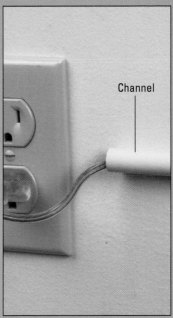

Channel

3 Plug an extension cord into a receptacle powered by a different circuit (one that is not already overloaded). If none is nearby, consider running an extension cord through a wall-mounted channel.

How much can a circuit handle?

The higher the amperage of a circuit, the more power it can handle. To figure out how many watts a circuit can take, multiply volts by amps. A circuit's safe capacity is only 80 percent of its total capacity. So a 120-volt, 15-amp circuit has a total capacity of 15 amps or 1800 watts (120 × 15 = 1800). A safe capacity for that circuit is 12 amps or 1440 watts.

Extension cord options

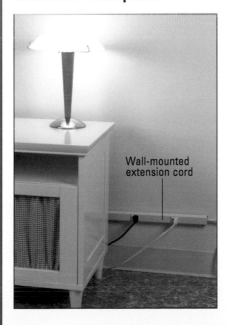

Wall-mounted extension cord

Various solutions are available to extend a circuit's reach without running new cable through walls. One option is a wall-mounted extension cord, which has one or two outlets per running foot. Raceway wiring is another option (pages 88–89), but it involves a little more work to install. Both are somewhat unsightly, though often they can be hidden behind furnishings.

WHAT IF...
A fuse blows?

If the metal strip is broken or melted but the window is clear, the fuse has blown because the circuit has overloaded—too much power was used at once (pages 24–25, 34–35). If the window is blackened, a short circuit is the culprit. Check the circuit's wiring for loose or damaged wiring (pages 40–41).

Overload

Short

PLUGS AND CORD SWITCHES

If a lamp cord and plug are brittle or damaged, rewire the lamp with a new cord that has an integrated plug *(page 55)*. If the plug has a cracked body or loose prongs but the cord is in good shape, install one of the replacement plugs shown here.

Cord maintenance

Always grasp the plug when you pull a plug out of a receptacle. If you tug on the cord, you may loosen or break wiring connections in the plug. Organize and position your cords to minimize tripping hazards.

PRESTART CHECKLIST

☐ **TIME**
About 10 minutes

☐ **TOOLS**
Phillips screwdriver, cutting pliers, long-nose pliers

☐ **SKILLS**
Cutting and twisting stranded wire; attaching stranded wire to terminals

☐ **PREP**
A clean, well-lighted work surface

☐ **MATERIALS**
Replacement plug, cord switch

Flat lamp plugs

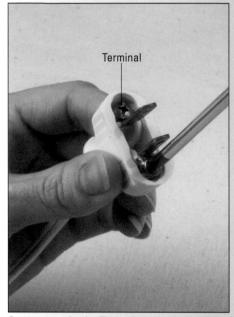

Terminal

Prong core

Plug body

Screw terminals: To replace a plug, snip the cord near the old plug, divide the cord, and strip ¾ inch of insulation from the end of each wire. Slip the wires through the replacement plug and connect them to the terminals. Tug to check the connections and make sure there are no loose strands.

Snap together plug: To add a squeeze-type replacement plug, snip off the old plug and feed the cord through the new plug body. Place the prongs over the cord and push the cord completely into the prong core. Squeeze the prongs tight. Slide the body up and snap it onto the core.

STANLEY PRO TIP

Neutral and hot wires

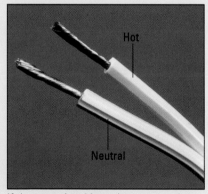

Hot

Neutral

If the neutral and hot wires on a cord get mixed up, a tool or light may be energized when the switch is off. The smooth wire on a cord is hot; connect it to the brass terminal. The wire with ridges (or ribs) is neutral; connect it to the silver terminal.

Replacement plug options

Flat

90°
angle

Industrial

Heavy-duty

Most replacement plugs connect in much the same manner as the plugs shown at left. The 90° plug allows you to position the cord in several different angles, making it easier to plug into tight spots.

Appliance plugs

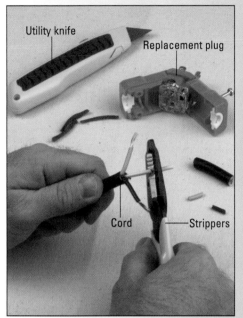

Utility knife
Replacement plug
Cord
Strippers

Terminal screw

1 For an appliance, choose a hefty plug with a grounding prong. Working carefully with a knife to avoid cutting into wire insulation, strip about 2 inches of sheathing from the end of the cord. Strip about ¾ inch from the ends of each wire and twist the wire strands tight *(page 48)*.

2 Slide the replacement plug's body onto the cord. Connect the wires to each of the terminals—black to hot (the narrower prong), green to ground (the round prong), and white to neutral (the wide prong).

3 Tug on the wires to see that the connections are firm and make sure there are no loose strands. Assemble the plug body and tighten the screws.

Rotary cord switches

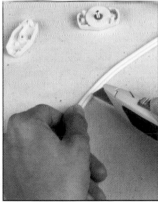

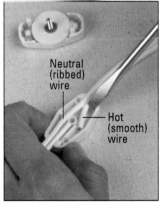

Neutral (ribbed) wire

Hot (smooth) wire

1 If a lamp switch is hard to reach, install a cord switch. To install a rotating (rotary) cord switch, first cut through the hot (smooth) wire, taking care not to nip the neutral (ribbed) wire.

2 Separate the wires about ¾ inch on each side of the cut. Push the wires into the body of the switch as shown, then screw the two parts of the body together.

Rocker cord switches

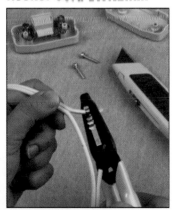

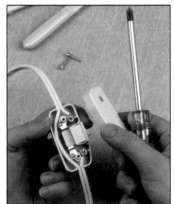

1 To install a rocker cord switch, snip the hot (smooth) cord without damaging the neutral (ribbed) cord. Separate the wires about 1 inch on each side of the cut. Strip about ¾ inch from the ends of each cut wire and twist the strands tight *(page 48)*.

2 Push the neutral wire into the switch's groove. Connect the stripped ends to the switch's terminals *(page 51)*. Snap the top part of the switch over the wires and tighten the screws.

LAMP SOCKETS AND SWITCHES

If a lamp doesn't come on even after you've changed the bulb, or if it flickers, check the cord (especially near the plug) for breakage. If you see no damage, unplug the lamp and examine the socket. Often, the problem is not the socket itself but the wire connections to it *(Step 3).*

The socket shown on these pages is the most common kind. Other types are made of plastic or porcelain and attach to the lamp or light fixture via screws or a nut and bolt. Take the old socket to a hardware store or home center for a replacement that fits.

PRESTART CHECKLIST

☐ **TIME**
About 20 minutes (not including shopping) to test and replace a socket

☐ **TOOLS**
Screwdriver, voltage tester, perhaps strippers and lineman's pliers

☐ **SKILLS**
Fastening wire to a terminal; testing for voltage

☐ **PREP**
A clean, well-lighted work surface

☐ **MATERIALS**
Replacement socket, switch

Contact tab

Terminal connection

Cardboard sleeve

1 **Unplug the lamp.** Before you replace a socket, pry the contact tab up with a screwdriver so that it makes stronger contact with the bulb's base. If a contact tab is rusty, scrape it with a slot screwdriver. Plug in again and test the lamp.

2 If the problem is not solved, **unplug the lamp** and remove the socket. Unscrew the small screw near the contact tab. Squeeze the socket shell and pull it out. (If the shell reads PRESS, put your thumb there when you squeeze.)

3 If there is a cardboard sleeve, slide it off. Pull up gently on the socket and examine the terminal connections. If you cannot fix the problem by tightening a terminal screw, loosen the screws, remove the wires, remove and test the socket.

TEST THE SOCKET
Check for faulty connections

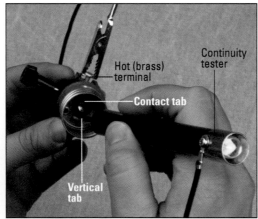

Continuity tester

Hot (brass) terminal

Contact tab

Vertical tab

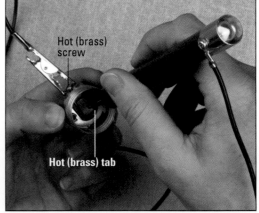

Hot (brass) screw

Hot (brass) tab

If the socket has a switch, attach the clip to the hot (brass) terminal and touch the probe to the vertical tab or the contact tab. The tester should glow with the switch on and not glow with the switch off. If you get other results, replace the socket.

If the socket does not have a switch, attach the clip to the hot (brass) screw and touch the probe to the brass tab, as shown. Then clip onto the neutral (silver) screw and touch the probe to the threads. If the tester does not glow in either test, replace the socket.

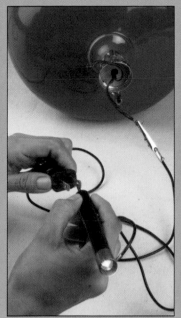

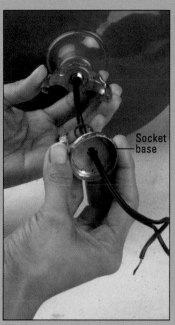

Socket base

Underwriters knot

4 If the socket tests OK, or if you replace the socket and that does not solve the problem, test the wires for continuity. If there is a break in continuity, rewire the lamp *(pages 62–63)*.

5 If the wire is knotted, untie it. If the socket base has a setscrew, loosen it. Unscrew and remove the socket base. Purchase a new socket that matches the old one.

6 Screw the new socket base into the lamp. Tighten the setscrew. Tie the cord in an Underwriters knot. Twist the wire strands tight with your fingers and connect them to the terminals *(page 51)*.

7 Slide on the cardboard sleeve (if there is one) and the socket shell. Push down to snap the shell onto the base.

WHAT IF...
A switch needs replacing on a lamp or ceiling fan?

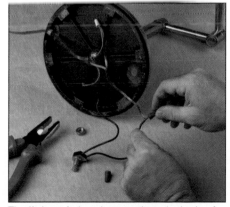

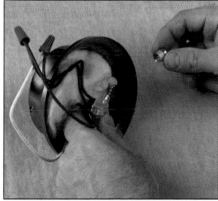

The little switches that attach to the body of a lamp or fixture are notoriously short-lived, but they are also easy to replace. To get at a fixture switch on a lamp, you may have to remove a metal or cloth cover on the bottom of the lamp base. Unscrew the nut, detach the wires, and replace the switch.

A pull-chain switch on a ceiling light or fan mounts in the same way as a lamp switch. To get at one, **shut off power to the circuit,** and remove the fixture's canopy *(page 37)*.

Fixture switch options

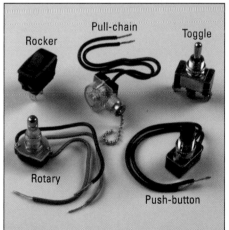

Rocker · Pull-chain · Toggle · Rotary · Push-button

You can usually replace one type of fixture switch with another—say, a toggle with a rocker or rotary switch. The hole in the lamp base is typically a standard size that accepts any of these.

REWIRING A LAMP

If the socket and the plug are ruled out as the cause of a lamp malfunction, then wiring must be the culprit. No matter what shape or size the lamp, the wiring is essentially the same: A cord runs from the plug to the socket. A multisocket lamp contains a sort of junction box, where the main cord is spliced to shorter cords that lead to individual sockets.

It is rarely a good idea to replace only part of a cord: The splice will be both unsightly and liable to unravel. It's usually not much more work to replace the entire lamp cord.

To divide, strip, and fasten cord wires to terminals, see *pages 48 and 51.*

PRESTART CHECKLIST

☐ **TIME**
About an hour to rewire a simple lamp

☐ **TOOLS**
Continuity tester, lineman's pliers, strippers, screwdriver

☐ **SKILLS**
Stripping wires and connecting them to terminals

☐ **MATERIALS**
Lamp cord with molded plug or a rewire kit containing a cord, and electrician's tape

Table or floor lamp

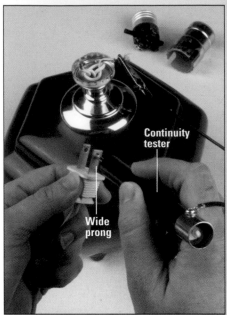

Continuity tester

Wide prong

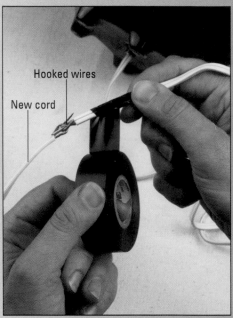

Hooked wires

New cord

1 Test wires for breaks in continuity. Attach a tester clip to the wide prong of the plug and touch the probe to the stripped neutral (ribbed) wire at the other end. Repeat for the narrow prong and the hot (smooth) wire. If the tester does not glow for both, replace the cord.

2 To replace the defective cord, begin by cutting the old cord. Strip about an inch off the ends of the old and new cord wires. Form hooks on all four wire ends and splice the old to the new in a splice that is thin enough to slide through the lamp. Wrap tightly and smoothly with electrician's tape.

Lamp rewire kit

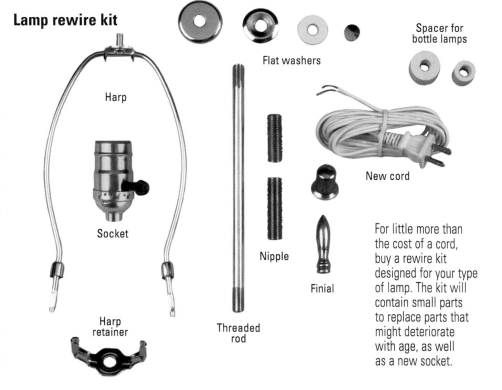

Harp

Socket

Harp retainer

Flat washers

Spacer for bottle lamps

New cord

Nipple

Threaded rod

Finial

For little more than the cost of a cord, buy a rewire kit designed for your type of lamp. The kit will contain small parts to replace parts that might deteriorate with age, as well as a new socket.

Desk lamp

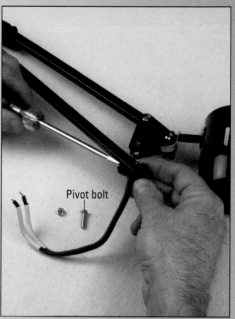

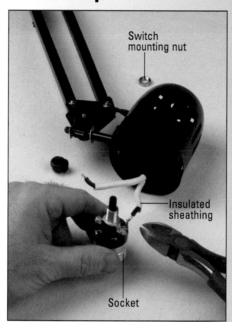

3 Feed the new cord into the base of the lamp while pulling the old cord through the top. Keep pulling until the new cord emerges. If rewiring a floor lamp, have a helper feed the cord into the base. Separate the cords; discard the old one.

1 **Unplug the lamp.** To remove the socket from a desk lamp, you may need to remove the nut from the twist switch or unscrew a mounting screw located near the contact tab *(page 60)*. Pull the socket out and disconnect the wires from the terminals.

2 Splice the new cord to the old and pull it through, as in Step 2 and Step 3 at left. Pulling may be complicated if the lamp has pivot points; it may require removing a nut and bolt to feed the wire through.

WHAT IF...
A lamp has two sockets?

If one socket on a multisocket lamp fails, test the socket. If that is not the problem, open the junction box cover and pull out the tangle of wires. Test the wires leading from the socket to the junction box for continuity *(Step 1 on page 62)*. If all the sockets fail to light, test the cord leading from the plug to the junction box.

STANLEY PRO TIP: **Halogen lamps**

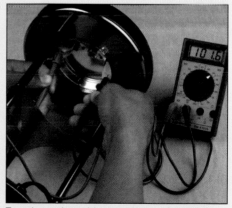

A halogen bulb gets very hot and may burn out if the lamp gets bumped while it is lit. Remove a bulb carefully, using a cloth, and find an exact replacement. If that does not solve the problem, test the socket.

Test the socket with a multitester *(page 47)*. If the reading is lower or higher than the lamp's rating, check the fuse in the lamp for proper amperage. Then test the wires for continuity. If these tests do not reveal a problem, the transformer is probably bad; replace the lamp.

FLUORESCENTS

A new fluorescent fixture is inexpensive and easy to install *(pages 96–97)*, so replacing rather than repairing is often the better option. Before you do, however, quickly check the components in this order: the tube, the starter (if any), the sockets, and the ballast.

Very old fluorescents have both a heavy ballast and a starter. More recent models have rapid-start ballasts and no starter. The latest models have electronic ballasts, which are nearly maintenance-free.

Fluorescent fixtures are often flimsy. Check that sockets are firmly seated and are not cracked. Tubes should fit snugly between the sockets.

An old delayed-start fluorescent flickers a few times before coming on as the starter delivers a burst of energy to get the tube going. A newer rapid-start fixture has a ballast that supplies extra power when turned on, so the light comes on immediately. A circuline fluorescent differs from rectangular models only in its shape.

Troubleshooting fluorescents

When faced with the following problems, work your way through the solutions one by one until the light works.

Does not light
Twist a tube to tighten it or replace the tube. If there is a starter, replace it. Replace a damaged socket. Replace the ballast or the fixture.

Tube is blackened
If only one end is black, turn the tube around. Replace the tube if both ends are black.

Flickers or takes a long time to light
Tighten, turn around, or replace a tube. If there is a starter, replace it. Replace the ballast or the fixture.

Hums and/or seeps black gunk
Don't touch the seepage with your fingers. Wear gloves. Tighten the screw securing the ballast. Replace a leaking ballast or the fixture.

Tubes

1 If a tube is black at both ends, replace it *(Step 2)*. If it flickers or does not come on, try rotating it in the socket until it seats firmly or until the light comes on.

2 To remove a tube, hold both ends and rotate until you feel it come loose at one end. Guide the pins out of the socket. To install a new tube, insert pins into one socket and guide the pins into the other socket. Rotate the tube a quarter turn, until you feel it seat or until it lights.

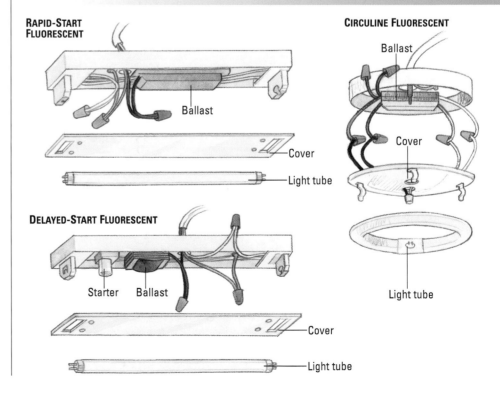

RAPID-START FLUORESCENT

Ballast
Cover
Light tube

DELAYED-START FLUORESCENT

Starter   Ballast
Cover
Light tube

CIRCULINE FLUORESCENT

Ballast
Cover
Light tube

Starters

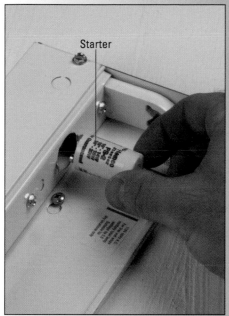

Starter

If a fixture has a starter, replace it every time you replace a tube. Be sure to buy a starter with the same serial numbers as the old one. If a tube is slow lighting up, tighten the starter. If that does not solve the problem, replace the starter. If the light still doesn't work, the ballast is to blame.

Sockets

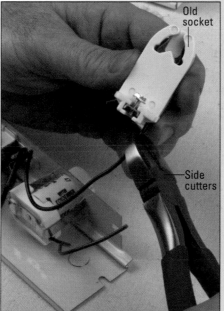

Old socket

Side cutters

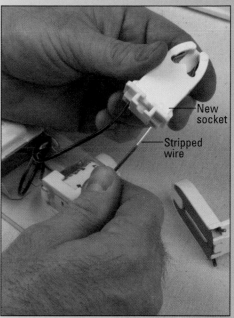

New socket

Stripped wire

1 Replace a socket if it is cracked or does not grab the tube firmly. Some sockets just slide out, while others are held in place by a screw. If you cannot remove the wires, cut them near the socket.

2 Buy a replacement to match the old socket. Strip ¾ inch of insulation from each wire end and push the wire end into the hole of the new socket. Push the new socket firmly to the fixture.

BALLAST
Install an exact replacement

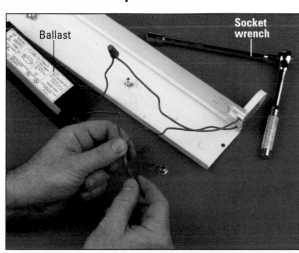

Ballast

Socket wrench

If all the other fixes fail, the ballast is the problem (see the troubleshooting box on *page 64).* A replacement ballast may cost about the same as a new fixture, but may be a bit less work to install. **Shut off power to the light.** Tag the wires for future reference. Disconnect wires, if possible, or cut them. Remove the ballast and install an exact replacement, wiring it just as the old ballast was wired.

Guard tubes from damage

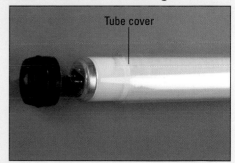

Tube cover

Fluorescent tubes are easily broken and are sensitive to cold. If your fixture lacks a cover and the tubes might get bumped, protect them with a clear plastic sleeve. Covers also help if the fixture has trouble starting in the cold.

CHANDELIER REPAIRS

Older chandeliers often need repair. Many were manufactured with little regard to the heat that the bulbs produce. Years of overheating have made the wire insulation brittle. A typical fixture has cord running through five or more tubes, allowing several opportunities for malfunctions.

Because they are near a hot bulb and surrounded by glass, sockets and the wires attached to them often deteriorate. If all the lights do not work, the stem wire probably needs to be replaced *(Step 4)*. If some of the wiring needs replacement, consider rewiring the entire fixture—it won't take much longer.

If only one light fails to come on, try pulling up the contact tab inside the socket *(page 60)*. Vacuum dust from the socket. If the bulb still does not light, pull out the socket and test it *(Step 2)*.

PRESTART CHECKLIST

☐ **TIME**
About three hours to dismantle, test, and run new wires in a chandelier

☐ **TOOLS**
Voltage tester, continuity tester, phillips screwdriver, wire strippers, long-nose pliers

☐ **SKILLS**
Testing for power and continuity, stripping and connecting wires

☐ **PREP**
Line up a helper to assist with removing the fixture. Lay a drop cloth on a work surface to cushion the fixture as you work on it.

☐ **MATERIALS**
Cord wire, electrician's tape

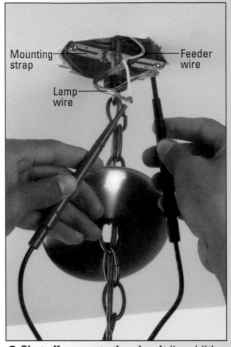

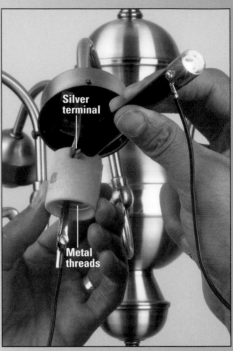

1 **Shut off power to the circuit** (in addition to flipping off the light switch). Support the chandelier so it won't fall down. Loosen the screws or screw collar holding the canopy in place and slide it down. Pull the wires apart and test for power *(page 46)*.

2 Attach a continuity tester clip to the metal threads inside the socket and touch the neutral (silver) terminal with the probe. Then clip onto the brass screw and touch the probe to the contact tab inside the socket. If the tester light does not come on for both tests, replace the socket *(page 61)*.

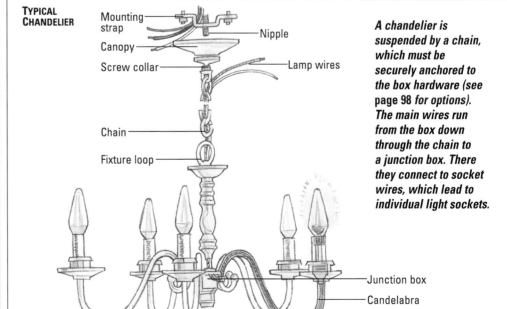

TYPICAL CHANDELIER

A chandelier is suspended by a chain, which must be securely anchored to the box hardware (see page 98 for options). The main wires run from the box down through the chain to a junction box. There they connect to socket wires, which lead to individual light sockets.

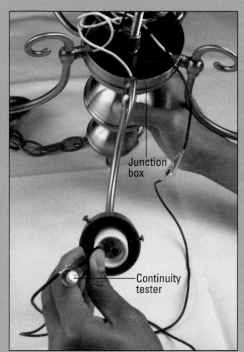

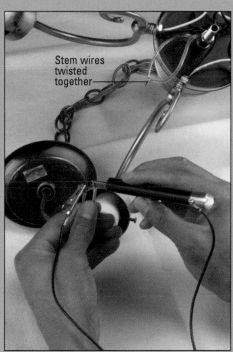

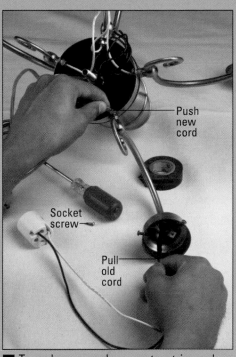

3 Disconnect the wires in the box, remove the chandelier, and place it on a work surface. Open the chandelier's junction box and pull out the wires. Test both the neutral (ribbed) and hot (smooth) wires for continuity.

4 To test the stem wires, twist them together at the junction box. At the other end, attach a continuity tester clip to one wire and touch the probe to the other wire. If the tester does not glow, replace the stem wires.

5 To replace a cord, separate, strip, and splice the old cord to the new. Pull the old wire through until the new wire appears *(pages 62–63)*.

STANLEY PRO TIP· **Accessing and pulling chandelier wires**

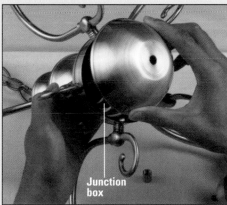

A chandelier's junction box is located in the center of the fixture. To open it, remove the nut at the bottom. Inside you will find a tight mass of wires. Space may be at a premium here, so after rewiring, cut the wires as short as you can. Use the smallest wire nuts possible.

Some chandelier junction boxes are crammed tight with wires. To figure out where a socket wire ends up in the junction box, tug the wires at the socket end and feel the wires at the other end.

Chandelier tubes may be narrow. Join the new cord (using lamp cord, which can withstand heat) to the old with a tight splice *(page 62)*; a bulky splice may stick. If you're still having trouble pulling wires through an old fixture, there may be corrosion in the tubes. Try blowing through the tubes, and run a single wire through the tube to remove any obstructions.

REPAIRING WIRING IN BOXES

A loose wall box can make working a switch or inserting a plug awkward— and put strain on the wiring. Firm up the box with mounting brackets or, if the box is against a framing member, by fastening it with a screw or two.

Wire insulation in a box—especially a ceiling fixture box, which gets very hot— becomes brittle more quickly than wiring inside a wall or ceiling. So even if the wires you see are badly worn, the wiring hidden in your walls is probably OK.

When doing work in boxes always **turn off power** and remove the device.

Wire repair tips

■ If bare wire shows below a wire nut, remove the nut, snip the bare wire(s) to shorten it slightly and reinstall the nut. If the wire is nicked, wrap electrician's tape tightly around the damaged area. If wiring is generally brittle and cracked, use heat-shrinkable tubing to cover all the wires.

■ If a wire's insulation is nicked near the point where it enters a box, it may be difficult to reach the damaged area with tape. Try slipping on a red plastic armored cable bushing *(page 41)*.

■ Whenever you untangle a wire splice or disconnect a wire from a terminal, you rebend a wire and thereby weaken it. If you have enough wire, snip off the old loop and start again.

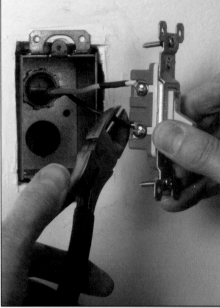

1 **Turn off power and test for power in the box.** Rather than disconnecting a device and then repairing wire ends, save time by simply cutting the wires just behind the terminals. Then strip and reconnect. Make sure remaining wires will be long enough—6 to 8 inches—before you cut.

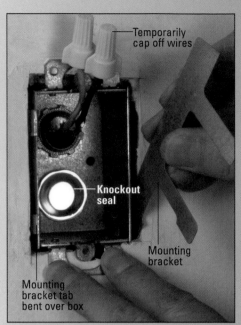

Temporarily cap off wires

Knockout seal

Mounting bracket

Mounting bracket tab bent over box

2 Stabilize a loose box with mounting brackets. On each side of the box, slip the bracket behind the wall material. Slide it down so both ends are behind the wall and bend the tabs into the box. (Or fasten it with screws—see *page 78).* If any knockouts are missing, push a knockout seal into place.

Evaluating old wire and cable

Old Romex

Knob-and-tube wiring

"Friction tape" splice

Old Romex or knob-and-tube wiring may have cloth insulation that can crack with age. Particularly with knob-and-tube, splices may be covered with clothlike "friction tape." As long as the insulation is sound and the splice is covered, it is safe. If a tape-covered splice is coming unraveled, remove the tape and twist on a wire nut.

Old wiring may be so dirty that you cannot tell hot (black) wires from neutral (formerly white) wires. It is important to find out—if you connect the neutral wire rather than the hot wire to a switch, power will always be present in the box, even when the switch is off. Gently clean portions of old insulation, using a cloth dampened with alcohol or soapy water, until you can tell which wire has white insulation.

Fixing wires in a ceiling box

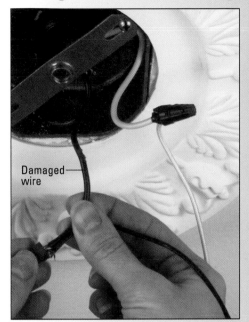

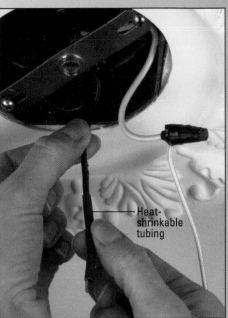

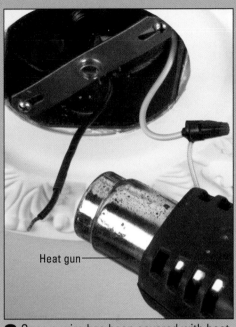

1 **Shut off power to the circuit.** Gently pull the wires out and unscrew the wire nuts. If you find thick tape instead of a wire nut, slice it with a knife, taking care not to damage the wire beneath.

2 Slide a piece of heat-shrinkable tubing over the wire as far as it will go. Cut the tubing to expose the stripped wire end.

3 Once a wire has been covered with heat-shrinkable tubing, direct a heat gun at the wire until the tubing has shrunk tight onto the wiring.

WHAT IF...
A box is set back?

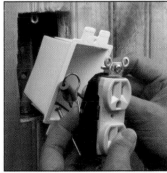

Codes require that a box be tightly enclosed to prevent an electrical fire from spreading. If a box's front edge is not flush with the wall or ceiling surface around it, slip in a box extender, available in various sizes and made of plastic (shown) or metal.

STANLEY PRO TIP

Clip and restrip

1 Wire that has been bent twice or more is liable to break. So whenever you install a device or fixture, cut off the previously stripped portion of the wires.

2 Strip the wire ends *(page 48)*, removing a ¾-inch piece of insulation if you will loop and attach the wire to a terminal, or a 1-inch piece if you will splice with a wire nut *(pages 49–51)*.

Grounding an old receptacle

Knockout slug

New ground wire

Fish tape

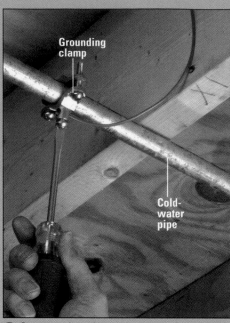

Grounding clamp

Cold-water pipe

1 If you have an old system with ungrounded receptacles and want to ground one receptacle, **shut off power to the circuit, test for power,** and pull out the receptacle. Pry out a knockout slug and then twist it back and forth to remove it.

2 Use the techniques shown on *pages 144–147* to make a pathway for a ground wire. Use one or two fish tapes to run a #12 green-insulated wire from the box to the service panel or to a cold-water pipe.

3 Connect the wire to the ground screw of the receptacle. Connect the other end to a cold-water pipe with a special grounding clamp.

STANLEY PRO TIP

Test a two-hole receptacle for grounding

If your system has two-hole receptacles, it is probably an ungrounded system. To make sure, shut off power, pull out a receptacle, and restore power. Insert one probe of a voltage tester into the hot (shorter) slot of the receptacle, and touch the other probe to the metal box. If the tester doesn't light, the system is not grounded. However, if it lights, the box is grounded; you can install a three-hole (grounded) receptacle and run a ground wire from the receptacle grounding terminal to a grounding screw in the box. Test the new receptacle for ground using a receptacle analyzer *(page 12)*.

Tricks for replacing cable

Wire insulation inside boxes (especially ceiling boxes, which get hot) deteriorates faster than wire wrapped inside cable. So even if you find a lot of brittle insulation inside a box, the wiring hidden inside your walls is probably OK. However, if you find brittle insulation in several boxes, call in a pro for an evaluation; the wiring in your house may need to be replaced.

Rewiring a house is usually a job for professionals, but if you work systematically and with your building department's approval, you may attempt it. The safest way is to pull and replace one cable at a time.

Running cable and connecting wires will probably be less than half the work. Cutting walls and ceilings to get at the cable, and patching and painting afterwards, will take much more time.

Start by replacing exposed cable (for example, in a basement or attic). Refer to *pages 144–147* for methods of running cable through walls.

In some cases, you may be able to pull cable through a wall or ceiling without damaging it. Once you've discovered where a cable leads (for example, between two receptacles) disconnect the cable at both ends. At one end, tightly tape the new cable to the old cable, making the splice as thin as possible so it can run through tight holes. Pull on the other end, and if you're lucky, the new cable will come through. Unfortunately sometimes there are tight turns or the cable is stapled, so this technique does not work, and you will have to cut into the wall or ceiling.

NEW DRYER CORD

Older 240-volt electric dryer receptacles have three prongs, attaching to three wires—two hots and one neutral. New codes require a four-prong receptacle, which connects to two hots, a neutral, and a ground wire.

If a dryer cord does not plug into your receptacle, hire a pro to change the receptacle, or change the cord yourself. The following steps show how to change from a three-wire to a four-wire cord. (Do not change from a four-wire to a three-wire. You will be eliminating a ground wire, which offers extra protection against shock.)

PRESTART CHECKLIST

□ **TIME**
About an hour to remove the old cord and install a new one

□ **TOOLS**
Screwdriver, drill, and perhaps strippers

□ **SKILLS**
Drilling a hole in metal; attaching wires to terminals

□ **MATERIALS**
A new dryer cord and a grounding screw with a head large enough to capture the cord's ground wire

1 Purchase a cord with a plug that fits the receptacle. See that the cord amperage rating matches the receptacle. **Unplug the dryer before beginning work.**

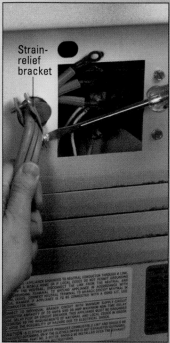

2 Remove the access panel at the back of the dryer. Loosen the screws to the strain-relief bracket and remove the old wires. Connect the black, red, and white wires from the new cord to the same terminals.

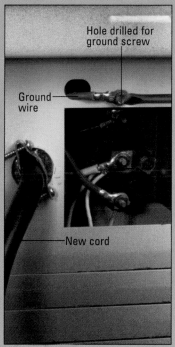

3 On the dryer's metal housing, drill a hole slightly smaller than the diameter of the screw shank. Feed the grounding screw through the ground-wire connector and finish tightening the screw.

SAFETY FIRST
240 volts pack a wallop

A shock from 120-volt wiring is painful but probably will not harm an adult. However, 240 volts are more dangerous. Even inserting a plug requires caution. To be safe, **shut off power to the circuit,** plug into the receptacle, and then turn the power back on.

STANLEY PRO TIP

Testing a 240-volt receptacle

If a 240-volt receptacle delivers no power or only partial power to an appliance, check the service panel to make sure power is on. Then very carefully make a live test: Insert the probes of a voltage tester into two slots at a time. You should get a reading of 120 volts in two positions (with one probe in the ground or neutral slot and one in a hot slot) and a reading of 240 volts in one position (with the probes in each of the hot slots). If you get different results, have a pro install a new receptacle.

REPAIRING A DOOR CHIME

If a chime or bell does not sound when you push the button, follow the steps shown on these pages: Check the button first, then the chime, then the transformer.

All these components are easily repaired or replaced. However, if the wiring is damaged inside walls, replacing it can be very difficult.

Power for a doorbell is supplied by a transformer, usually attached to a metal electrical box in some out-of-the-way location, such as a basement, crawlspace, garage, or inside a cabinet. Work carefully—other components, such as thermostats, might have similar-looking transformers. Follow the wires to be sure.

Doorbell wires may be color-coded, but there is no predicting which color goes to which button. Often all the wires are the same color.

Because the bell circuit operates on low voltage, you do not need to turn off power while testing the button or chime. However, the transformer is connected to 120 volts. **Shut off power** before working on the transformer.

PRESTART CHECKLIST

☐ **TIME**
About two hours to diagnose and repair most problems, not including time spent buying the new part

☐ **TOOLS**
Screwdriver, strippers, perhaps a multitester

☐ **SKILLS**
Stripping wires; attaching wires to terminals; using multitester

☐ **MATERIALS**
Short length of wire, perhaps a new button, chime, or transformer

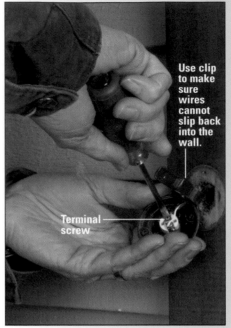

1 Detach the button from the wall. If the mounting screws are not visible, you may need to snap off a cover to reach them. To remove a small round button, pry it out with a screwdriver. Clean away any debris. Make sure wires are not broken. Tighten terminal screws.

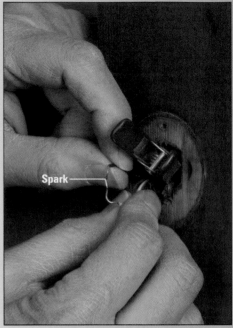

2 If that does not solve the problem, detach the wires from the terminals. Hold each wire by its insulation and touch the bare wires together. If you get a tiny spark and the chime sounds, replace the button. If you get a spark and the chime does not sound, test the chime (*Step 4*). If there is no spark, check the transformer (*Step 5*).

SINGLE CHIME SYSTEM

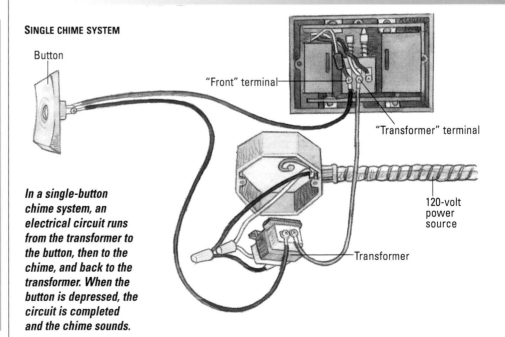

In a single-button chime system, an electrical circuit runs from the transformer to the button, then to the chime, and back to the transformer. When the button is depressed, the circuit is completed and the chime sounds.

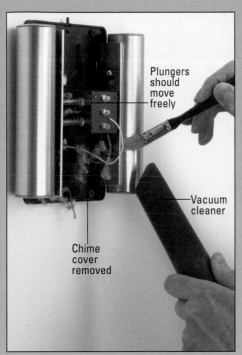

Plungers should move freely

Vacuum cleaner

Chime cover removed

Multitester

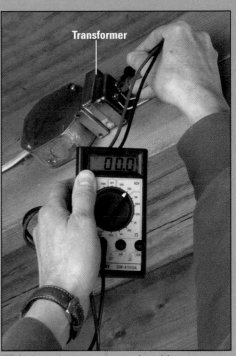

Transformer

3 If a chime does not sound or has a muffled sound, remove the cover and clean any dust or gunk. Make sure the wires are firmly connected to the terminal screws. If there is corrosion on the connections, detach and clean the wires and terminals with steel wool or light sandpaper.

4 Set a multitester to a low AC reading and touch the probes to "front" and "trans" terminals, then to "rear" and "trans." If you get a reading that is close to the chime's printed voltage rating, power is entering the chime. That indicates the chime mechanism is not functioning and needs replacing.

5 If there is no power at the chime, test the transformer. Remove the thin wires. Touch the probes of the multitester to both terminals. If it reads more than 2 volts below the transformer's rating, replace the transformer.

Wireless options

Wireless chime

Battery-powered button

Wireless add-on chime

Sending unit

A wireless chime installs easily. Put a battery in the button and attach it to the outside of the house. Then plug the chime into an electrical receptacle.

To add a second chime to your system, buy a wireless add-on chime. Place the sending unit inside the existing chime and connect its wires to the terminals. Plug the wireless chime into an electrical receptacle and mount it on the wall.

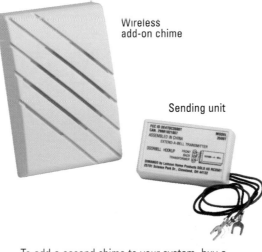

CHIME NEEDS REPLACING
Find a new chime with the same voltage rating

Before removing a chime, tag the wires so you know where they go. Loosen the terminal screws and remove the wires. Remove the mounting screws. Pull the chime out, carefully threading the wires through the hole in the chime.

Purchase a new chime of the same voltage rating as the transformer. (The voltage rating is usually printed on the chime unit.) Make sure the chime housing is large enough to cover any imperfections in the wall. Slip the wires through the opening in the housing, mount it to the wall, and connect the wires.

Repairing a door chime (continued)

 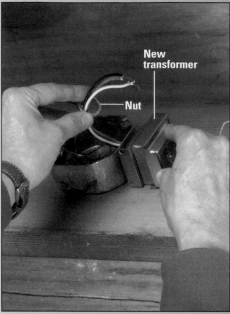 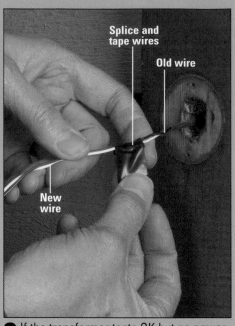

6 Before you buy a new transformer, make sure the box it is attached to has power. If it's attached to a receptacle box, insert the tester probes in the receptacle slots. If it's attached to a junction box, carefully remove the cover and test the wires (page 136). **Remember, these are 120-volt wires.**

7 If the transformer doesn't work, buy a new one with the same voltage rating. **Shut off power** to the circuit. Open the box and disconnect the transformer wires. Remove the nut that clamps the transformer to the box and pull out the transformer. Wire and clamp the new transformer.

8 If the transformer tests OK but no power reaches the chime or a button, the wiring is damaged. You may be able to attach new wire to the old and pull the new wire through. If you can't rewire, install a wireless chime (page 73).

TWO-CHIME SYSTEM

In a two-button system, a separate wire runs from the chime to the transformer to create a complete circuit for both buttons.

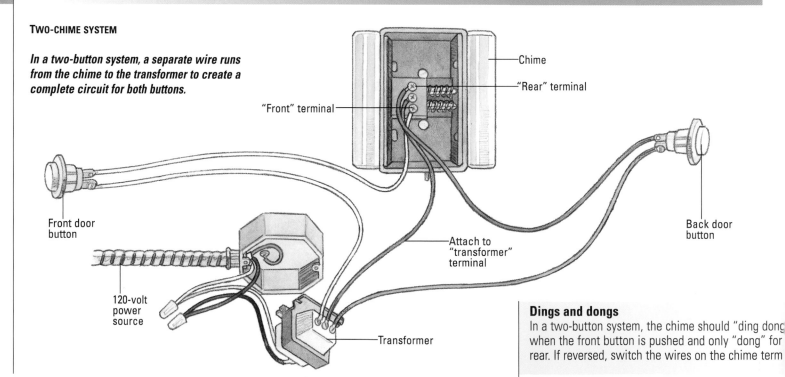

Front door button

120-volt power source

Transformer

"Front" terminal

Chime

"Rear" terminal

Attach to "transformer" terminal

Back door button

Dings and dongs
In a two-button system, the chime should "ding dong" when the front button is pushed and only "dong" for rear. If reversed, switch the wires on the chime term

THERMOSTATS

A thermostat senses when the air temperature is a degree or two above or below the desired level and switches the heating or cooling system on or off accordingly.

If a thermostat is attached to an electrical box and has standard house wires connected to it, it is a line-voltage unit. If it malfunctions, **shut off power to the circuit,** remove it, and take it to a dealer for a replacement.

A low-voltage thermostat like the one shown here receives power from a transformer, much like that for a door chime. The transformer is typically located on or near the heating or cooling unit. Replace the transformer if it does not deliver power *(pages 73–74)*. In a typical setup, two wires control the heater and two control the air conditioner. If there are more wires, consult a heating and cooling pro.

PRESTART CHECKLIST

☐ **TIME**
Less than an hour for most repairs

☐ **TOOLS**
Screwdriver, soft brush, strippers

☐ **SKILLS**
Stripping wire; making connections

☐ **MATERIALS**
Short length of thin-gauge wire, perhaps a replacement thermostat or transformer

Inner cover   Contact

1 On a low-voltage thermostat, pull off the outer cover and loosen screws to remove the inner cover. Clean away dust with a soft brush. Gently lift the control lever and clean the contact beneath it. Replace the covers and test.

2 If it still doesn't work, test for power. Strip the ends of a short wire and touch the terminals marked W and R. If they spark and the heating unit comes on, the thermostat is broken and should be replaced. If nothing happens, check the transformer *(page 73)*.

WHAT IF ...
The room temperature is far different from the setting?

If the thermostat is sending the wrong message to the heating unit or air conditioner, it may be out of plumb. Use a string with a small weight near the two alignment marks. If they do not line up, loosen the mounting screws and twist the thermostat.

STANLEY PRO TIP

Installing a new thermostat

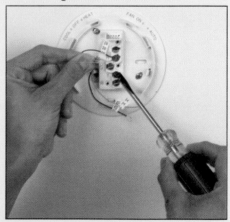

Replacing a thermostat is not difficult. Tag the wires before removing the old unit. Make sure the new thermostat is plumb (see box at left) and drive mounting screws. Attach the wires, inner cover, and outer cover.

SWITCHES & RECEPTACLES

It's not unusual for a switch to be flipped on and off tens of thousands of times before it malfunctions—pretty good for a device that may cost less than a dollar. When one wears out, replacing it is a simple job.

This chapter shows how to replace a standard single-pole switch and presents other switches that meet the needs of special situations. These handy devices, such as dimmers and motion-sensor switches, are just as easy to install as a standard switch.

Receptacles have no moving parts and can last even longer than switches, provided they are not abused. Replacing one is just as easy as putting in a switch.

Always turn the power off and test a receptacle for power before you remove the cover plate. Once the box is open, test again for power *(page 46)*. See *pages 36–37* to learn how to safely open boxes to access a switch or receptacle.

Use the tools and skills shown in the previous chapters. To complete these projects, you should be able to strip wire insulation, splice wires, and connect wire ends to terminals.

Working in a box
Wires inside a box may be short, and space may be tight. Pull out the device and straighten the wires to make working in the box easier. Take your time. A mistake could force you to cut a wire for a second or third time, making it even shorter. If you do need to lengthen a wire, use a pigtail *(page 79)*.

After you have pulled a device out of a box, examine the wiring before you loosen terminal screws. If you do not understand the wiring, you may find it explained on *pages 21 or 43*. If the wiring is complicated, tag each wire as you unhook it with a piece of tape that tells you where it should be reattached. Work methodically to ensure a safe and successful installation. Call in a professional if you are still confused.

Replacing and upgrading switches and receptacles call for just a few simple skills.

CHAPTER PREVIEW

Problems with cover plates
page 78

Replacing single-pole switches
page 79

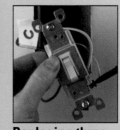
Replacing three-way switches
page 80

Installing a dimmer switch
page 81

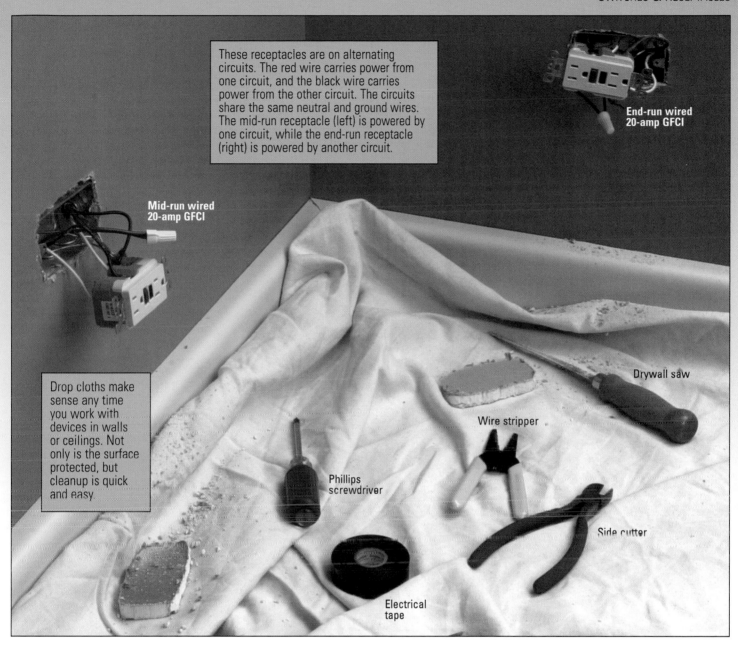

These receptacles are on alternating circuits. The red wire carries power from one circuit, and the black wire carries power from the other circuit. The circuits share the same neutral and ground wires. The mid-run receptacle (left) is powered by one circuit, while the end-run receptacle (right) is powered by another circuit.

End-run wired 20-amp GFCI

Mid-run wired 20-amp GFCI

Drop cloths make sense any time you work with devices in walls or ceilings. Not only is the surface protected, but cleanup is quick and easy.

Drywall saw

Wire stripper

Phillips screwdriver

Side cutter

Electrical tape

Special-duty switches
page 82

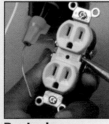

Combination switches
page 84

Replacing a receptacle
page 85

GFCI protection
page 86

Surge protection
page 87

Raceway wiring
page 88

PROBLEMS WITH COVER PLATES

Cover plates are the last line of defense between human hands and live wires. A cracked (or ugly) plate is quickly replaced, and it only takes a few minutes to straighten a device that is out of plumb. (Use a torpedo level if you don't trust your ability to eyeball it.)

Cover plates are available in many styles and can be made of plastic, wood, metal, glass, and ceramic. Cost varies according to style and material, but even a plain, inexpensive plate can be easily dressed up.

One option is paint. With the cover plate installed, use a roller that is slightly damp with paint, so paint does not seep into the receptacle slots.

It is also possible to wrap a cover plate with wallpaper or a small art reproduction.

PRESTART CHECKLIST

☐ **TIME**
About 10 minutes to adjust or replace a cover plate

☐ **TOOLS**
Screwdriver with a small slot head, drill, level

☐ **PREP**
Lay a towel or small drop cloth on the surface below the device

☐ **MATERIALS**
Have on hand plenty of receptacle and switch cover plates—they're inexpensive

Phillips screwdriver

1 If a cover plate is crooked or doesn't cover the wall completely, note which direction it needs to move. **Shut off power to the circuit** and remove the plate. (A receptacle is shown here, but this will also work with switch plates.)

2 Loosen the screws that hold the device to the box. Slide the device until it is plumb, tighten the screws, and place the cover plate on. (If you have a small level, hold it firmly against the device to check its alignment.)

Oversize plates

If a standard–size cover plate cannot cover damage to a wall, a slightly oversized plate may do the trick.

Oversize

Normal size

WHAT IF...
A box needs straightening?

Occasionally a box may be so out of plumb that you cannot straighten the device. To straighten it, **shut off the power** and pull the device off to the side. Drill a hole in the side of the box and drive a drywall screw through the hole and into a nearby stud. Be careful not to nick any wires.

REPLACING SINGLE-POLE SWITCHES

If a switch fails to turn on a light, or if its toggle feels loose, replace it.

A single-pole switch is the most common type of switch. It has two terminals (not counting the ground), and its toggle is marked with ON and OFF. If three wires attach to it (not counting the ground), it's a three-way switch: see *page 80* for more on those.

Replace a single-pole with an exact match, or install a dimmer or special switch *(pages 81–83)*.

PRESTART CHECKLIST

☐ **TIME**
About 20 minutes to replace a single-pole switch

☐ **TOOLS**
Screwdriver, strippers, side cutters, long-nose pliers, voltage tester

☐ **SKILLS**
Stripping wires and fastening them to a terminal

☐ **PREP**
Lay a towel or small drop cloth on the surface below the switch

1 **Shut off power to the circuit** so that the switch cannot turn the light on. Remove the cover plate. Unscrew and pull the switch out gently. Test to make sure there is no power in the box.

2 Check the wires and terminals. If they look like they've been handled before, cut and restrip. Otherwise loosen the terminal screws and pull off the wires.

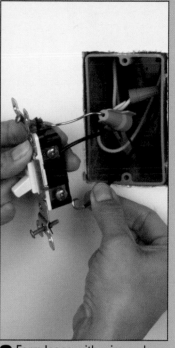

3 Form loops with wire ends, wrap clockwise around terminals, and tighten screws. Wrap device with electrician's tape to cover terminal screws and any bare wire. Reinstall switch and cover plate.

REFRESHER COURSE
Cut and restrip wire ends

1 To make sure a wire won't break after being bent several times, cut off the bare end using a stripper or side cutters.

2 Place the wire in the proper size hole on the strippers, give a slight twist and slide the insulation off. Bend the wire into a loop.

STANLEY PRO TIP

Pigtail short wires

If the feed wires in the box aren't long enough to easily connect a device, don't try to pull more slack into the box—you might damage the wires. Instead make a pigtail—a 6-inch-long wire stripped at both ends *(page 51)*. Splice one end to the incoming wire and connect the other end to the terminal.

Ensure grounding: If your system has metal boxes and no ground wire so that sheathing acts as the ground *(page 42)*, remove the little cardboard or plastic washers from screws to make a firm contact between the device and the box.

Testing
To test for power, see *pages 46–47*. To attach wires to terminals, see *pages 50–51*.

REPLACING THREE-WAY SWITCHES

If a switch does not have ON and OFF written on its toggle and has three terminals (not counting the ground), it is a three-way. Two three-way switches can control the same fixture. With a three-way switch, you may turn the light on or off by flipping the toggle either up or down.

If one or both of a pair of three-ways fails to control the light, replace the faulty switch or switches. If the toggle is wobbly, replace the switch.

If you keep track of which wire goes where, replacing a three-way is not much more difficult than replacing a single-pole switch *(page 79)*. If you forget to tag the wires, however, the proper connections can be difficult to figure out.

PRESTART CHECKLIST

☐ **TIME**
About 25 minutes if you remember to tag the wires; possibly much longer if you forget

☐ **TOOLS**
Screwdriver, side cutters, voltage tester, strippers, long-nose pliers

☐ **SKILLS**
Stripping wires and joining them to terminals

☐ **PREP**
Lay a towel or small drop cloth on the surface below the switch

☐ **MATERIALS**
One or two three-way switches, wire and wire nuts for pigtails, electrician's tape

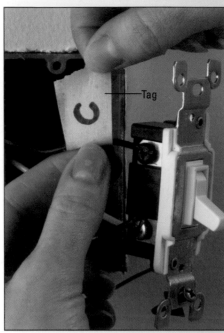

Tag

1 **Shut off power,** remove the cover plate, pull out the switch, and **test for power** *(page 46).* A three-way switch has a common terminal, a different color than the other two traveler terminals. Tag the wire that connects to the common terminal.

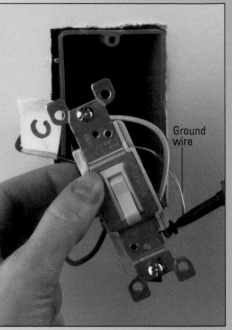

Ground wire

2 Cut and restrip wire ends *(page 69)* and form them into loops. Connect the ground wire. Connect the tagged wire to the common terminal and the other two wires to the traveler terminals (it doesn't matter which wire goes to which traveler terminal).

STANLEY PRO TIP

If you forget to tag wires

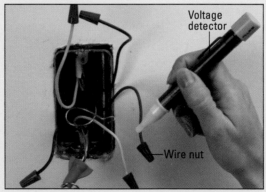

Voltage detector

Wire nut

Separate all the wires and place a wire nut on the end of each. Restore power to the circuit. Use a voltage detector to find out which wire is hot. If none is hot, flip the toggle on the other three-way switch and check again. **Shut off power.** Connect the hot wire to the common terminal and the other two wires to the other two terminals.

WHAT IF...
It's a four-way switch?

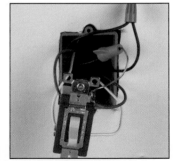

If three switches control the same fixture, two are three-ways and one is a four-way switch. A four-way has four terminals (plus a ground). Before removing the switch, tag each wire. Two wires connect to input terminals; two to output terminals. If the wires aren't tagged, it will take a pro to hook up the switch.

INSTALLING A DIMMER SWITCH

In addition to the common rotary dimmer, you can opt for a sliding dimmer like the one shown here or a dimmer that looks like a toggle switch.

Do not use a standard dimmer switch for a ceiling fan—you'll not only damage the fan, but the switch as well. Instead install a dimmer made specifically for fans. If two three-way switches control a fixture, you can replace only one of them with a three-way dimmer switch.

Cut and restrip wire ends before splicing them to the new switch (page 69).

PRESTART CHECKLIST

☐ **TIME**
About 20 minutes to replace a single-pole switch with a dimmer switch

☐ **TOOLS**
Screwdriver, side cutters, voltage tester, lineman's pliers, strippers

☐ **SKILLS**
Stripping and splicing stranded wire to solid wire

☐ **PREP**
Lay a towel or small drop cloth on the surface below the switch

☐ **MATERIALS**
Dimmer switch, wire for pigtails, wire nuts (they may come with the switch), electrician's tape

1 **Shut off power to the circuit.** Remove the cover plate, pull the switch out, and **test to make sure there is no power** (page 46). Loosen the terminal screws and remove the wires. Cut and restrip the wires.

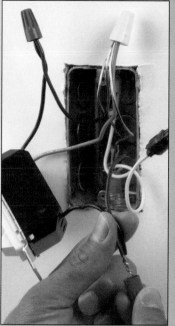

2 If two cables enter the box, connect the grounds. Splice the white wires together. Splice each black lead to each black wire. One cable entering the box indicates it is at the end of the circuit.

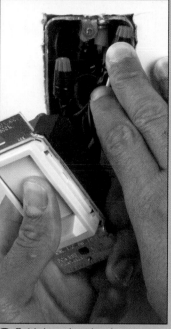

3 Fold the wires back as you push the dimmer into the box. It is bulkier than a regular switch, so the box may be a little crowded.

WHAT IF ...
A three-way dimmer is needed

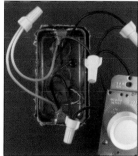

You can use a three-way dimmer for one of the switches—the other must be a toggle. Wire a dimmer as you would a regular switch, except splice wires rather than connecting to terminals.

ONE CABLE
End-line wiring

If only one cable enters the box, splice one lead to the black wire and one lead to the white wire (which should be marked with black).

STANLEY PRO TIP

Handle the wattage

An inexpensive dimmer switch that is rated for 600 watts can handle most ceiling fixtures. However, if that switch will control a large chandelier, add up the watts of all the bulbs; you may need a switch with a higher wattage rating.

SPECIAL-DUTY SWITCHES

The simplest way to improve a home's lighting is to install a switch that does more than turn the lights on and off. This project is usually no more complicated than installing a standard switch.

Examine a switch carefully before buying it. Some special-duty switches are available as three-ways (page 80) and can be installed only if you have two cables entering the switch box (see Pro Tip on opposite page).

Installing a special switch is similar to installing a dimmer (page 81). **Shut off power to the circuit before removing the switch.** Connect the switch's ground wire to the house ground. To be sure that wires will not break after being rebent, cut and restrip all wire ends before you connect them to the new switch (page 69).

PRESTART CHECKLIST

☐ **TIME**
About 25 minutes to remove an existing switch and install a special switch

☐ **TOOLS**
Screwdriver, side cutters, strippers

☐ **SKILLS**
Stripping wire; splicing stranded to solid wire

☐ **PREP**
Lay a towel or small drop cloth on the surface below the switch

☐ **MATERIALS**
Special-duty switch, wire nuts (they may come with the switch), electrician's tape

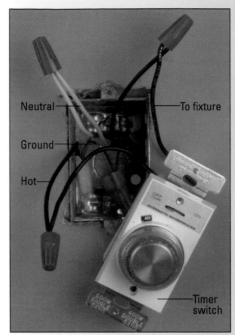

Timer switch: A timer switch turns lights on and off once a day. Most commonly it is used for outdoor lights. Connect the grounds and splice the neutral (white) wires to the white lead. Splice each black lead to a black wire.

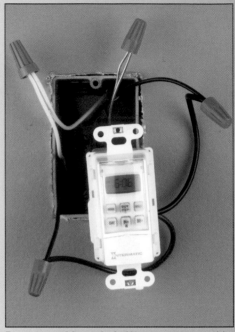

Programmable switch: Use a programmable switch to turn lights on and off more than once a day. It can fool a potential robber into thinking people are at home while they are away on vacation. Wire this switch just as you would a dimmer switch (page 81).

Remote-control switch

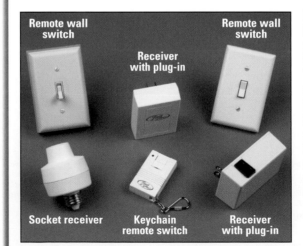

If you have a fixture controlled by a pull-chain switch and would rather use a wall switch, consider installing one of these devices. They operate by remote control, so you don't have to run cable through walls. To install one, open the fixture and wire the receiving unit, following the manufacturer's instructions. Put a battery in the sending unit, which contains the switch. Mount it anywhere on the wall.

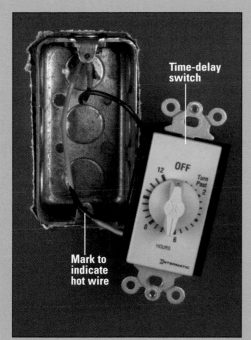

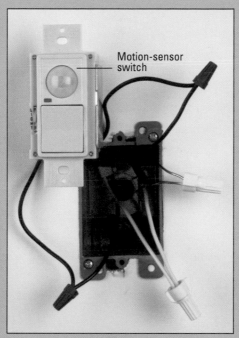

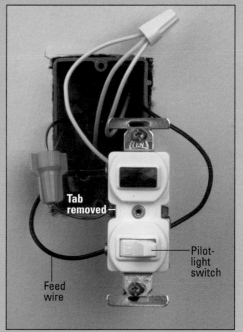

Time-delay switch: With a time-delay switch, crank the dial to turn the fixture on and set it to turn off after a specified time. This is useful for fixtures that are risky or expensive to run—a bathroom vent fan or a space heater, for instance. Wire it as you would a dimmer switch *(page 81)*.

Motion-sensor switch: A motion-sensor switch turns its light on when it senses movement in the area, then turns the light off after a specified time. (Some models allow you to determine how long the light stays on.) Wire it as you would a dimmer switch *(page 81)*.

Pilot-light switch: A pilot-light switch has a small bulb that glows when the device, such as a fan, is turned on. Connect the white wires to the silver terminal (you may need a pigtail) and connect the grounds. Attach the feed wire to the brass terminal without a connecting tab and connect the other black wire to the other brass terminal.

STANLEY PRO TIP

Some switches need two cables in the box

There are two ways to wire a switch *(page 43):* Through-switch wiring brings power into the switch box and then out to the fixture. End-line wiring brings power to the fixture; a single cable runs from the fixture to the switch box, and the white wire should be marked black. If a switch has more than two leads, it can be installed only if two cables enter the box.

Other switches

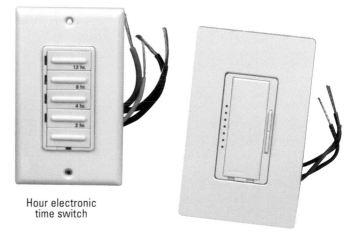

Plug-in timer

Hour electronic time switch

Touch-control dimmer

Browse the electrical department of a home center to find even more special-duty switches. A plug-in timer (left) turns a floor or table lamp on and off at set times. A 20-amp hour timer switch (center) lets you run an attic fan or pool filter motor for 2, 4, 8, or 12 hours. A touch-control dimmer (right) turns the light up, down, on, or off with the tap of a finger.

COMBINATION SWITCHES

These devices combine two functions. Correctly installed, they are just as safe as two individual switches.

Combination switches are always installed with through-switch wiring and never with end-line wiring. That means you will find two or three cables entering the box *(page 43)*.

Before removing a malfunctioning special switch, tag the wires—and the old switch as well—so you can remember exactly where each wire goes. Purchase a switch to match the old one; ask a salesperson if you are not sure.

Shut off power to the circuit before removing the old switch. To be sure that rebent wires will not break, cut and restrip the wire ends before you connect them.

PRESTART CHECKLIST

☐ **TIME**
About 30 minutes to remove an old combination switch and replace it

☐ **TOOLS**
Screwdriver, side cutters, strippers, long-nose pliers

☐ **SKILLS**
Stripping wire; connecting wire to terminals

☐ **PREP**
Lay a towel or small drop cloth on the surface below the switch

☐ **MATERIALS**
Combination switch, electrician's tape, wire for pigtails

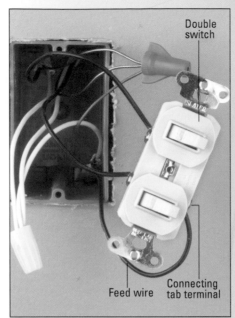

Double switch: Squeeze two switches into the space of one. Three cables enter the box: one brings power, the other two run to separate fixtures. Connect the grounds and splice all the neutral (white) wires together. Attach the feed wire to a terminal with the connecting tab. Connect the other two black wires to terminals on the side with no tab.

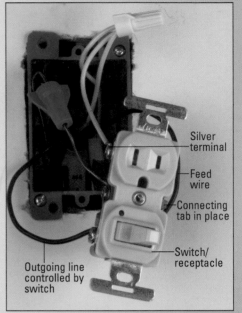

Unswitched plug: To make the plug always hot (not controlled by the switch) on a switch/receptacle, start by connecting the grounds. Attach a white pigtail to the silver terminal and splice all the neutral (white) wires together. Connect the feed wire to a terminal with the connecting tab. Screw the other black wire onto the brass terminal on the side with no connecting tab.

WHAT IF ...
A switch controls a receptacle?

To have a middle-of-the-run receptacle controlled by the switch, connect the grounds. Make a white pigtail and connect it to a chrome terminal on the side of the device that doesn't have a connecting tab. Splice all the white wires together. Attach the black feed wire to the brass terminal that is not attached to the connecting tab. Attach the outgoing black wire to one of the black terminal screws next to the connecting tab.

Feed wire
This is the wire (usually black or red) that brings power into the box.

Grounding
For information on connecting ground wires, see *page 42*.

REPLACING A RECEPTACLE

A new receptacle is inexpensive and easy to install, so don't hesitate to replace one that is cracked or caked with paint. If a receptacle fails to deliver power, **shut off power to the circuit,** pull the receptacle out, and make sure all the wires are firmly connected to its terminals.

Install a grounded (three-hole) receptacle only if it will be connected to ground *(page 42)*. If the wires connected to it are #14, install a 15-amp receptacle; if the wires are #12, install a 20-amp model.

If wiring is complicated, tag wires with pieces of tape to make clear which wire goes where.

PRESTART CHECKLIST

☐ **TIME**
About 30 minutes to remove an old receptacle and install a new one

☐ **TOOLS**
Screwdriver, side cutters, strippers, long-nose pliers

☐ **SKILLS**
Stripping wires and joining them to terminals

☐ **PREP**
Lay a towel or small drop cloth on the surface below the receptacle

☐ **MATERIALS**
Receptacle, electrician's tape

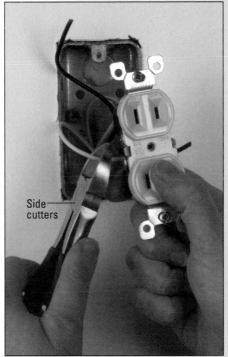

Side cutters

1 **Shut off power to the circuit.** Remove the cover plate and the mounting screws, and gently pull out the old receptacle *(pages 36–37)*. **Test for power.** Loosen the terminal screws and remove wires, or use side cutters to cut the wires.

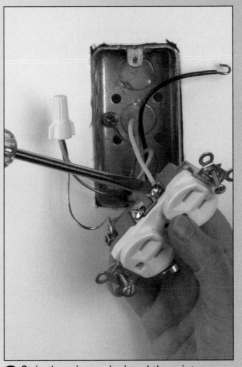

2 Strip the wire ends, bend them into loops, and connect them to the terminal screws. Connect the hot (black or colored) wires to brass terminals and the neutral (white) wires to silver terminals. Connect the grounds.

Spec-rated receptacles

Most homeowners turn to the bargain bin for their receptacles. Those work just fine. But if a receptacle often gets bumped, or if people yank on cords when pulling plugs out, consider upgrading to a spec-rated (commercial) receptacle.

Making connections
For tips on connecting wires to terminals, see *pages 50–51*.

WHAT IF...
A receptacle is on two circuits?

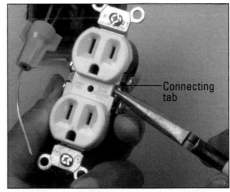

Connecting tab

If more than two wires connect to a receptacle, look at the tab that connects the two hot (brass) terminals. If it is broken off, the receptacle is split, meaning either that it is on two circuits or that one half is switched *(page 43)*. Break off the tab on the replacement receptacle before wiring it.

GFCI PROTECTION

If electricity goes astray (as in a shock or a short), there will almost always be a change in the flow of current between the hot and neutral wires. A ground fault circuit interrupter (GFCI) shuts itself down immediately upon sensing any such change. Install a GFCI wherever a receptacle might get wet, such as in a bathroom, near a kitchen counter, or outdoors.

Note that GFCIs can malfunction so that they provide power but not safety. To make sure one is still protecting you, check it at least once a month by pushing the "test" button.

PRESTART CHECKLIST

☐ **TIME**
About 25 minutes to remove a receptacle and install a GFCI

☐ **TOOLS**
Screwdriver, side cutters, strippers

☐ **SKILLS**
Stripping and splicing wire

☐ **PREP**
Lay a towel or small drop cloth on the surface below the receptacle

☐ **MATERIALS**
GFCI receptacle, wire nuts, electrician's tape

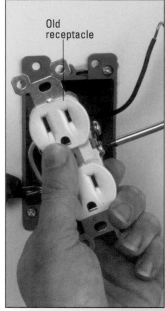

Old receptacle

1 **Shut off power to the circuit.** Remove the cover plate, pull the receptacle out, and **test for power** (pages 36–37). Cut and restrip the wire ends (page 69).

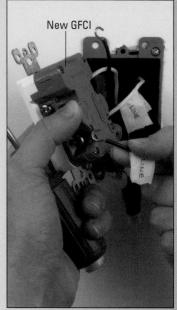

New GFCI

2 If you wire a GFCI into the middle of a circuit, all the receptacles down the line will also be protected by it. Connect the wires that bring power into the box to the LINE terminals and the wires that go out from the box to other receptacles to the LOAD terminals.

3 Wrap the device with tape and push it back into the box. Because a GFCI is bulkier than a standard receptacle, take extra care folding the wires into the box behind it.

WHAT IF...
Only one receptacle needs protection?

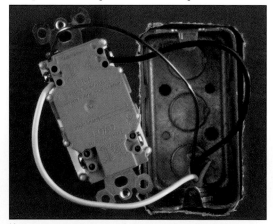

If you want to protect only one receptacle and not others down the line, connect only to the LINE terminals. If the receptacle is in the middle of the run (page 43), add bypassing pigtails (page 51) to feed the other receptacles.

STANLEY PRO TIP

Finding LINE and LOAD wires

To protect all the receptacles on a circuit, install a GFCI at the beginning of the circuit run (pages 27). If you don't know which wires bring power into the box and which lead to other receptacles, remove the wires, spread them out so they do not touch each other, and cap with wire nuts. Restore power and use a voltage tester to find out which is the hot wire. Connect it and its companion neutral wire to the LINE terminals. Connect the other wires to the LOAD terminals.

SURGE PROTECTION

Utilities provide power that generally is steady and constant. Your lights may flicker occasionally due to a drop in power that lasts less than a second. This is normal and does no damage. Less common, the power coming into your house may suddenly increase, or surge, for an extremely short time. This will not damage most electrical components but may harm a computer, modem, or other electronic equipment.

Telephone lines also may carry unwanted current surges. In fact modems are damaged by surges more often than items plugged into household receptacles.

A surge arrester senses any increase in voltage and directs it to the ground wire so it can flow harmlessly into the earth. Surge protection works only if your household electrical system is grounded *(page 26)*.

For most homes, all that's needed is a good quality plug-in surge protector (also called an arrester or suppressor) or two. For your office, choose a protector that includes a phone connection to safeguard the modem. If you have state-of-the-art audio/visual equipment, plug those components into a surge protector as well.

Lightning protection

In rural areas, houses can sometimes be damaged by lightning. The devices shown here will not protect your electrical system against a lightning strike. Consult with a local electrical contractor to see if you should install lightning protection.

A bolt of lightning hitting your house can cause a fire. For protection, install a lightning rod mounted on the roof, fastened to a wire that runs into the ground. When a bolt of lightning strikes the house, the rod directs much of the power into the earth.

If lightning strikes overhead power lines near your house, the burst of power can fry your service panel or house wires and fixtures. Surge arresters mounted in the service panel are designed to direct excess voltage to the house ground. Consult with contractors and your local building department to see if a device like this could make your home safer.

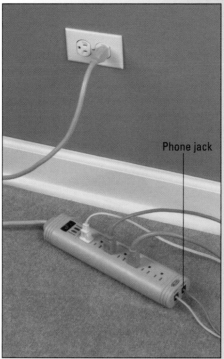

Phone jack

Simple protection: A simple power strip like this not only protects against surges, but also makes it easy to organize your cords.

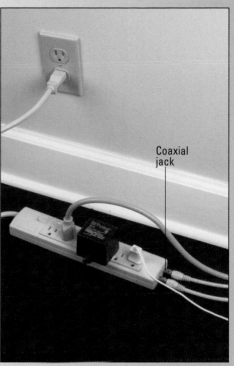

Coaxial jack

Protect a TV: This surge protector has a coaxial jack to protect a TV from a surge through the cable.

Whole-house surge protector

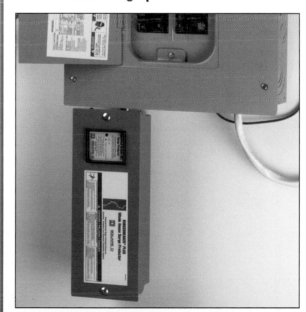

To protect all receptacles and lights from surges, have a whole-house surge protector installed. It is wired directly into the service panel.

Fully protecting an electrical system from a direct lightning strike is not possible. However, this device may keep your wires from harm since lightning damage is not usually caused by direct strikes. It will help protect sensitive electronic equipment from damage due to a power surge traveling through local service lines.

RACEWAY WIRING

If you need a new receptacle or a new light and switch, the usual procedure is to run cable inside walls. That is a complicated, messy job. In fact cutting and patching walls takes much more time than the wiring. Wall-mounted raceway wiring eliminates that trouble. The drawback to raceway wiring is the unsightly channel mounted on the wall. If used in a living area, however, raceway can be hidden behind furnishings.

Planning the job

Choose plastic raceway (as shown here) or metal raceway, which can be painted. Have a salesperson help you assemble all the raceway parts you need: a starter box, channel, clips, cover plates, and elbows if you need to turn a corner. You'll also need enough black, white, and green wire for the length of your run. Use #14 wire for a 15-amp circuit and #12 wire for a 20-amp circuit.

PRESTART CHECKLIST

☐ **TIME**
About three hours to install two new receptacles

☐ **TOOLS**
Drill, screwdriver, level, strippers, side cutters, hacksaw, lineman's pliers

☐ **SKILLS**
Stripping, splicing, and connecting wires to a terminal; cutting metal or plastic channel; driving screws into a wall

☐ **PREP**
Spread drop cloths on the floor

☐ **MATERIALS**
Raceway components, plastic anchors, wire nuts, electrician's tape, screws

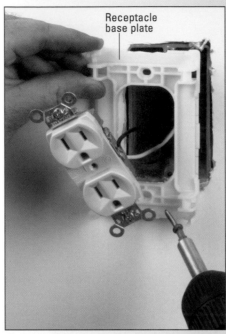

1 **Shut off power** to the circuit and pull out the existing receptacle (pages 36–37). **Test for power.** Screw the base plate to the electrical box.

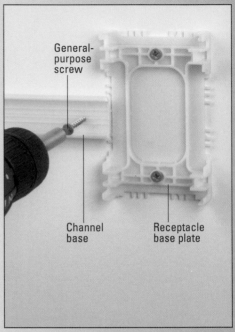

2 Attach receptacle base plates wherever you want a new receptacle. With a hacksaw, cut pieces of channel to fit between the plates. Screw them to the wall. Where possible, drive screws into studs for solid mounting; otherwise, use plastic anchors to attach screws to wallboard.

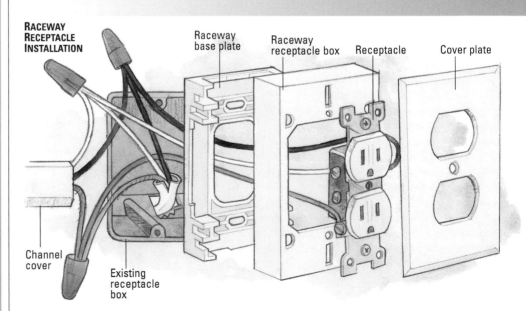

Raceway components include a starter box, receptacle box, channel, and clips. Use green-insulated wire for the ground.

Do your codes allow raceway?
Check your local building codes to see whether raceway is permitted. You may be required to use metal rather than plastic parts.

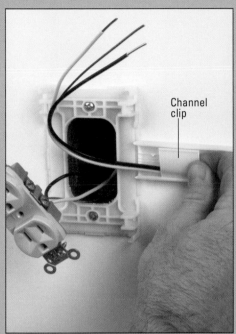

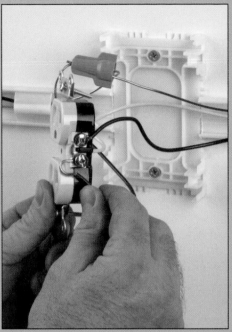

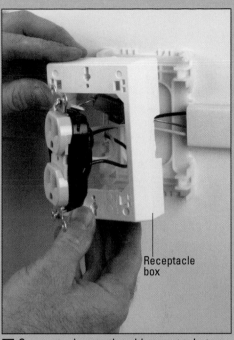

Channel clip

Receptacle box

3 Insert black, white, and green wire into the channels and secure them with the clips provided. Leave about 8 inches of wire at each receptacle box or starter box.

4 Connect wires to the new receptacles—black wires to brass terminals, white wires to silver terminals, and green wires to ground.

5 Connect wires to the old receptacle to supply power. Snap on the covers for the channel. Attach the covers for the new receptacle boxes and install cover plates.

Metal raceway

Metal components cost a bit more, but they withstand more abuse than plastic, and they can be painted. Install the parts on the wall, then push wires through the channels.

Stripping and joining
For tips on stripping and joining wires, see *pages 48–51.*

SUPPLY POWER
Options for connecting to existing wires

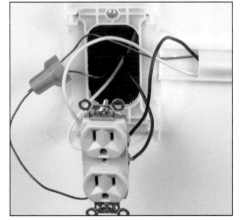

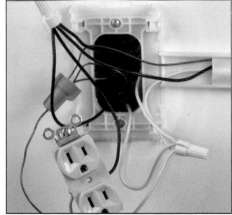

End-of-run: If the existing receptacle is at the end of a run *(page 43),* connect the raceway wiring to the two open terminals—black to the brass terminal, white to the silver terminal. Pigtail the ground *(page 42).*

Middle-of-run: If the existing receptacle is in the middle of a run *(page 43),* remove wires from two of the terminals and connect to terminals with pigtails, as shown.

LIGHTS & FANS

No matter how old your electrical system, it is always possible—and usually easy—to remove an old wall or ceiling fixture and install a new one. A new fixture can dramatically change the appearance of a room. You can replace a ceiling light with a plain light, a chandelier, track lighting, or even a ceiling fan. See *pages 92–93* for more lighting options.

Mounting hardware
If your home was built after World War II, attaching a new fixture will be easy. Mounting hardware has changed little, and the new fixture should come with all the parts you need. Simply attach a strap to the ceiling box, and perhaps a center stud as well. Splice the wires, screw the fixture to the strap or the stud, and you are done.

If you have an older home, the old fastening hardware may not line up with the new fixture. Fortunately home centers carry adapters to solve this problem.

If the new fixture's canopy (the part that snugs up to the ceiling) is smaller than the old one, you may have to paint or patch the ceiling. A medallion *(page 95)* can hide the problem and save work.

Installing a ceiling fan or a heavy chandelier calls for removing the electrical box and installing a heavy-duty "fan-rated" box *(pages 102–103)*.

Wiring a light or fan
Shut off power before removing an existing fixture. Test the box for power after removing the fixture *(pages 7, 46)*. To ensure a conductive and long-lasting splice, cut and restrip old wire ends *(page 69)* before joining them to the stranded leads *(page 49)* of new fixtures.

Wiring a light or fan is straightforward: Splice white lead to white wire, black to black, and connect the grounds. Installing a new fixture where there was none before is more involved and best left to a professional electrician or someone with experience running new cable. Running cable through walls is a time-consuming and complicated task.

Installing a new light fixture is an easy way to make a dramatic change in any room.

CHAPTER PREVIEW

Choosing lights
page 92

Installing flush-mounted lights
page 94

Installing fluorescents
page 96

Installing pendant lights
page 98

Wall lights are wired just like ceiling lights, only the mounting hardware differs. A center stud or a swivel strap allows the light to be adjusted so it is plumb. Outdoor fixtures have foam or rubber gaskets to seal out moisture.

To avoid straining the wires, cut and bend a coat hanger to support the fixture while you attach the wires.

Replacing a light fixture is an easy upgrade that usually takes no more than an hour or two. A porch light is no exception. Shut off power. Work on a stable ladder if the fixture is out of reach.

Installing track lights
page 99

Installing a ceiling fan box
page 102

Attaching a ceiling fan
page 104

Adding under-cabinet lights
page 107

Installing Euro-style lights
page 109

Adding a porch light
page 111

CHOOSING LIGHTS

A light fixture's packaging tells how high in wattage the bulb or bulbs can be. Installing bulbs of higher wattage will damage the fixture, and the bulbs will burn out quickly.

An existing light may seem adequate, but often a room benefits from a brighter light. Buy a new fixture that provides more light than the old one. Install bulbs of lower wattage if it turns out to be too bright.

In living and dining rooms, you may want bright light at some times, and a mellow effect at other times. If so, install a dimmer switch *(page 81)*.

Canopies to cover
After removing an old fixture, measure its canopy—the part that attaches to the ceiling. If the new fixture has a smaller canopy, you will have to paint and maybe patch the ceiling. Or you may purchase a medallion, a round decorative piece that covers up ceiling imperfections *(page 95)*.

Pendant lights
The lower a light hangs down, the more attention it commands and the more focused its light becomes. Most pendant lights hang by chains; the lamp cord runs through the links to the fixture. Some modern versions have a decorative cable, and some use a pipe, through which the cord runs. A pendant light may be a chandelier with many arms and bulbs, or it may have a single bulb surrounded by a shade or a globe.

Chandeliers have numerous bulbs, often encased in decorative glass. A chandelier that hangs over a dining room table should be a foot or so narrower than the table and hang about 3 feet above the table. Control a chandelier with a dimmer switch to achieve both brilliant and subdued effects.

If you don't like the look of newer style chandeliers, seek out a dealer who specializes in refurbishing old fixtures. An older chandelier that is completely rewired will be as reliable as a new unit.

A one-piece pendant light is often used in an entryway. Hang it in the center of the room, at least 6½ feet from the floor, so people won't bump their heads.

A pendant light with a shade directs most of its light at a table or counter directly

Lantern-shaped pendant

Globe pendant

Chandelier

below, although it can also provide general illumination if the shade is translucent. A small fixture can be hung as low as 24 inches above a tabletop. Just make sure the bulb will not shine directly into people's eyes when they are seated at the table.

Flush-mounted lights
A flush-mounted light fastens against the ceiling or wall. A ceiling-hugging fixture in the middle of a room may be all that is needed to light a bedroom or small dining room. Wall-mounted fixtures are ideal for illuminating bathrooms, especially near a vanity mirror. Sconces work well in hallways.

Most flush-mounted fixtures use standard incandescent bulbs, but energy-saving fluorescents and halogens are available. A "semiflush" fixture hangs down a few inches and casts light upwards at the ceiling, for a more even distribution of light.

If you cannot find a light fixture that is both pleasing and affordable, the best choice

Over-mirror fixture

Swivel halogen lamp

Semiflush-mounted fixture

Flush-mounted fixture

Wall sconce

Decorative wall sconce

Two-light wall sconce

may be to buy an inexpensive flush-mounted fixture and paint its canopy to match your ceiling color.

Sconces and other wall-mounted fixtures install much like ceiling lights, except they mount on a wall. Such fixtures typically attach to a box, using a strap and nipple (page 95) so they can be leveled easily.

If a sconce will be mounted less than 7 feet above the floor, purchase one that doesn't stick out too far from the wall. Some sconces shine upward and provide ambient lighting; others point out or down

to illuminate stairs or provide subtle lighting in a hallway.

Other types
Sleek fixtures that hang from wires or twist in whimsical shapes add a contemporary look. They use low-voltage halogen bulbs, which save energy but get very hot.

In addition to the lights shown here, consider fluorescent (pages 96–97) and track lighting (pages 99–101). To light the area in or under a cabinet, see pages 107–108.

Recessed canisters need new cable
In some cases a recessed canister light can replace a single fixture. Typically, though, canisters are installed in a series. That means running new cable through walls and ceilings—an advanced procedure best left to the pros or experienced do-it-yourselfers.

INSTALLING FLUSH-MOUNTED LIGHTS

Replacing a ceiling fixture is a simple job. The hardware that held the old fixture typically can be reused to attach the new. If not, a new fixture most often comes with all the hardware needed to install it.

When buying a fixture, make sure it is designed to provide the amount of light you want in a room. Compare its wattage with the old fixture. Don't install bulbs that exceed recommendations, or you will dangerously overheat the fixture and its box. Choose a fixture with a canopy large enough to cover any imperfections in the ceiling, or use a medallion *(page 95)*.

If possible, ground the new fixture. If it is being installed in a metal box, connect the fixture ground lead to the box and to the house ground wire. Check local building codes. Wires in a ceiling box may have cracked or brittle insulation due to overheating. See *page 69* to repair them.

PRESTART CHECKLIST

☐ **TIME**
About half an hour to remove a fixture and install a replacement, as long as there are no problems with the hardware

☐ **TOOLS**
Screwdriver, strippers, side cutters, voltage tester, ladder

☐ **SKILLS**
Stripping wire; splicing stranded wire to solid wire

☐ **PREP**
Spread a drop cloth on the floor below; set up a stable, nonconductive ladder

☐ **MATERIALS**
Replacement fixture, wire nuts (the ones that come with the fixture may be too small), electrician's tape

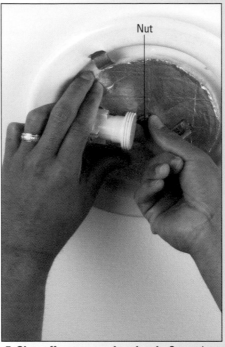

1 **Shut off power to the circuit.** Open the fixture *(page 37)*. Remove the nut or screws holding the fixture to the box and pull the fixture down. Remove the wire nuts and **check for power in the box** *(page 46)*. Pull the leads off the house wires and remove the fixture.

2 If the existing mounting hardware will not fit the new fixture, or if it doesn't have a grounding screw, remove it and attach a new strap to the box.

STANLEY PRO TIP: **Attaching to older boxes**

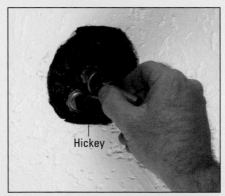

An older "pancake" box like this may have a ⅜-inch pipe running through the middle. To install a center-mount or pendant fixture, use a hickey, which has two sets of threads, one for the pipe attached to the pancake box and the other for a center stud. A hickey is helpful for wiring chandeliers because it has an opening through which a cord can run.

If the pipe protrudes too far, purchase a mounting strap with a hole large enough to accommodate the pipe. Or attach the strap off center by drilling pilot holes in the box and driving sheet-metal screws through the slots in the strap and into the box. However, make sure the fixture's canopy is large enough to cover the box.

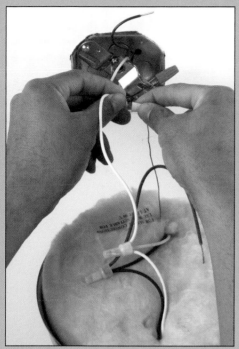

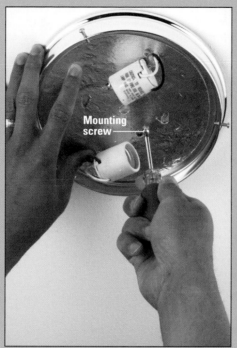

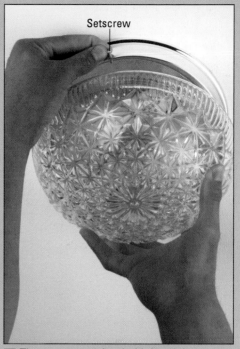

3 If the fixture is heavy, support it with a coat hanger wire while you work *(page 91)*. Connect the ground wire. Splice white lead to white wire and black to black. Wrap the wire nuts with electrician's tape. The insulation may be difficult to work around, but don't remove it; it's a safety feature.

4 Fold the wires up into the box. Start one mounting screw, then the other, then tighten them. If the fixture has keyhole-shaped screw holes, attach the screws to the box; slip the fixture over the large holes. Rotate the canopy so the screws fit into the smaller slots, and tighten the screws.

5 The setscrews that hold the globe may already be in the base or may have to be installed. Push the globe to raise the lip above all the setscrews, then hand tighten all the setscrews evenly.

WHAT IF...
The new fixture's canopy doesn't cover the old hole?

If the new canopy is not large enough to cover up holes or unpainted portions of the ceiling—or simply to add a decorative touch—purchase a medallion. Hold it against the ceiling while you wire the fixture. Before tightening the canopy, see that the medallion is centered.

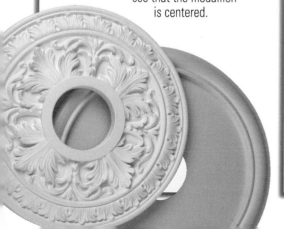

MOUNTING SCREWS
Installing a center-mounted fixture

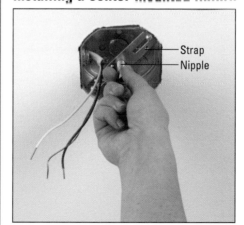

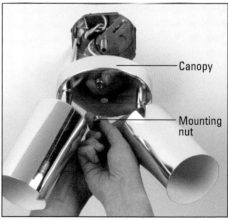

1 Some fixtures mount with a nipple (short threaded pipe) and a nut in the center, rather than two screws. Install a strap and screw in a nipple. If the nipple that comes with the fixture is too short or too long, purchase another one.

2 After wiring the fixture, slide the canopy up so the nipple pokes down through the center hole. Screw on and tighten the mounting nut.

INSTALLING FLUORESCENTS

Fluorescent lighting is inexpensive to run, but the most common tubes produce light that has a cold, industrial feel. For a little more money, buy tubes labeled "warm" or "full spectrum," which produce light that is much more suitable for a home. Adding a translucent lens diffuses the light and reduces the glare.

It is not difficult to replace an incandescent fixture with a fluorescent one. However, if your goal is simply to save energy costs, a simpler solution is to install a fluorescent bulb in an incandescent fixture *(page 56)*.

An existing fluorescent light might have cable running directly into it, with no electrical junction box. That's okay— the fixture's housing is usually considered adequate for protecting spliced wires.

Because fluorescent fixtures are bulky, enlist a helper when removing an old fixture and installing a new one.

PRESTART CHECKLIST

☐ **TIME**
About an hour to remove a fixture and install a new fluorescent

☐ **TOOLS**
Screwdriver, drill, strippers, side cutters, voltage tester, lineman's pliers, ladder

☐ **SKILLS**
Stripping and splicing wires; driving screws

☐ **PREP**
Spread a drop cloth on the floor beneath the light; set up a stable ladder

☐ **MATERIALS**
New fluorescent fixture, wire nuts, screws, electrician's tape

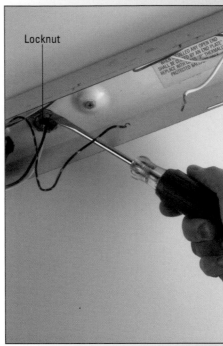

Locknut

1 **Shut off power to the circuit.** Remove the wire nuts and untwist the house wires from the fixture wires (or snip and restrip them—*page 70).* Loosen and remove the locknut that holds the cable clamp to the fixture.

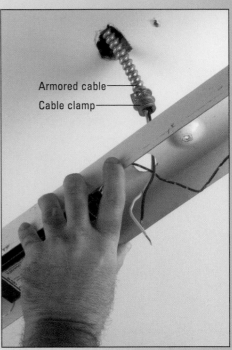

Armored cable
Cable clamp

2 Remove the screws holding the fixture in place—usually there are several driven into ceiling joists. Support the fixture as it comes loose and guide the wires out through the hole. Note the locations of the ceiling joists. Mark the new fixture to line up screws with joists when you install it.

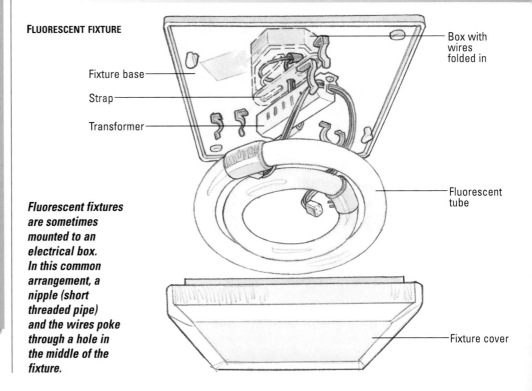

FLUORESCENT FIXTURE

Fixture base

Strap

Transformer

Box with wires folded in

Fluorescent tube

Fixture cover

Fluorescent fixtures are sometimes mounted to an electrical box. In this common arrangement, a nipple (short threaded pipe) and the wires poke through a hole in the middle of the fixture.

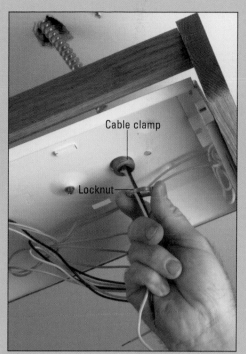

Cable clamp

Locknut

3 With a hammer and screwdriver, punch open a precut knockout hole in the top of the fixture, then twist off the piece with pliers. Thread the wires through the hole and attach the cable clamp to the fixture with the locknut.

4 Have a helper hold the fixture up against the ceiling. Drive the screws into joists.

5 Wire the fixture. Connect the ground wires together and to a grounding screw on the fixture. Splice white fixture wire to white house wire and black to black. Install the fixture tubes and cover.

Circuline fixture

A round fluorescent fixture is usually mounted to a box. Thread the house wires through the hole in the middle and splice them to the fixture wires. Start driving both mounting screws into the electrical box, then tighten.

WHAT IF...
The defective fixture is in a suspended ceiling?

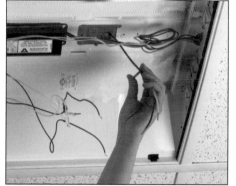

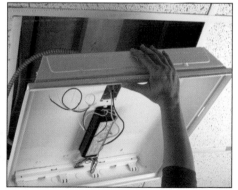

1 To replace a fluorescent fixture in a suspended ceiling, **shut off power to the circuit.** Remove the ceiling panels around the fixture. Remove the diffuser, disconnect the wires, unscrew the locknut, and pull out the cable (Steps 1 and 2 above). With a helper, lift the old fixture out and set the new fixture in place in the ceiling frame.

2 Clamp the cable and splice the wires, as in Steps 3 and 5. Replace the ceiling panels, install tubes, and slip on the diffuser.

INSTALLING PENDANT LIGHTS

Replacing a flush ceiling fixture with a pendant light (chandelier) is usually a simple project. Study the pendant's mounting system before you buy it and make sure you have all the parts you'll need.

To adjust the height of a fixture that hangs by a chain, remove or add links. Use two pairs of pliers to open and close them. On other types, you may need to cut a hanging cable or alter the length of a cord and tighten a locknut.

If the pendant light is heavy, make sure the box is strong enough to hold it; it may require a fan-rated ceiling box *(pages 102–103)*.

PRESTART CHECKLIST

☐ **TIME**
About two hours to remove an existing fixture and install a new pendant fixture

☐ **TOOLS**
Screwdriver, long-nose pliers, strippers, side cutters, lineman's pliers, voltage tester, nonconducting ladder

☐ **SKILLS**
Stripping wire; splicing stranded wire to solid wire

☐ **PREP**
Spread a drop cloth on the floor; set up a stable ladder

☐ **MATERIALS**
New pendant fixture, wire nuts, electrician's tape

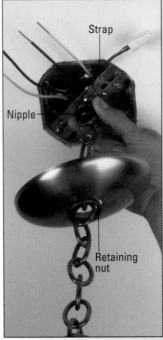

1 **Shut off power to the circuit** and remove the old fixture *(page 94)*. Screw a nipple into a strap so the nipple hangs down about ¾ inch. Screw on the fixture's retaining nut.

2 Thread wires up through the chain. Cut and strip the wire ends. Splice the ribbed wire to the house's white wire and the other wire to the black house wire. Connect the grounds.

3 Fold the wires into the box. Slide the canopy up against the ceiling, and tighten the canopy nut.

STANLEY PRO TIP

All on board?

It's easy to get a pendant fixture installed, only to find a part has been left out. Work carefully and install parts in order. On a fixture with a chain, be sure to slide the canopy onto the chain, then thread the wires all the way through the chain and retaining nut before making electrical connections.

Get the height right
If people will walk under a pendant light, it should be at least 6½ feet high.

WHAT IF...
The fixture has a down rod or retaining ring?

A pendant light with a solid down rod or a round cord typically attaches to the canopy with two hold-down nuts, one on either side of the canopy. The canopy attaches to the box with two screws.

Some lightweight pendant fixtures with chains are not screwed into the box. The chain is secured to the canopy by means of a retaining ring. Nuts attach the canopy to the box.

INSTALLING TRACK LIGHTS

Track lighting offers plenty of options for style, layout, and design. You can install the track in a straight line, or form a T, L, or H shape *(page 100).* Choose from among a variety of lamp styles. Place them anywhere on the track and point them in any direction. You can even use two or more types of lights, some for general illumination and others to highlight work areas or spotlight a work of art.

At some point the track must cross over a light fixture box to grab power via a mounting plate. Sketch your planned installation and show the drawing to a salesperson, who can help assemble all the parts required: track, mounting plate, lamps, and other fittings. Chances are a kit will supply everything needed.

PRESTART CHECKLIST

☐ **TIME**
About four hours to remove an old fixture and install about 8 feet of track with a turn or two, as well as several lamps

☐ **TOOLS**
Screwdriver, tape measure, strippers, drill, side cutters, voltage tester, lineman's pliers, stud finder, nonconducting ladder

☐ **SKILLS**
Measuring accurately; driving screws into joists; stripping wire; splicing stranded wire to solid wire

☐ **PREP**
Spread a drop cloth on the floor and set up one or two ladders. A helper will come in handy when installing long pieces of track.

☐ **MATERIALS**
Parts for the track system (see illustration), plastic anchors, screws, wire nuts, electrician's tape

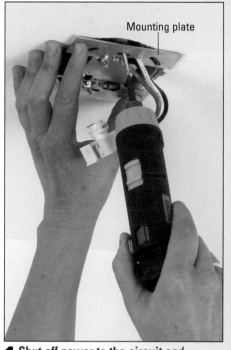

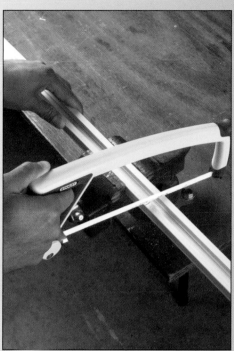

Mounting plate

1 **Shut off power to the circuit** and remove the existing light fixture *(page 94).* Splice the mounting plate leads to the house wires—green to ground, white to white, and black to black. Fold the wires up into the box. Screw the mounting plate snugly to the box.

2 If necessary, cut pieces of track to length. To cut a track, hold it firmly in place. If you use a vice, take care not to bend the metal. Cut with a hacksaw that has a metal-cutting blade. Support the waste side of the piece when nearing the end of a cut so it does not fall and bend the track.

TRACK LIGHTING SYSTEM

The mounting plate live-end connector supplies power to the track, which carries power via two strips of wire to the lamps.

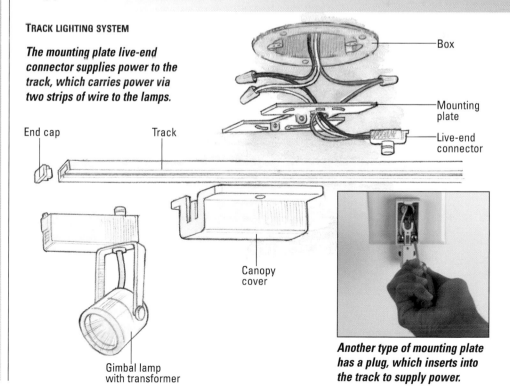

Box

Mounting plate

Live-end connector

End cap

Track

Canopy cover

Gimbal lamp with transformer

Another type of mounting plate has a plug, which inserts into the track to supply power.

Installing track lights *(continued)*

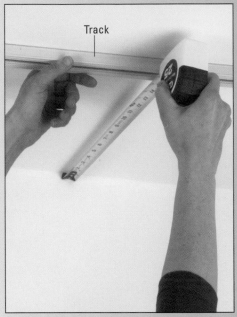

Track

3 With a helper holding one end of the track, push the track up against the mounting plate. Secure it by tightening the setscrews.

4 With a helper holding one end of the track, measure at two points along the track so it is parallel to the nearest wall. If the track configuration includes any 90-degree angles, use a framing square to mark a guide line.

5 Locate joists with a stud finder. Drive a screw into every joist the track crosses. If the track runs parallel to the joists, drill holes every 16 inches, tap in plastic anchors, and drive screws into the anchors.

TRACK CONFIGURATIONS

With various lamp directions and types of bulbs, track lighting can supply general illumination, task lighting, or accent lighting.

On your own

To install track lighting by yourself, make two T-braces out of 1×2s. Cut the uprights to the height of the ceiling, the cross pieces about 2-feet long. Position the track, wedge the braces underneath, and fasten the track to the ceiling.

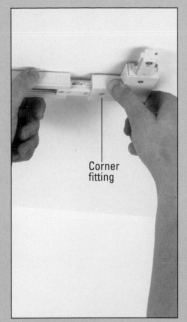

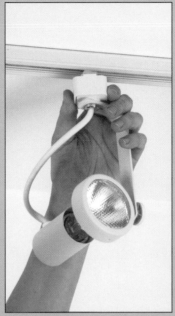

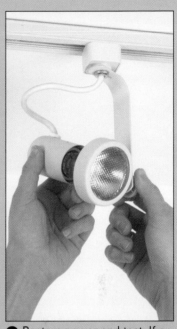

6 If the track has to turn a corner, slide the fitting onto the track piece just installed. Slide the next piece onto the connector, measure to see that it is parallel to the nearest wall, and anchor it to the ceiling.

7 Once all the pieces are installed, place end caps on all the track ends. Push the live-end connector plug into the track; twist it to make contact with both strips of metal in the track. Attach the canopy cover.

8 Insert the plug of a lamp into the track and twist to tighten. To move a lamp along the track, loosen it first—do not force it while it is still attached.

9 Restore power and test. If a lamp does not work, remove it and twist it back on again. Once it works, adjust the lamp to direct the light where needed.

FITTINGS
Any shape you need

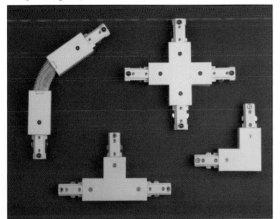

In addition to the "L" fitting shown above, other fittings allow you to form different shapes. A flexible fitting turns to most any angle. With each fitting you use, make sure the exposed ends of all the tracks have end caps, or the track will not energize.

Available lamps

Cylinder and bell lamps partially hide the bulb, while gimbal rings let them hang out. Low-voltage halogen lamps use less energy, but are expensive and become hot when they're on.

INSTALLING A CEILING FAN BOX

Ceiling fans are heavy, and they vibrate. So if one is connected to a standard electrical box, there is a good chance that it will come loose and perhaps come crashing down.

The first step in adding a ceiling fan is to check out the existing electrical box. **Shut off power to the circuit**, and remove the existing ceiling fixture *(page 94)*. Test to confirm that the power is off.

Most building codes require ceiling fans to be mounted onto special fan-rated boxes *(opposite)*, which are made of metal or strong plastic and have deep threaded holes for the mounting screws. The box must be mounted firmly, either by attaching it directly to a framing member or by using a fan-rated brace *(Step 1, page 103)*.

Replacing a ceiling box is a messy job. Work carefully to avoid cutting through wires hidden in the ceiling.

PRESTART CHECKLIST

☐ **TIME**
About two hours to remove an old ceiling box and install a new one

☐ **TOOLS**
Screwdriver, hammer, drill, pry bar, utility knife, flashlight, wrench or groove-joint pliers, perhaps a reciprocating saw

☐ **SKILLS**
Cutting drywall, prying boxes out without damaging surrounding ceiling or wall

☐ **PREP**
Spread a drop cloth on the floor below; set up a ladder

☐ **MATERIALS**
Fan-rated box, box brace

Remove old box

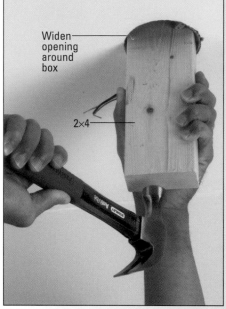

Widen opening around box

2×4

Pry bar

1 Use a knife (not a saw) to cut through the drywall or plaster all around the old box. The box should be attached to a joist with screws or two horizontally driven nails. Force the box loose by hammering a 2×4 into it.

2 Insert a flat pry bar between the box and the joist. Pry the box away from the joist. You may need to pry out a staple anchoring the cable to the joist. Work carefully to avoid unnecessary damage to the ceiling.

WHAT IF...
There is another type of box in the ceiling?

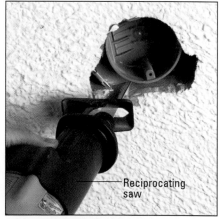

Reciprocating saw

Older pancake boxes are mounted with screws driven into a framing member. Remove the screws and pry out the box.

If a box is too firmly mounted to be knocked free, cut a hole in the ceiling just large enough so you can see the mounting nails and the cable. Carefully cut through the nails with a reciprocating saw.

Install a new box

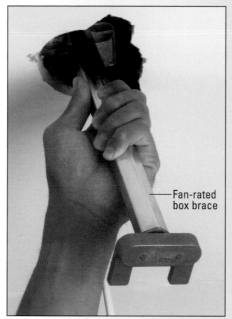

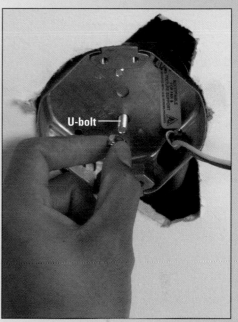

3 Pry out the box's mounting nails and pull the box down from the ceiling. Disconnect the cable from the box. The box shown has a slot that the cable slides through; pry the tab and pull the cable out. If the box has a cable clamp, remove the locknut *(page 96).*

Poke the tab to release the cable.

1 To install a braced box, slip the brace through the hole. Rotate the shaft of the brace clockwise until it touches a joist on either side, and its legs rest on top of the drywall or plaster.

Fan-rated box brace

2 Tighten the brace with a wrench or groove-joint pliers. Attach the U-bolt to the brace and slide the box up through it. Tighten the nuts.

U-bolt

Available fan boxes

Fan-rated plastic box attaches to joist

Pancake box with joist attachment

Pancake fastens directly to joist

If a strong framing member is positioned directly above the box's hole, a pancake fan box or a box with a joist bracket through its center may be the easiest to install.

WHAT IF...
You can work from above?

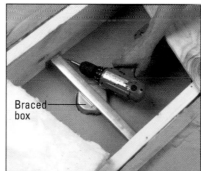

Braced box

If you can get at the attic space above the ceiling box, go there to disconnect the old box. Install a braced box.

Don't depend on plaster lath: If you have a plaster ceiling, make sure you attach a box to a joist—not the ⅜-inch-thick pieces of lath, which have very little strength.

Screw the fan plate to a ceiling joist

Here's an option that eliminates the need for a new box. Screw the fan's mounting plate *(page 104)* directly to a nearby joist. The plate will be off center, so you may need a medallion *(page 95)* to cover the hole.

ATTACHING A CEILING FAN

Although a ceiling fan is a complex fixture with lots of parts, each step of installation is fairly simple. The most challenging task is assembling the parts in the right order.

Make sure your ceiling box is fan-rated and strongly attached to framing (*pages 102–103*).

If there is three-wire cable (with black, white, red, and ground wires) running from the fixture box to the switch box, you can install a standard fan/light switch (*page 106*).

With two-wire cable (see *page 21* for the wiring possibilities), use one of the following means of controlling the fan and the light:

■ Have the wall switch control both the fan and the light; turn one or the other off using the fixture's pull-chain switches.

■ Install a wireless remote-control switch for the fan (*page 105*).

■ Purchase a fan that has a special fan/light switch that works with two-wire cable (these are expensive).

PRESTART CHECKLIST

☐ **TIME**
About four hours to install a ceiling fan and switch

☐ **TOOLS**
Screwdriver, drill, strippers, voltage tester, lineman's pliers, nonconducting ladder

☐ **SKILLS**
Stripping wire; splicing stranded wire to solid wire

☐ **PREP**
Spread a drop cloth on the floor below; position a ladder

☐ **MATERIALS**
Ceiling fan, wire nuts, electrician's tape

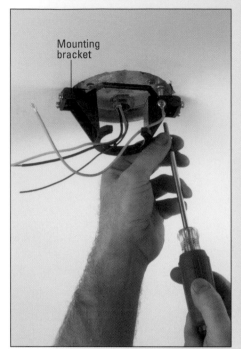

1 **Test that there is no power in the box.** Secure the fan mounting bracket to the ceiling fixture box with screws. If rubber washers are provided, be sure to install them between the bracket and the box.

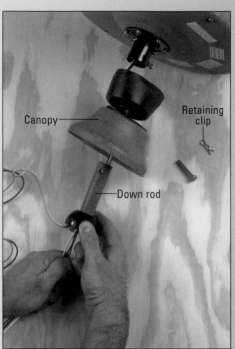

2 Slide the down rod through the canopy, slip on the decorative cover, and pull the wires through. Slip the down rod over the motor housing and fasten with the retaining clip. Tighten the assembly.

CEILING FAN

In this typical arrangement, the down rod and ball hanger nest in the mounting bracket, so it can vibrate without shaking the bracket. If you want the fan to hang down farther, purchase a down rod extender.

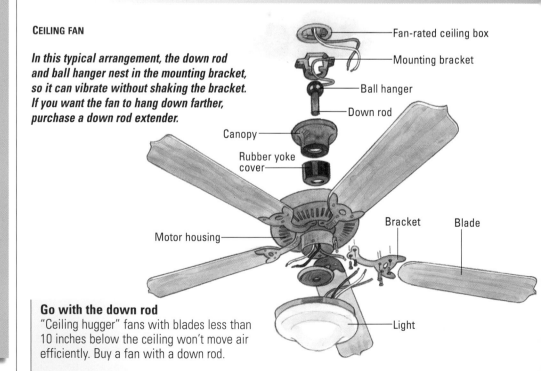

Go with the down rod
"Ceiling hugger" fans with blades less than 10 inches below the ceiling won't move air efficiently. Buy a fan with a down rod.

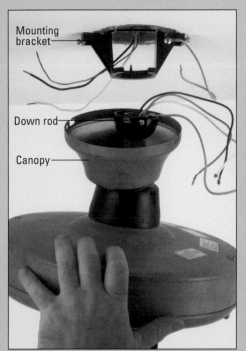

Mounting bracket

Down rod

Canopy

3 Carefully lift the assembled fan and hook the ball-like end of the down rod into the mounting bracket. Don't allow wires to get caught between the brackets and the end of the down rod. This ball and socket arrangement lets the fan unit swing slightly.

4 Wire the fan. The black lead controls the motor and the blue or striped lead controls the light. If you have two-wire cable, splice both to the black house wire. Splice white lead to white wire and connect the grounds.

Fan blade

Canopy setscrew

Fan bracket

Cordless drill with phillips bit

5 Fold the wires into the box. Push the canopy against the ceiling and secure it to the mounting bracket with the setscrews provided. Screw a fan bracket onto each fan blade. Attach each fan bracket to the underside of the motor. Make sure all the screws are tight.

Wireless remote control

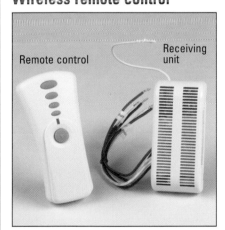

Remote control

Receiving unit

A wireless remote-control fan/light switch controls both the fan and the light from anywhere in the room. It has two parts. Wire the receiving unit according to its instructions and tuck it inside the canopy. The sending unit is battery-powered.

Fan light options

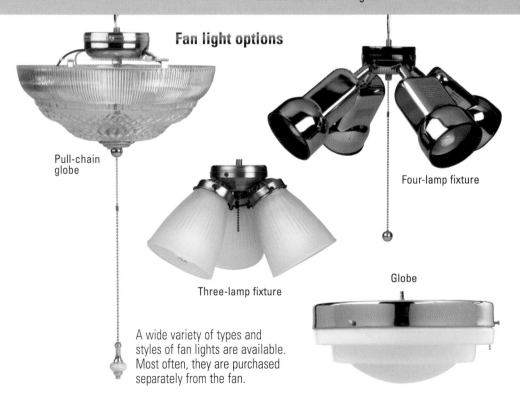

Pull-chain globe

Three-lamp fixture

Four-lamp fixture

Globe

A wide variety of types and styles of fan lights are available. Most often, they are purchased separately from the fan.

Attaching a ceiling fan (continued)

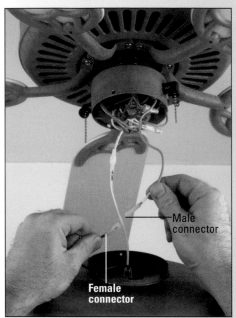

Male connector

Female connector

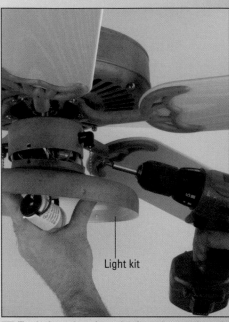

Light kit

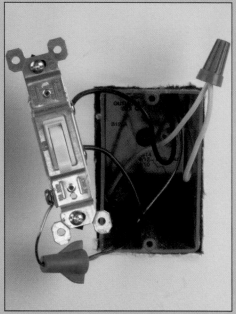

6 Remove the plate on the bottom of the fan and wire the light kit. The model shown above uses plug-together connectors. Some fans require that wires be spliced.

7 Tuck the wires into the housing and push the light kit onto the fan. Tighten the screws to secure it. Install the lightbulb(s) and globe.

8 In this arrangement, a standard single-pole switch turns the fan and the light on and off at the same time. To turn one or the other off, use the pull-chain switch. Do not install a standard dimmer for a fan—it will damage the fan.

Fan switch options

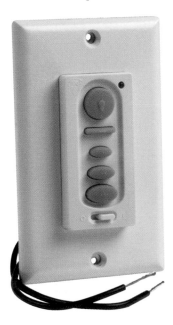

If you installed a fan only with no light kit, a push button fan control (left) operates the fan at different speeds.

With more expensive ceiling fans, switches are available that have separate controls for the fan and the light, though they require only two-wire cable.

STANLEY PRO TIP

Balancing the fan

If the fan wobbles, check the blade bracket screws and tighten, if needed. Measure down from the ceiling to each blade; replace any that are warped. If that doesn't solve the problem, remove the blades and turn on the motor. If it wobbles without the blades, make sure the down rod is assembled correctly. If the fan still wobbles, purchase a fan balancing kit, which uses small weights to evenly distribute the load. Finally the motor itself may be defective and may need to be replaced.

WHAT IF...
There is three-wire cable?

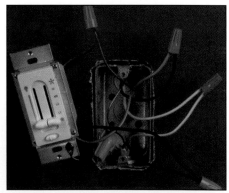

In this configuration, two-wire cable brings power into the switch box, and three-wire cable runs from the switch box to the fixture box. Connect the grounds. Splice the black lead to the black feed wire. Splice the light lead to the other black wire, and the fan lead to the red wire. Splice the white wires together.

ADDING UNDERCABINET LIGHTS

The easiest way to light up counter space is to install low-voltage halogen lights on the underside of wall cabinets. Halogens can also help create a dramatic display area inside glass-fronted cabinets.

The most common type of halogen is called a puck light because of its shape, but other shapes are available. Buy a kit that includes lights, cord, a transformer, and a cord switch. Some models allow you to hook up several more lights, if needed.

Halogens get very hot. Locate them out of children's reach or where they won't be accidentally touched. In areas where heat can build up—such as inside a cabinet—install bulbs of lower wattage.

Plan the locations of the lights and the plug-in unit and work out the least conspicuous route for the cord. Either staple the cord under a cabinet or shelf, or drill small holes and run the cord inside the cabinets and out of sight.

If you want to control halogens from a wall switch, install a switch/receptacle (page 108).

PRESTART CHECKLIST

☐ **TIME**
About two hours to install five or six halogens with transformer and switch

☐ **TOOLS**
Screwdriver, drill, strippers, stapler, and a hammer

☐ **SKILLS**
Drilling holes; driving screws

☐ **PREP**
Spread a towel or small drop cloth on the surface below

☐ **MATERIALS**
Halogen light kit, including lights, a plug-in unit, transformer, cord, and switch

1 Position each lighting unit as recommended by the manufacturer. Check that the mounting screws provided won't pierce through to the inside of the cabinet. Fasten each fixture in place.

2 When all the fixtures are in place, run connecting wires between them; then connect the source line that runs from the lights to a receptacle. Some kits come with plugs already installed. Coil any excess wire and hide it near the back of the cabinet.

INSTALLING UNDERCABINET PUCK LIGHTS

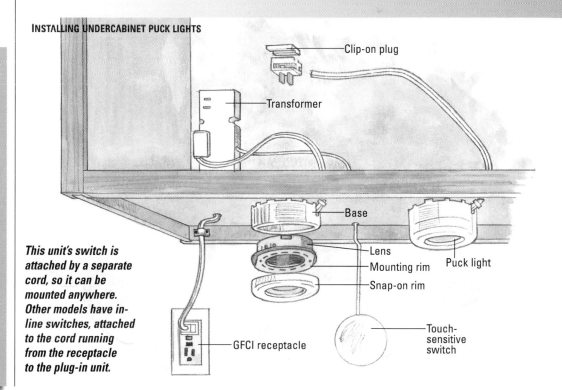

This unit's switch is attached by a separate cord, so it can be mounted anywhere. Other models have in-line switches, attached to the cord running from the receptacle to the plug-in unit.

Adding undercabinet lights *(continued)*

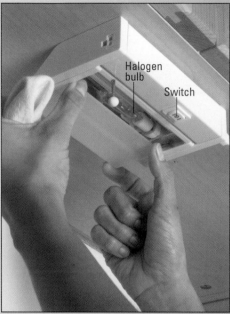

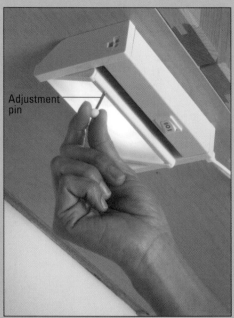

3 Fasten the connecting cords to the underside of the cabinet. Use the staples provided with the kit, or plastic-coated or round-topped staples. Don't use standard metal square-topped staples; they may cut the cord.

4 Slide back the lens covering. Holding the halogen bulb with a cloth, install it in the fixture. Replace the lens.

5 Plug in the main cord and turn the lights on with the switch. On the model shown above, the direction of the lamp can be adjusted by holding an attached pin and swiveling the lamp housing.

STANLEY PRO TIP: **Wiring a switch/receptacle**

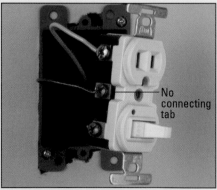

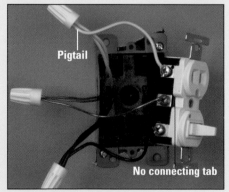

Shut off the power. Remove the old receptacle *(page 85)*. Connect the ground *(page 42)*. Connect the black wire to the brass terminal that does not have a connecting tab and connect the white wire to the silver terminal on the same side. The switch will turn the receptacle on and off.

If the receptacle is in the middle of the run, with two cables entering the box *(page 85)*, splice the black wires and the white wires to pigtails. Then connect them to the brass and silver terminals on the side that does not have a connecting tab.

Rope lights

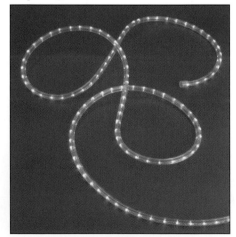

Rope lights are especially easy to install. Just staple them where you want, using the plastic staples supplied, and plug them in. Install an in-line cord switch *(page 59)*, or plug into a switched receptacle (left).

INSTALLING EURO-STYLE LIGHTS

High-tech-looking Euro-style lights are readily available at lighting stores and home centers. They look complicated, but they are easy to install.

Use one of these fixtures to replace an existing light fixture, as shown on these pages, or buy a unit that simply can be plugged into a receptacle.

Low-voltage halogens save on energy use. But halogen bulbs get very hot, so keep them out of the reach of children and well away from combustible surfaces, such as curtains.

The fixture uses a transformer that steps voltage down—typically to 8 to 20 volts. However, you will be hooking it up to standard household wiring, so be sure to **shut off power** before working. To remove an existing light fixture, see *page 94*.

PRESTART CHECKLIST

☐ **TIME**
About two hours to remove a ceiling fixture and install a Euro-style light

☐ **TOOLS**
Screwdriver, drill, voltage tester, stud finder, strippers, lineman's pliers, nonconducting ladder

☐ **SKILLS**
Attaching hardware with screws; stripping wire; splicing stranded wire to solid wire

☐ **PREP**
Spread a drop cloth on the floor below

☐ **MATERIALS**
New light fixture, wire nuts, electrician's tape

1 **Shut off power to the circuit.** Remove an existing light fixture *(page 94)* and splice the transformer leads to the house wires.

2 Measure carefully and try to position the rod holders under a joist. Attach the holders with screws long enough to reach through drywall or plaster and fasten at least ½ inch into the joist. Use plastic wall anchors if no joist is available.

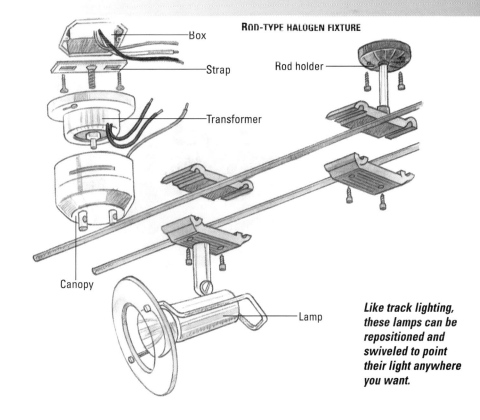

ROD-TYPE HALOGEN FIXTURE

Box, Strap, Transformer, Canopy, Lamp, Rod holder

Like track lighting, these lamps can be repositioned and swiveled to point their light anywhere you want.

Installing Euro-style lights *(continued)*

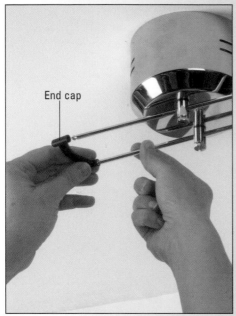

End cap

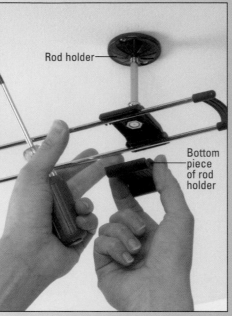

Rod holder

Bottom piece of rod holder

3 Mount the transformer and canopy to the ceiling box strap *(page 94)*. Slide the rods through the canopy rod connectors. Slip an end cap onto the two rods at either end.

4 Remove the bottom piece from each rod holder, snap the rods up into the grooves, and screw the bottom piece back into place.

5 Attach each lamp the same way that you clamped the rods to the rod holders. Slide the lamp into position before completely tightening the screw.

Stylish options

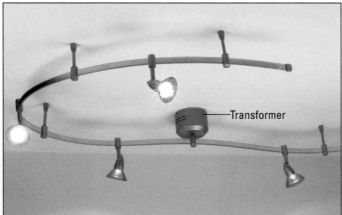

Transformer

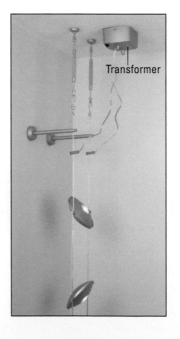

Transformer

With a track that can be bent into curves, the halogen fixture above is as decorative as it is functional. The transformer can be mounted anywhere along the track, and the track can be cut to any desired length. Lights straddle two vertical wires (right), which deliver low-voltage current. Lights can slide up or down and rotate on an axis. The same unit can be installed horizontally.

REFRESHER COURSE
Switch/receptacle for plug-in transformers

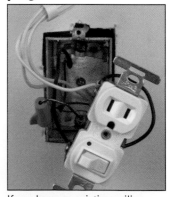

If you have no existing ceiling fixture, buy a unit that plugs into a receptacle. *Page 84* shows how to replace a receptacle with a switched plug, so you can control the light with a wall switch.

ADDING A PORCH LIGHT

Porch lights add safety and security to an entryway, as well as a pleasing decorative accent. They illuminate stair steps and house numbers, and they give you a clear look at your visitors before you open the door.

As with the installation of most new light fixtures, running the cable is the hardest part of the job. See *pages 142–149* for how to run cable through finished walls. In addition, you'll need to tie in to a source of power and install an interior light switch *(pages 160–161)*. For how to wire two fixtures to one switch, see the diagrams on *pages 162–163*.

PRESTART CHECKLIST

☐ **TIME**
About 6 hours to run cable, install two fixtures and a switch

☐ **TOOLS**
Voltage tester, drill, ¼-inch bit, saber saw, fish tape, drywall saw, screwdriver, strippers, long-nose pliers, lineman's pliers

☐ **SKILLS**
Locating studs; cutting into siding; stripping, splicing, and connecting wires to terminals; installing boxes; running cable into boxes

☐ **MATERIALS**
Fixture(s), outdoor box(es), 2-wire cable, interior switch box, switch, electrician's tape, wire nuts, bent coat hanger

Installing the box and fixture

Old work box

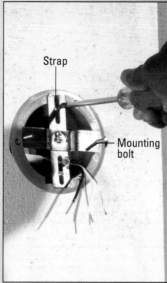
Strap
Mounting bolt

Coat-hanger support

1 Before wiring the switch, use a fish tape to pull the switch cable out through the box opening. Strip 8 inches of insulation and clamp the cable to the box. (For two lights, run cable and install the second box. See *page 163* for how to wire.) Install the box.

2 Strip the individual wires, removing about ¾ inch of insulation. Attach the mounting strap (typically provided with the light fixture) so the mounting bolts are positioned to hold the light fixture.

3 Support the fixture with coat hanger wire. Connect the ground. Splice white lead to white wire and black to black. Fold the wires into the box and install the fixture onto the mounting bolts. Caulk around the base. Wire the switch *(page 160)*, install a bulb, and test.

Cutting a hole for the box opening

1 Using a ¼-inch bit, drill a finder hole and use a bent wire to check that the box is not positioned over or too near a stud. (If it is not possible to move the box, cut the opening and chisel out the stud.)

2 Check for any pipes or cables in the wall. If clear, trace the outline of the box on the siding. Use a saber saw to cut an opening for the box.

REFRESHER COURSE
Install a programmable switch

For convenience and security, wire porch lights with a programmable switch. Set them to go on at dusk and off at bedtime. For added security, program the lights to stay on until dawn. Such switches have override options for turning the light on and off at will.

PLANNING NEW ELECTRICAL SERVICE

Anytime you install new electrical cable—adding just one receptacle or installing wiring for a remodeled kitchen—you are adding new service to your system. Because you may be increasing the demand on circuits or adding entire circuits, new service calls for careful planning.

Put your plans on paper
The first step is to make rough drawings that depict the lighting and electrical service you want to achieve. *Pages 114–117* show typical electrical systems for a kitchen, a bathroom, and utility rooms. Your installations will vary; these pages serve as a guide to help calculate how many circuits of which amperages

are needed. Start planning cable runs that can be routed with minimal damage to the walls.

Next figure out whether your existing service can support new electrical lines. You may simply be able to connect to existing circuits. Or you may need to add a circuit or two to your existing service panel, or install a subpanel or a new service panel. *Pages 122–123* guide you through those calculations.

Why codes count
The importance of building safety codes can't be overemphasized. First, codes protect you and everyone in your home from shock and fire. Second, they provide common ground for everyone who works

on electrical systems. When someone else works on your home's wiring after you, he or she will be able to understand the system.

Check local codes
Pages 118–119 describe requirements throughout much of the country. However, codes can vary from town to town, so contact your local building department when planning a project. Have your rough drawings and finished plans reviewed by the department. See *pages 124–125* for tips on drawing plans that an inspector will be able to read easily. Follow the department's instructions and schedule inspections, if needed. Do no work until you are sure it will be approved.

Adding new service calls for carefully assessing demand and making detailed project plans.

CHAPTER PREVIEW

Wiring a kitchen
page 114

Wiring a bathroom
page 116

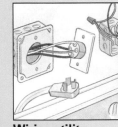

Wiring utility rooms
page 117

Codes often encountered
page 118

Jobs that involve running new cable typically require a permit.

Post your work permit in a highly visible location.

Once you have presented acceptable plans to your building department, you will receive a work permit. Follow the inspection schedule and instructions to the letter.

Loading circuits for safety
page 120

Checking out your basic service
page 122

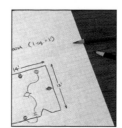

Drawing plans
page 124

WIRING A KITCHEN

Electrical services abound in modern kitchens: lights on the ceiling; lights in, on, and under cabinets; counter receptacles with the capacity to run six or seven appliances at once; and separate circuits for appliances, such as the refrigerator, dishwasher, and microwave. All in all, a medium-size kitchen may require six, seven, or more circuits.

Types of lighting
General lighting (or ambient lighting) is usually provided by ceiling-mounted fixtures. Consider fluorescent fixtures with "daylight" tubes and opaque lenses to disperse the light. Or install a series of recessed canister lights or incandescent fixtures.

If you use a track fixture for general lighting, shown on the opposite page, you'll get better illumination if you run several tracks around the room rather than having a single track in the middle. That way the light comes from several different directions.

Cove lighting mounts on top of wall cabinets and points upward, providing general lighting and creating a halo effect.

Area lighting focuses on a certain spot while also providing some general illumination. A recessed canister light equipped with a spotlight bulb, for instance, may shine down on the sink. Be sure to position it so the person doing dishes does not cast a shadow over the work area.

Pendant shade lights, as shown, are ideal area lights placed over a dining table or a counter. Position them over the center of the table or counter and adjust the heights so they do not shine in people's eyes.

Task lighting directs a beam of light at a work surface. The position of task lighting is critical: It must be in front of the worker to eliminate shadows, but it must not shine in the worker's eyes. Fortunately a perfect location is available in almost every kitchen: the underside of wall cabinets. Undercabinet lights are available as fluorescent or low-voltage halogen fixtures.

Accent lighting shines a spotlight on an object, such as a wall hanging. As shown, small fluorescent lights inside a glass-doored cabinet draw attention to a collection of fine china and crystal.

Consider installing a grow-light pointed at decorative or culinary plants. The one shown here shines on an herb garden positioned in front of the window. A typical grow-light cannot supply plants with all the rays they need, but it can be a supplement.

Light switches
Think carefully about the location of switches. If you put four or five next to each other, people may be confused about which switch controls which light. Where possible, position switches near their lights.

Be sure that you can turn on lights easily, no matter which door or entryway you use. Often the most convenient arrangement is to use three-way switches so that a single light or series of lights can be controlled by two different switches *(pages 164–167)*.

The lights in a kitchen typically are on a single 15-amp circuit.

Receptacles
Codes often require that a refrigerator receptacle be on a separate circuit because a blown circuit breaker or fuse could lead to food spoiling. A microwave oven may need its own circuit too, depending on its size and power.

Most codes require two circuits for countertop receptacles. In some areas the receptacles must be ground fault circuits (GFCI receptacles, *page 153)* and must be on 20-amp alternating circuits *(page 156)*. In other areas the required arrangement is to have two 15-amp circuits with non-GFCI receptacles wired with split circuits so the two plugs are connected to two different circuits *(page 157)*. Check local codes.

Appliances
An electric range, cooktop, or oven must be wired to a dedicated 120/240-volt circuit *(page 154)*. Other appliances are 120-volt.

Under the sink there must be a receptacle for the garbage disposer. It may be split so that one plug is switched and the other is always hot *(page 158)*, allowing you to plug in a garbage disposer and a hot-water dispenser. Or the disposer may be hard-wired into a switched box. The switch is usually placed on the wall near the sink.

A dishwasher may have its own circuit, or it may be on the same circuit as the garbage disposer. A range hood *(pages 185–187)* typically is hardwired.

Over-sink canister light

Cove lighting

Grow-light

Switch for garbage disposer

Wire for dishwasher and disposer under the sink.

Track lighting

Inside-cabinet light

Pendant light

Light for desk area

Undercabinet lights

20 amp GFCI

Receptacle for appliances used on island

This kitchen combines ambient track and cove lighting, area lighting from a recessed spotlight and pendant light, and task lighting from undercabinet halogens and fluorescents. Halogens placed inside a cabinet provide accent lighting.

WIRING A BATHROOM

Even a relatively large bathroom tends to be damp. Light fixtures must be watertight, ventilation must be effective, and the receptacles should be ground fault circuit interrupters.

Circuits
The lights and fan must be on a different circuit from the receptacle(s). Some codes require that bathrooms have their own circuits; others permit bathrooms to share circuits with receptacles or lights in other rooms. In some locales all bathroom wiring—including the lights—must be GFCI-protected *(pages 153 and 231).*

The vent fan
To satisfy codes and for your comfort, a bathroom needs a fan that effectively pulls moist air out and sends it outside. *Pages 188–191* show how to install one. Some local codes require that the fan always comes on when the light is on; others allow you to put the fan on its own switch.

Usually there is a vent/light fixture in the middle of the ceiling, which may be controlled by one or two switches. Some fixtures also include a heating unit or a night-light. A bathroom heater—whether it is a separate unit or a part of a fan/light—may use so much electricity that it requires its own circuit.

Lights
In addition to a light or fan/light in the middle of the ceiling, plan to put lights over the sink, where they can shine on a person standing at the mirror. A strip of lights above the mirror is a common arrangement, but most people find that two lights, one on each side of the mirror, illuminate a face more clearly. A mirror light's switch may be by the entry door or near the sink.

A tub or shower does not need to be brightly lit, but people shouldn't have to shower in the dark. Install a recessed canister light with a waterproof lens made for shower areas.

Receptacles
Install at least one 20-amp GFCI receptacle within a foot or so of the sink. Position the receptacle so a cord does not have to drape over the sink when someone is using a blow dryer.

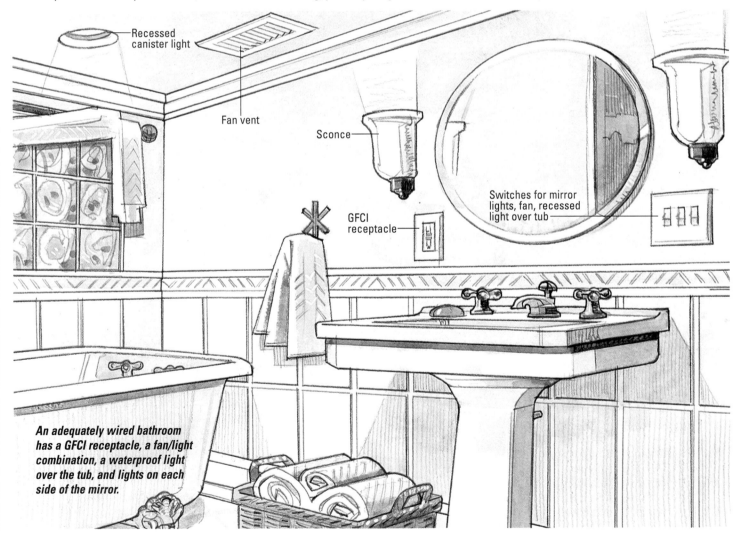

Recessed canister light

Fan vent

Sconce

GFCI receptacle

Switches for mirror lights, fan, recessed light over tub

An adequately wired bathroom has a GFCI receptacle, a fan/light combination, a waterproof light over the tub, and lights on each side of the mirror.

WIRING UTILITY ROOMS

Work areas tend to be informal, with unfinished walls and exposed framing. Unfortunately the wiring is sometimes just as informal with exposed cable, overloaded receptacles, missing coverplates, and a tangle of extension cords.

Safe utility wiring

Attach all boxes firmly, and staple or strap cables so they are taut and out of harm's way. Although some codes allow it, exposed NM cable is unsafe in an area where people work. Replace it with armored cable or conduit *(pages 130–135).*

Make sure there are enough receptacles placed in convenient locations to avoid the need for long extension cords. You shouldn't have to use three-way adapters. If the area is damp, install GFCIs.

Wiring a workshop

People will be wielding tools and moving large pieces of lumber, so take special care in placing the receptacles. In a large shop with serious power tools, add up the amperages to see if one or two dedicated circuits are needed *(pages 120–121).* Position a receptacle near each stationary power tool, such as a table saw or drill press. Scatter plenty of other receptacles so you can plug in hand power tools without using extension cords.

Provide plenty of overhead lighting. Large fluorescent fixtures do the trick easily and inexpensively. Install lenses to cover the tubes to prevent breakage. For work that requires close scrutiny, plug in desk lamps.

Wiring a laundry room

Codes are very specific about laundry room requirements. Use common sense when positioning receptacles so that cords are well away from the folding table.

If the dryer is electric, you need a separate 120/240-volt receptacle *(pages 154–155).* If the dryer is gas, it can plug into a receptacle on the same circuit as the washer. There should be an extra receptacle so you won't have to reach back and unplug the washer or dryer when you need power.

The receptacles in a laundry room must be on a dedicated 20-amp circuit. The lights, however, can share a circuit with lights in another room.

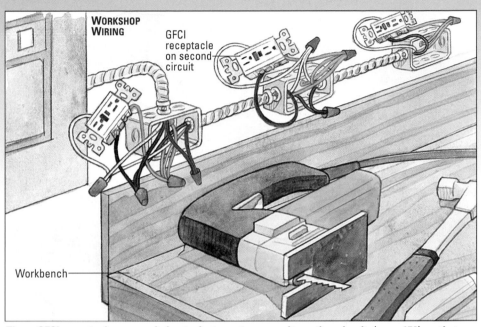

These GFCI receptacles, spaced about a foot apart, are on alternating circuits (page 156) so that there is little chance of overloading.

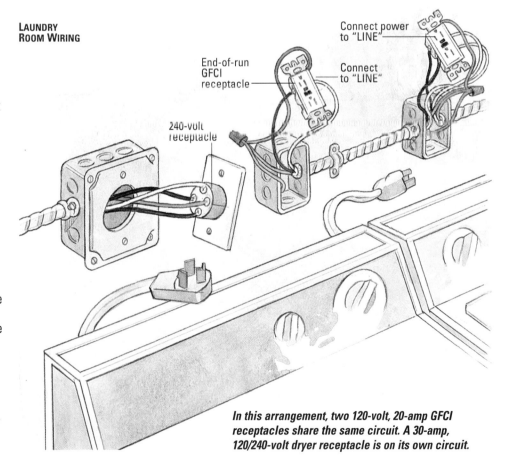

In this arrangement, two 120-volt, 20-amp GFCI receptacles share the same circuit. A 30-amp, 120/240-volt dryer receptacle is on its own circuit.

CODES OFTEN ENCOUNTERED

If you're simply replacing an existing fixture, switch, or receptacle, there's usually no need to contact the building department. But when you run new electrical cable for new service, whether wiring several circuits or adding just one receptacle, be sure to work with a building inspector and comply with all local codes.

National and local codes
Professional electricians often refer to the National Electrical Code (NEC), a massive volume that describes national codes for residential and commercial wiring. You don't need to buy this book, but you may need to refer to a library copy from time to time.

Local building departments often modify the NEC, and it is local codes that you must satisfy. It's not unusual for adjacent towns to have very different codes; for instance, one may allow plastic boxes while another requires metal boxes.

The charts in this section present many of the most important code requirements. However, they are not exhaustive. **Have your wiring plans approved by a local inspector before you begin work.**

If existing wiring does not meet contemporary local codes, chances are that your building department will not require

you to change the wiring. Usually only the new work must be up to code. However, if the old wiring is unsafe, you should change it. An extensive remodeling project may also require you to bring the entire house up to current codes.

Loading and grounding circuits
Any plan, however simple or complex, must start with two considerations. First, make sure the new service will not overload a circuit. *Pages 120–121* explain how.

Second, see that all receptacles and appliances are safely grounded. Local codes will probably require that switches and light fixtures also be grounded. Grounding provides protection against shock in case a wire comes loose or an appliance or device malfunctions. Check using a receptacle analyzer *(page 12)*.

All receptacles and appliances must be attached to a ground wire (or metal sheathing) that runs to the service panel. The most common methods of grounding are shown below. Check with local codes to find out which method they approve.

A thick ground wire should emerge from the service panel and clamp tightly to a cold-water pipe or grounding rods driven into the ground outside the house.

Common code requirements

Here are some of the most common general requirements for home electrical systems. Keep in mind that local building departments may have different demands.

■ **Boxes:** Plastic electrical boxes are common throughout much of the United States and Canada; some localities require metal boxes. Buy large boxes so wires won't be cramped *(page 17)*. Attach them firmly to a framing member whenever possible or use remodel boxes that clamp to the wall surface *(pages 142–143)*.

■ **Receptacles, fixtures, and appliances:** All new receptacles and appliances must be grounded. Fixtures and appliances should be approved by the Underwriter's Laboratory (UL).

■ **Cable:** Nonmetallic (NM) cable is the easiest to run and is accepted by most building departments. Wherever cable will be exposed rather than hidden behind drywall or plaster, armored cable or conduit may be required. See the chapter Installing Cable & Boxes for the correct ways to install cable so it is protected against harm.

■ **Circuits:** Most 120-volt household circuits are 15 amps, and all lights must be on 15-amp circuits. In kitchens and utility areas, 20-amp circuits may be required. To make sure your circuits aren't overloaded, *see pages 120–121*.

■ **Wire size:** Attach #14 wire to 15-amp circuits and #12 wire to 20-amp circuits. If cable runs exceed 500 feet, you may need to increase wire size. Consult your building department.

■ **Service panels:** As long as you do not need to add a new circuit *(pages 230–231)*, your existing service panel, even if it is an old fuse box, will probably be sufficient. If you add circuits, you may need to upgrade the panel or add a subpanel *(pages 232–233)*. Check with an inspector.

REFRESHER COURSE
Grounding methods

If the box is plastic, connect the ground wire to the receptacle only. For a middle-of-run receptacle (shown) splice the ground wires together and connect to the receptacle with a pigtail.

With a metal box, attach ground wires to both the receptacle and to the box using a grounding screw. Use a pigtail and a grounding wire nut.

Systems that use armored cable or metal conduit may have no grounding wire. The sheathing or conduit provides the path for ground, so it must be connected firmly at all points.

STANLEY PRO TIP

Working with the electrical inspector

Filing for a permit and working with an electrical inspector may seem unnecessary, but the inspection process ensures safe and reliable electrical service. Most inspectors know their business; pay attention and follow their instructions to the letter. You will benefit from the sound advice.

■ **Find out if your building department requires a licensed electrician** to perform new electrical installations. Some departments require a homeowner to pass a written or oral test before doing certain types of work.

■ **Make a rough sketch and materials list** for the project before you start drawing plans; then find out as much as possible about local codes. Find out what kind of cable and boxes are required. Are there any specific requirements for the room you will be wiring? The building department may have pamphlets answering your questions, or an inspector may be able to answer them over the phone.

■ **The inspector's job is not to help you plan, but to inspect.** An inspector may be willing to offer advice, but don't ask, "What should I do?" Instead propose a plan using the information in this chapter and present it for feedback.

■ **Draw up professional-looking plans** *(pages 124–125)*, as well as a complete list of materials. Make an appointment with the inspector to go over your plans. Listen attentively and take notes. Be polite and respectful, but don't be afraid to ask questions if you don't understand.

■ **Schedule inspections.** There will probably be two: one for the rough wiring and one for the finished job. Don't call the inspector in until the required work is completely finished—inspectors hate having to come back for a reinspection. Above all, do not cover up any wiring until the inspector has signed off on it. If you install drywall before the rough electrical inspection, you may have to tear it off.

Electrical codes room by room

Some codes apply to the entire house; others apply to specific rooms. Here are some general guidelines. Local codes may vary. These requirements usually apply only to new installations—older wiring does not have to comply as long as it is safe. These requirements make good sense and are not overly strict. Wiring that does not meet these standards would be either awkward or unsafe to use.

Bedrooms, living room, dining room
Every room in a house must have a wall switch located near the entry door, which controls either a ceiling fixture or a switched receptacle. All ceiling fixtures must be controlled by a wall switch and not by a pull chain. Receptacles must be no more than 12 feet apart, and there must be at least one on each wall. If a section of wall between two doors is wider than 2 feet, it must have a receptacle. Light fixtures must be on 15-amp circuits. Usually receptacles are allowed to share a circuit with lights. But a heavy electrical user, such as a window air-conditioner or a home theater, may need to be on a dedicated circuit.

Hallways and stairways
All stairways must have a light fixture controlled by three-way switches at the bottom and top of the stairs. Hallways may also need a light controlled by three-ways. A hallway longer than 10 feet must have at least one receptacle.

Closets
There should be at least one overhead light, controlled by a wall switch rather than a pull-chain. The light must have a globe rather than a bare bulb; a bulb can get hot enough to ignite clothing, stacked blankets, or storage boxes.

Attached garage
There must be at least one receptacle—not counting receptacles used for laundry or other utilities. There should be an overhead light (in addition to a light that is part of a garage door opener) controlled by at least one wall switch.

Kitchen
Here things can get pretty complicated; see *pages 114–115*. Many codes call for two 20-amp small appliance circuits, controlling GFCI receptacles placed above countertops. Other codes call for 15-amp split-circuit receptacles. The refrigerator, microwave, garbage disposer, and dishwasher may or may not need to be on separate circuits. The lights should be on a separate 15-amp circuit.

Bathroom
Codes require that all receptacles be GFCI-protected. Any light fixture should have a sealed globe or lens to shut out moisture. A fan/light/heater may pull enough amps to require its own circuit.

Outdoors
For standard-voltage wiring, codes call for either waterproof underground feed (UF) cable or conduit, or both. The depth at which the cable must be buried varies depending on local codes. Special waterproof fittings and covers are called for. For low-voltage lighting, standards are less strict; usually no permit is needed for installation.

LOADING CIRCUITS FOR SAFETY

When adding only a few receptacles, lights, or a small appliance, tap into an existing circuit. Grab power from a nearby receptacle, junction box, switch box, or ceiling fixture box *(pages 136–137)* and run cable to the new electrical box. First make sure that you won't overload the circuit.

Indexing circuits

An index telling which electrical users—lights, receptacles, and appliances—are on each circuit should be posted on the inside of a service panel door. However, this index may not be accurate. Whenever evaluating a circuit, **test to make sure which electrical users are on the circuit.**

If there is no index, make one. Shut off one circuit and test to see which lights, receptacles, or appliances have been turned off. Write down the results. Repeat for all the circuits until you have covered all electrical users in the house. Draw up the index and tape it to the service panel.

Indexing circuits is easier with two people, one stationed at the service panel while the other tests plugs, lights, and appliances and writes down the findings. Walkie-talkies or cell phones ease communications.

Figuring the load

Once you've identified all the users on a circuit, total up the wattage. If the wattage is not printed on an item's label, there should be an amperage rating (amps). For 120-volt users, multiply the amps times 120 to get the wattage. For example, a 4-amp tool uses 480 watts ($4 \times 120 = 480$).

Add the wattage of all the bulbs in each fixture. For each receptacle include the appliances or tools that are commonly plugged into them. (Don't forget the vacuum cleaner.) Also include hardwired appliances, such as a dishwasher. Once you've totaled all the electrical users on a circuit, determine if adding new services will overload the circuit. The box (above right) shows how to make this calculation. If grabbing power from a nearby box will overload its circuit, try another circuit. If no convenient circuit has enough available capacity, install a new circuit *(pages 230–231).*

Major appliances such as electric ranges and dryers use dedicated 240-volt circuits. Only one user is connected to each circuit.

Calculating safe capacity for a circuit

To find the total capacity of a circuit, multiply amps times volts (usually 120). Most local codes demand that all the users on a circuit must not add up to more than 80 percent of total capacity. This 80-percent figure is the circuit's "safe capacity."

15-amp circuit
total capacity: 1800 watts
safe capacity: 1440 watts (12 amps)

20-amp circuit
total capacity: 2400 watts
safe capacity: 1920 watts (16 amps)

30-amp circuit
total capacity: 3600 watts
safe capacity: 2880 watts (24 amps)

REFRESHER COURSE
Home electrical circuits

Power from the utility company enters the service panel, where it is divided into individual "branch" circuits, each of which supplies power to specific lights, receptacles, or appliances. In each circuit, a black or colored hot wire carries power out to the user, and a white neutral wire completes the circuit by carrying power back to the service panel.

Some household electrical systems are orderly with each circuit covering a clearly defined area of the house. Others are helter-skelter—a single circuit may travel across the house or up two floors. Disorganized wiring is not necessarily unsafe, but it may take extra time to figure out what's going on when you add new service or track down a problem.

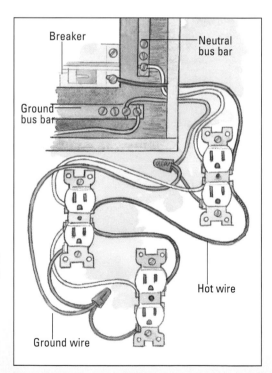

Breaker

Neutral bus bar

Ground bus bar

Hot wire

Ground wire

Appliances and tools that need special attention

To find the wattage of a 120-volt appliance or tool, look at its nameplate. If it tells only the amps, multiply times 120 to get the wattage. For example, a table saw that pulls 11 amps uses 1320 watts (11 × 120 = 1320). Here are some typical wattages; yours may vary considerably. (All 240-volt appliances should be on dedicated circuits, so you never need to figure whether they can fit in a circuit.)

Television, 350 watts

Table saw, 800–1400 watts

Window air-conditioner, 700–1600 watts

Electric range, 4000–4500

Microwave, 600–1500 watts

Dishwasher, 1000–1500 watts

Garbage disposer, 400–850 watts

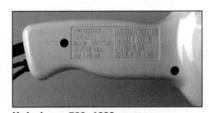
Hair dryer, 500–1200 watts

Refrigerator, 800–1200 watts

REFRESHER COURSE
Ways to relieve an overloaded circuit

If a circuit often blows a fuse or trips a breaker, it means too many appliances, lights, or tools are sharing it. List the wattage ratings of all the electrical users on the circuit. Add up the numbers; the total will probably exceed the safe capacity (left).

The solution may be as simple as plugging an appliance into a nearby receptacle that is on another circuit. If that is not possible, install a wall-mounted extension cord (center) or protective channel (right) so you can plug the device into a receptacle located on another circuit.

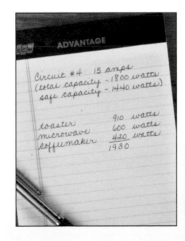

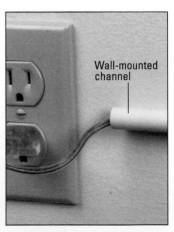

Wall-mounted extension cord

Wall-mounted channel

CHECKING OUT YOUR BASIC SERVICE

Installing a new circuit is not difficult. First make sure that your service panel can handle the extra load. A service panel with too many circuits is dangerous.

Fuse boxes rarely have space for new circuits. If you have a fuse box and need new service, replace it with a new service panel or install a subpanel *(pages 232–233).*

If you see an available slot in a breaker box, either an open space or a knockout that can be removed, chances are you can simply install a new breaker there and run cable to it. If there is no open space, local codes may allow you to replace a single breaker with a tandem breaker, which supplies power to two circuits *(pages 230–231).*

Make sure you will not overload your service panel. A panel's total amperage is printed near or on the main circuit breaker, which controls all the circuits in the panel. Most breaker boxes are 100, 150, or 200 amps. Add the amperages of all the individual breakers in the box. The total may be more than twice the total amperage of the box. For example, a 100-amp service panel may have circuits that add up to over 200 amps. This is normal.

Take your total amperages and the name of the service panel manufacturer with you to meet with the inspector to ask about adding another circuit. Or compute your home's power needs using the chart at right.

Evaluating a home's total loads

A 60-amp service is probably too little for a modern home unless it is small. If a home is under 3,000 square feet and does not have central air-conditioning or electric heat, 100-amp service should be enough. A home larger than 2,000 square feet with central air or electric heat probably needs 200-amp service.

1. Calculate your total needs. First multiply the square footage of all the living areas times three watts. This is the total lighting and receptacle needs.

2. Add 1500 watts for each kitchen small-appliance circuit and laundry-room circuit.

3. Add the wattages for all appliances that are on their own circuits, such as an electric dryer, water heater, or range; or a window air-conditioner. (Check the nameplates and remember that watts = volts times amps.)

4. Add the three numbers up. Figure the first 10,000 watts at 100 percent and the remaining watts at 40 percent.

5. Add the wattage of either the heating unit or the central air-conditioner—whichever is greater.

6. Divide this figure by 230. This figure tells how many amps a home needs.

Example
Here's a sample calculation for a 2,000-square-foot home with central air:

1. 2,000 square feet × 3 =	6000 watts
2. Two kitchen small-appliance circuits plus a laundry-room circuit: 3 × 1500 =	4500 watts
3. Water heater: 5000 watts	
Dishwasher: 1200 watts	
Electric dryer: 5500 watts =	11700 watts
	22200 watts
4. First 10000 at 100 percent =	10000 watts
Remaining 12200 at 40 percent =	4800 watts
Subtotal =	**14880 watts**
5. Central air =	4000 watts
Total =	**18800 watts**
6. Total divided by 230 =	÷ 230
(100-amp service will be enough for this home.)	**81 amps**

REFRESHER COURSE
Inspecting a service panel

A service panel should be located out of children's reach, but where adults can get to it easily. Any exposed cables leading to it should be firmly attached to the wall and clamped tightly to knockout holes in the panel. If there are any open holes, cover them with a "goof plug" (available at hardware stores).

If a #14 wire is connected to a 20-amp circuit breaker or fuse, replace the breaker or fuse with one that is 15 amps to prevent the wire from overheating. In most cases, a 20-amp fuse or breaker should be connected to a #12 wire; a 30-amp fuse or breaker should be connected to a #10 wire.

Wires should run in a fairly orderly way around the perimeter of the panel. If you find a hopeless tangle, call in an electrician for an evaluation. Also call in a pro if you find melted or nicked wire insulation, any signs of fire, or extensive rust.

In an older home, there's a good chance that a service panel has had new wiring added over the years—perhaps by a pro, perhaps by an amateur. So check out all the connections.

Small fuse box: A 60-amp fuse box may be found in an older home that has not had its wiring upgraded. It can supply power to only one 240-volt appliance and is probably inadequate for a home larger than 1,200 square feet.

Medium size service: A 100-amp service panel provides enough power for a medium-sized home, even if it has several 240-volt appliances and central air-conditioning (opposite page).

Large capacity: Many newer homes and some older large homes have a 150- or 200-amp service panel. Unless the home is a mansion, there is virtually no way to overload it.

STANLEY PRO TIP: **Making room in a service panel**

Knockout tab

If a service panel has an unused slot for a circuit breaker, installing a new breaker is easy. Poke and twist out the knockout tab and install the new breaker (pages 230–231).

Tandem breaker

If there is no open space, codes may permit you to replace a single breaker with a tandem breaker, which supplies two circuits while taking up only one space. Ask an inspector.

Add capacity with a subpanel

Subpanel

If you can't fit new breakers into the service panel, either hire a pro to install a new service panel or add a subpanel. Pages 232–233 show you how to do this.

DRAWING PLANS

Carefully drawn plans help show the building inspector that you've thought through your project. And spending an extra hour or two with pencil and paper will help you spot potential problems before you begin tearing into walls, saving you time and expense in the long run.

A drawing must include the locations and types of all fixtures, switches, receptacles, hardwired appliances, and cables. On an attached sheet, provide a complete list of materials.

Drawing plans

Get a pad of graph paper, a straightedge, a compass, and several colored pencils if you will be installing several circuits. Make a scale drawing of the room, including features such as counters and cabinets.

First make a rough drawing. Use the symbols shown below or get a list of symbols from your local building department. Make a quick freehand drawing, using colored pencils to indicate each circuit. Are the switches in convenient locations? Are all the circuits correctly loaded *(pages 120–121)*? Do you have enough receptacles, and will they be easy to reach? Once you've made your final decisions, draw a neat, final version of the plan.

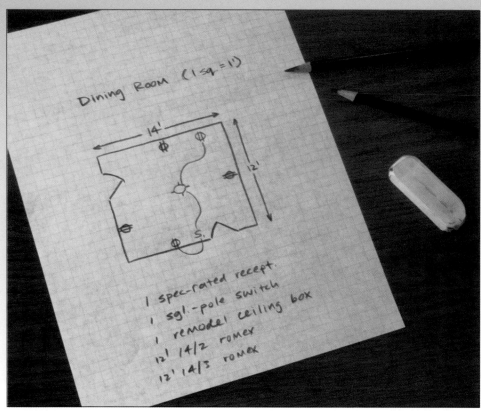

A simple extension of an existing circuit— in this example, adding a receptacle and a switched light fixture—is easy to draw.

Don't take the task lightly: Use the correct symbols and make the drawing clear and neat.

Electrical symbols

Duplex receptacle	240-volt receptacle	Ceiling light fixture	Split-wired duplex receptacle	Fourplex receptacle
Wall light	Wall junction box	Ceiling fan	Vent fan	Switched receptacle
Fluorescent ceiling light	Recessed canister light	GFCI receptacle	Indoor telephone	Television jack
Service panel	S Single-pole switch	S_P Pilot light switch	S_3 3-way switch	S_4 4-way switch

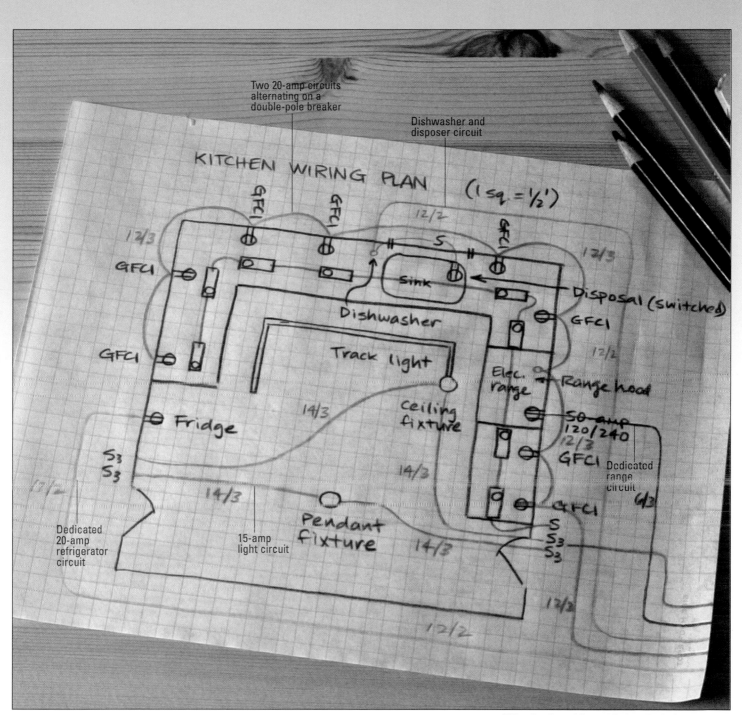

Two 20-amp circuits alternating on a double-pole breaker

Dishwasher and disposer circuit

KITCHEN WIRING PLAN (1 sq. = ½')

GFCI
GFCI
12/2
12/3
GFCI
S
12/3
GFCI
Sink
Disposal (switched)
GFCI
Dishwasher
12/2
GFCI
Track light
Elec. range
Range hood
Ceiling fixture
14/3
Fridge
50-amp 120/240
12/3
GFCI
Dedicated range circuit
S₃
S₃
14/3
GFCI
Dedicated 20-amp refrigerator circuit
14/3
Pendant fixture
15-amp light circuit
14/3
S
S₃
S₃
12/2

Safe capacity
To make sure the planned circuits won't be overloaded, check *page 120* for how to calculate safe capacity.

Photocopy the floor plan
For complex projects, draw your floor plan, then make several photocopies. This allows you to sketch out several trial plans.

This plan for wiring a kitchen includes a 15-amp circuit for lights, some controlled by three-way switches. A 20-amp refrigerator circuit has been added, as well as two 20-amp small-appliance circuits and a 20-amp circuit for the dishwasher and garbage disposer. The range has its own circuit.

INSTALLING CABLE & BOXES

In a typical wiring project, installing cable and boxes can take four or five times as long as making the connections. It's important to plan cable runs and box placement carefully.

Getting the right materials

All the materials you plan to install need the approval of your local building department. Local electrical codes will determine the type of cable you need, as well as whether the boxes should be plastic or metal. Buy boxes that are as large as possible or consult *page 17* to make sure your boxes are large enough for the wires they will hold.

Cable, boxes, receptacles, and switches are not expensive and can be returned if you do not use them. So buy more than you think you need to save trips back to the home center. Purchase plenty of the little items needed for a project too—straps or staples, nail guards, electrician's tape, and wire nuts of several sizes.

Plan your work

Be sure you understand exactly how each installation will be wired. Consult the specific projects described in this book. Follow them from start to finish. Draw a plan and make a materials list. Have them approved by your local building department. Buy all the materials you need and store them in an uncluttered space so you can easily get at what you need when you need it.

The order of work

Determine how you will connect to power *(pages 136–137)*. When working in exposed framing (in a new addition, or if the drywall or plaster has been removed), first install the boxes, then drill holes and run the cable *(pages 138–141)*.

If you are working in finished walls and ceilings, first cut holes for the boxes *(page 142)*. Run the cable through a basement or attic, or fish it through the walls *(pages 144–147)*. Then install the boxes *(page 143)*.

Here's how to install the backbone of a new circuit—boxes to hold devices and cable to carry power.

CHAPTER PREVIEW

Stripping and clamping NM cable
page 128

Armored cable
page 130

Metal conduit
page 132

PVC conduit
page 134

Pulling wires through conduit
page 135

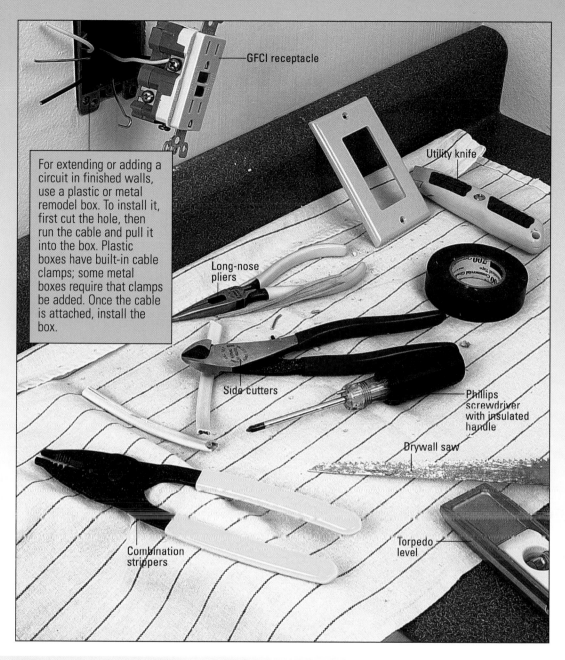

GFCI receptacle

Utility knife

Long-nose pliers

Side cutters

Phillips screwdriver with insulated handle

Drywall saw

Torpedo level

Combination strippers

For extending or adding a circuit in finished walls, use a plastic or metal remodel box. To install it, first cut the hole, then run the cable and pull it into the box. Plastic boxes have built-in cable clamps; some metal boxes require that clamps be added. Once the cable is attached, install the box.

To attach a new receptacle or switch, start by removing sheathing from cable (pages 128–131) and strip wire ends— 1 inch for a splice, or ¾ inch for a terminal connection—using a pair of combination strippers. Poke the stripped wires into the box and clamp the cable. If you need to splice two or more wires, hold them side by side, grab their ends with a pair of lineman's pliers, and twist them together to form a uniform spiral. Snip off the end and twist on a wire nut of the correct size (page 19). To connect a wire to a terminal, use long-nose pliers or a wire-bending screwdriver to form a clockwise loop in the wire end. Slip the loop over a loosened terminal screw, squeeze the wire tight to the screw threads, and tighten the screw.

 Grabbing power *page 136*

 Installing boxes in framing *page 138*

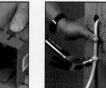 **Running cable in framing** *page 139*

 Working with metal studs *page 141*

 Installing boxes in finished walls *page 142*

 Running cable through finished rooms *page 144*

 Patching walls *page 148*

STRIPPING AND CLAMPING NM CABLE

Nonmetallic cable (NM cable) is easy to work with and inexpensive, so it's not surprising that it is the most common type of cable used in household wiring.

NM cable is usually sold in lengths of 25, 50, or 100 feet, or more. When in doubt, buy the larger package—it doesn't cost much more and it may come in handy later.

NM's plastic sheathing does not offer much protection to the wires, so keep it out of harm's way. If the cable might get wet, install UF (underground feed) cable, which encases wires in molded plastic. Wherever cable will be exposed—in a garage or basement—many local codes call for armored cable or conduit *(pages 130–135)*.

Codes call for running NM through the center of studs so that drywall nails cannot damage it. If the cable is less than 1¼ inches from the edge of a framing member, install a protective nailing plate *(page 140)*. Some codes require metal plates even if the cable is in the center of a stud.

Take care not to damage wire insulation when working with NM cable. Slit the sheathing right down the middle using a sharp utility knife. To avoid slicing the wire insulation, don't cut too deep. Or use the sheathing stripper shown below.

When cutting cable to length, leave yourself an extra foot or two. If you make a mistake while stripping, you can recut the cable and try again.

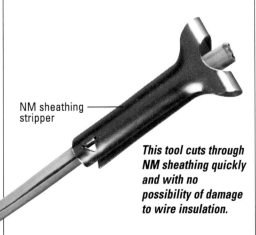

NM sheathing stripper

This tool cuts through NM sheathing quickly and with no possibility of damage to wire insulation.

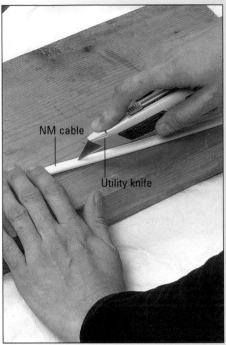

NM cable
Utility knife

1 Lay the cable on a flat work surface, such as a small sheet of plywood. Starting 8–10 inches from the end, insert the tip of a utility knife blade into the center of the cable, pushing just hard enough to cut through the sheathing.

Pierce sheathing without nicking wires

2 Slice the sheathing, exerting even pressure. You'll feel the tip of the knife rubbing against the bare ground wire as you slice. With practice, you can cut evenly and quickly without damaging wire insulation.

WHAT IF ...
You have three-wire cable?

NM cable that holds three wires (plus the ground) is round rather than flat. If you cut through the sheathing too deeply, you'll hit insulated wire rather than the ground wire. Practice cutting through the sheathing. Always examine the wires for damage after removing the sheathing.

REFRESHER COURSE
Grounding NM cable

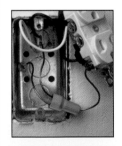

If the box is metal, code requires it to be grounded. The surest method is to connect both the device and the box to the ground wire using pigtails.

If the box is plastic, simply connect the ground wire to the device's grounding terminal.

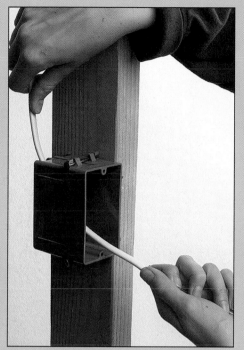

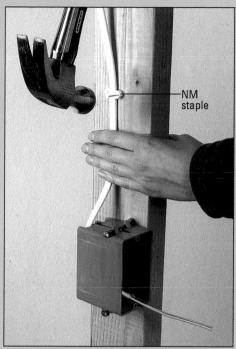

3 Pull back the plastic sheathing, as well as the paper that wraps the wires, exposing 6–8 inches of wire. Use a pair of side cutters to snip back the sheathing and paper. If you use a utility knife, cut away from the wires to avoid cutting or nicking the insulation.

4 Insert the wires into the box. With this type of plastic box, push the wires through a hole, which has a tab that grabs the cable. Check that about ½ inch of sheathing is visible inside the box. Other types of boxes use other clamping methods.

5 Wherever possible, staple NM cable firmly to a framing member, out of reach of nails. Cable should be stapled within 8 inches of the box and every 2–4 feet along the run of the cable. Check your local building codes.

Other clamping methods

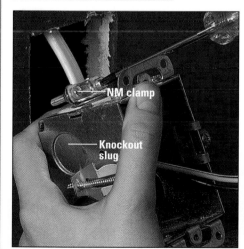

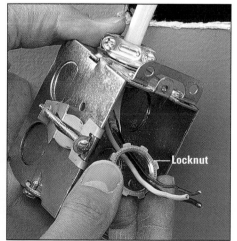

Clamp on box: Remove a knockout slug from a metal box and fasten an NM clamp in the hole. Insert the clamp and tighten the locknut. Insert the cable through the clamp; tighten the screws.

Cable first: Remove the locknut from the cable clamp and fasten the clamp to the cable. Then insert the cable with clamp body into the box, slide on the locknut, and tighten it.

Built-in clamps: Some boxes have built-in clamps. Slide in the cable and tighten the screws.

ARMORED CABLE

Some municipalities require either armored cable or conduit *(pages 132–135)*, rather than NM. Even if your local codes do not demand it, you may choose to install armored cable for added safety, especially wherever cable will be exposed.

Pluses and minuses
The coiled metal sheathing that wraps armored cable protects its wires from puncture by nails, unless a nail hits it dead-center. (Even conduit cannot offer absolute protection against a direct hit.) You may want to run armored cable behind moldings where it comes near nails *(pages 144–145)*. Armored cable costs more than NM, takes longer to strip and clamp, and can't make tight turns. With some practice, you can install armored cable nearly as quickly as NM.

BX cable has no ground wire *(page 131, lower right)*, is common in older homes, and is still available in some areas. Local code may limit use of BX to no more than 6 feet; then ground wire must be used. MC cable has a green-insulated ground wire, used like the bare ground wire in NM cable.

1 Bend the cable about 10 inches from its end and squeeze with your hand until the coils of the armor come apart. If you can't do this by hand, use pliers or employ one of the other cutting methods shown below.

2 Firmly grip the cable on each side of the cut and twist until the split-apart armor coil pops out, away from the wires. Use two pairs of pliers if you can't do this by hand.

REFRESHER COURSE
Grounding MC cable

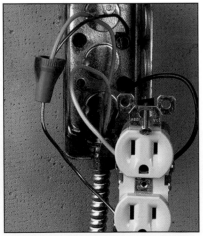

MC cable has a ground wire. Attach it the same way you would the ground wire in NM cable *(page 128)*, except strip the green insulation first.

Other cutting methods

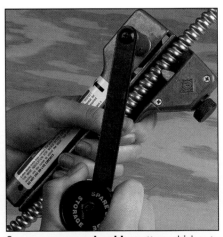

If the method shown in the steps above seems too difficult, try cutting the cable with a **hacksaw.** Cut through just one of the coils and no more, so you won't damage any wires. Then twist and pull off the waste piece.

Or use an **armored-cable cutter,** which cuts at just the right depth. Adjust it for the size of cable, slip in the cable, and turn the crank.

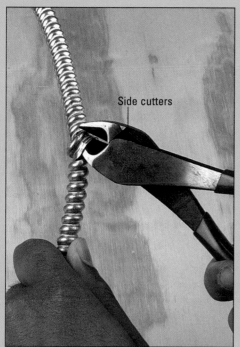

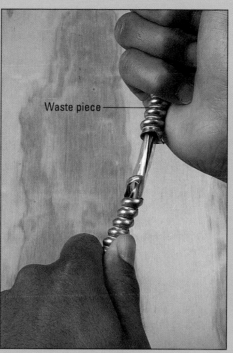

Side cutters

Waste piece

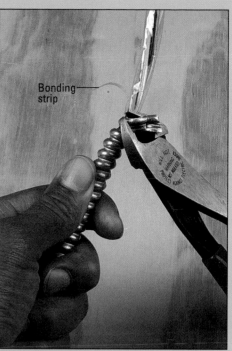

Bonding strip

3 Using side cutters, cut the exposed coil of sheathing. You may have to grab the coil with the side cutters and work it back and forth to open and make the cut.

4 If you are cutting a piece to length, slide back the sheathing and cut through the wires. Otherwise slide the waste piece off and throw it away.

5 Cut off any sharp points of sheathing, using side cutters. Remove the paper wrapping and any thin plastic strips. If the cable is BX, it will have a thin metal bonding strip. Cut it to about 2 inches.

STANLEY PRO TIP: **Clamping armored cable**

Bushing

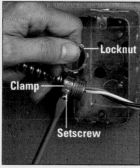

Locknut

Clamp

Setscrew

Knockout slug

Locknut

1 If the cable did not come with a bag of little bushings, purchase some. Slip a bushing over the wires and slide it down into the sheathing so it protects wires from the cut end of the armor.

2 Use an armored-cable clamp, which has a single setscrew. Remove the locknut and slide the clamp over the wires and down onto the bushing. Then tighten the setscrew.

3 Remove the knockout slug from the box. Guide the wires and the clamp through the hole. Slip the locknut over the wires and screw it onto the clamp. Tighten the nut by levering it with a screwdriver or tapping it with a screwdriver and hammer.

BX cable with a bonding strip

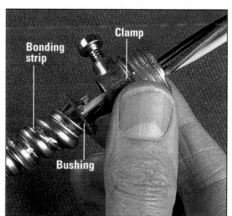

Clamp

Bonding strip

Bushing

The metal sheathing of BX cable acts as the ground; a thin metal bonding strip helps ensure a conductive connection. Before putting on a cable clamp, wrap a strip 2 inches long around the sheathing.

METAL CONDUIT

Conduit offers superior protection and safety for wires. Even if local codes permit NM or armored cable in a basement, garage, attic, or crawlspace, consider installing conduit to protect wiring.

Choosing conduit

Metal conduit comes in several thicknesses. For most interior home installations, EMT (also called thinwall) is strong enough. Outdoors, use intermediate metal conduit (IMC), or PVC conduit *(page 134)*. PVC is sometimes used indoors as well.

Metal conduit may serve as the path for grounding, or local codes may require you to run a green-insulated ground wire. If you use PVC pipe, you definitely need a ground wire, either green-insulated or bare copper. **If there will be no ground wire, take extra care that all the connections in metal conduit are firm; one loose joint could break the grounding path.**

Conduit fittings

A conduit bender, used by professional electricians, is a fairly expensive tool that takes time to master. Unless you will be running lots of metal conduit, you'll save time by buying prebent fittings. A coupling joins two pieces of conduit end to end. A sweep makes a slow turn through which wires can slide easily. A pulling elbow makes a sharper turn.

The setscrew fittings shown here are commonly used with EMT conduit; they provide joints that are firm but not waterproof. For weathertight joints, use IMC conduit and compression fittings *(page 219)*.

Flexible metal conduit

Flexible metal conduit, also called Greenfield, is like armored cable without the wires. It's not cheap, so it is typically used only in places where it would be difficult to run conduit.

When installing a hardwired appliance, such as an electric water heater or cooktop *(page 229)*, buy an electrical "whip," which is a section of armored cable equipped with the correct fittings for attaching to that specific appliance.

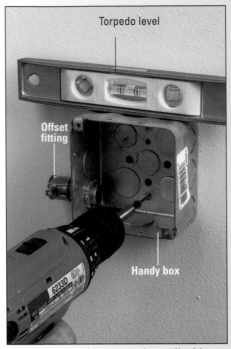

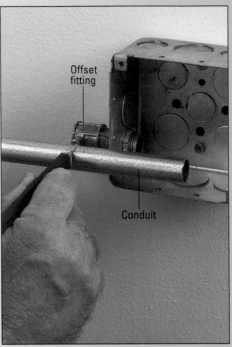

1 Anchor metal boxes to the wall with screws. For exposed wiring, use "handy boxes," which have rounded edges and metal covers. An offset fitting allows the conduit to run tight up against the wall.

2 Once the boxes are installed, measure the conduit for cutting. The surest method is to hold a piece in place and mark it, rather than using a tape measure. Remember that the conduit will slide about an inch into each fitting.

Metal conduit

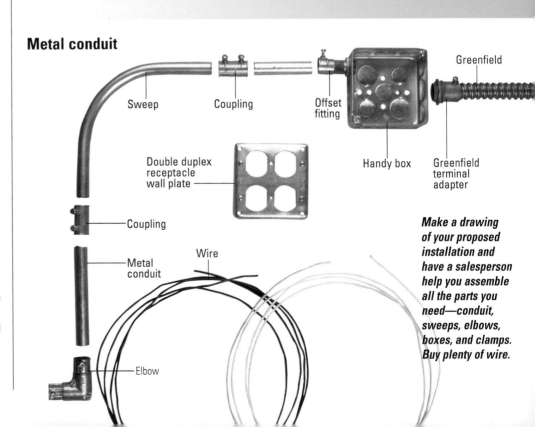

Make a drawing of your proposed installation and have a salesperson help you assemble all the parts you need—conduit, sweeps, elbows, boxes, and clamps. Buy plenty of wire.

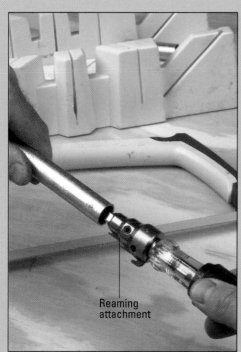

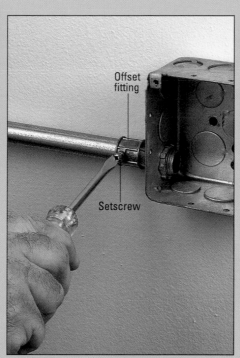

3 Cut the conduit to fit with a hacksaw. Do not use a tubing cutter, which creates sharp edges inside the conduit that could damage wire insulation. Remove the burrs inside and out. A conduit-reaming attachment on a screwdriver makes this easy.

4 Slide the conduit all the way into a fitting and tighten the setscrew. Test to make sure the connection is tight. (If you will not be installing a ground wire, these connections are critical for grounding.)

5 Anchor the conduit with a one- or two-hole strap at least every 6 feet and within 2 feet of each box. The larger the conduit, the closer the straps need to be. Check with local codes. Screws should be driven into joists or studs, not just into drywall.

Conduit that's large enough

Make sure the wires have ample room inside the conduit to slide through easily. Local codes have detailed regulations regarding conduit size, but in general, ½-inch conduit is large enough for five or fewer wires; ¾-inch conduit is used for more than five wires. When in doubt, or if you might run more wire in the future, buy the larger size—it doesn't cost much more.

Anchoring conduit
Anchor conduit with one- or two-hole straps every 6 feet and within 2 feet of each box.

A pulling elbow every fourth turn

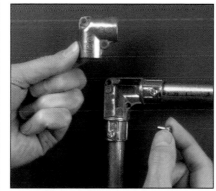

Every time you make a turn, it gets harder for the wires to slide through. If the conduit will make more than three turns before entering a box, install a pulling elbow so you can access the wires. Never make a splice here, just use it as an access point when pulling wires.

STANLEY PRO TIP: **Anchoring to masonry**

To attach boxes and straps to concrete, block, or brick, buy masonry screws and the correct masonry bit. Level the box and drill pilot holes.

Drive a masonry screw into the pilot hole, being careful not to overtighten it. The combination of proper hole and screw provides a much more secure attachment than a plastic anchor.

PVC CONDUIT

Plastic conduit is nearly as durable as metal conduit and it costs less. Some local codes permit it for exposed indoor wiring as well as for outdoor installations *(pages 216–223).*

When installing PVC, connect four or five pieces in a dry run, then dismantle and glue the pieces together. When making a turn, take care that the elbow or sweep is facing in exactly the right direction when you glue it. Once the glue sets, there's no way to make adjustments. Work in a well-ventilated area when using PVC primer and cement; the fumes are powerful and dangerous.

Consult your local codes for the correct PVC cement. You may be required to apply purple-colored primer to every piece before you apply the cement. **Always run a green-insulated ground wire through PVC pipe.**

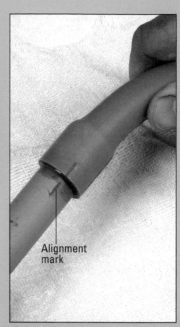

Backsaw

Miter box

Alignment mark

Primer

Alignment mark

1 Install PVC boxes, then measure and mark the conduit for a cut. Cut with a backsaw and miter box, or a hacksaw, or a circular saw equipped with a plywood blade.

2 Use alignment marks to ensure that the pieces will face in the right direction. Apply PVC primer (if needed) and cement to the outside of the conduit and to the inside of the fitting.

3 Immediately push the conduit into the fitting, twisting slightly to align the marks. Hold the pieces together for about 10 seconds; wipe away excess cement.

Flexible nonmetallic conduit

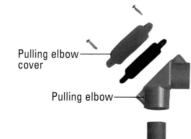

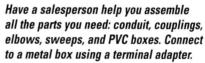
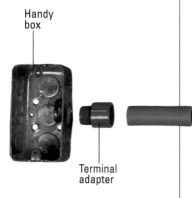

Pulling elbow cover

Pulling elbow

Coupling

PVC box

Handy box

Radius elbow

Terminal adapter

Have a salesperson help you assemble all the parts you need: conduit, couplings, elbows, sweeps, and PVC boxes. Connect to a metal box using a terminal adapter.

Flexible nonmetallic conduit

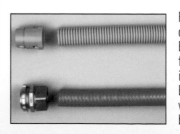

Flexible plastic tubing is a convenient way to channel wiring. Blue corrugated EMT tubing is used for indoor installations; moisture-impermeable tubing is used outdoors. Both come in long coils. Check to see whether these products are allowed by your local codes.

PULLING WIRES THROUGH CONDUIT

If wires travel less than 6 feet through conduit and make only one or two turns, you may be able to simply push them through. For longer runs, use a fish tape.

If wires become kinked while you work, they will get stuck. So have a helper feed the wire carefully from one end of the conduit while you pull at the other end. If you must work alone, precut the wires (leave yourself an extra 2 feet or so) and unroll them so that they can slide smoothly through the conduit.

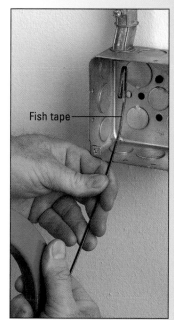

Fish tape

1 At a box or pulling elbow, push the fish tape into the conduit and thread it back to the point of entry.

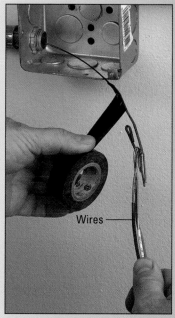

Wires

2 Strip 6 inches of insulation from one wire, 8 inches from another wire, 10 inches from a third wire, and so on. Fold the wires over the fish tape as shown and wrap tightly with electrician's tape.

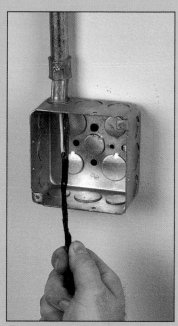

3 Pull smoothly, using long strokes to avoid stopping and starting. If the wires get stuck, back up a foot or so and start again.

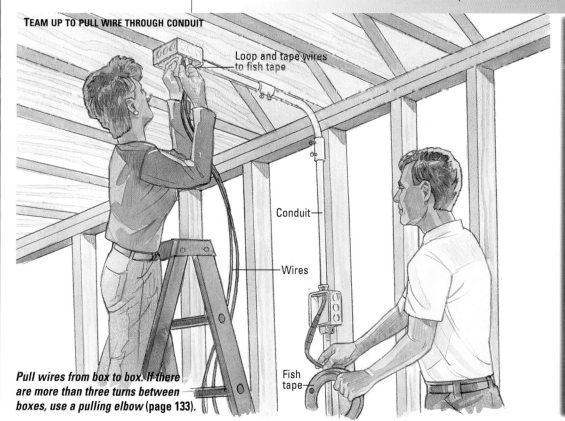

TEAM UP TO PULL WIRE THROUGH CONDUIT

Loop and tape wires to fish tape

Conduit

Wires

Fish tape

Pull wires from box to box. If there are more than three turns between boxes, use a pulling elbow (page 133).

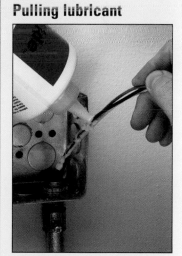

STANLEY PRO TIP

Pulling lubricant

If the pulling gets tough, try squirting some pulling lubricant on the wires. Don't use soap, detergent, oil, or grease, which can damage wire insulation.

GRABBING POWER

When planning new electrical service, begin by deciding where you can tap into power. If you are adding a couple of receptacles or lights, it is usually easiest to grab power from a nearby receptacle or junction box. First, however, make sure the new service will not overload the circuit (pages 120–121).

If nearby boxes are on circuits that do not have enough available wattage for the new service, try a box farther away. If no circuit is usable or if the new service needs its own circuit, run cable all the way to the service panel and connect to a new circuit breaker (pages 230–231).

If you need to run cable through walls and ceilings to get at power, see pages 142–149.

PRESTART CHECKLIST

☐ **TIME**
About two hours to connect new cable to an existing receptacle or junction box (not including cutting a pathway for the cable and patching walls)

☐ **TOOLS**
Voltage tester, drill, saw, hammer, close-work hacksaw, screwdriver, strippers, long-nose pliers, lineman's pliers

☐ **SKILLS**
Stripping wire and connecting wire to terminals; running cable through walls; prying and cutting nails

☐ **PREP**
Spread a drop cloth or towel on the floor. Run cable to the box from which you will grab power (pages 139–147).

☐ **MATERIALS**
New cable, wire nuts, electrician's tape, cable clamps, remodel box

Voltage tester

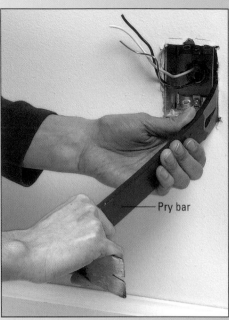

Pry bar

1 To grab power from a receptacle, make a load list to verify that there is room on the circuit for new service. **Shut off power to the circuit and test that power is not present.** Disconnect the receptacle.

2 If the box is inside a wall, either cut a hole in the wall to get at the box or pull the box out. Pry with a flat pry bar, then remove the nails or cut through them with a close-work hacksaw.

Grabbing power from a junction box and switch

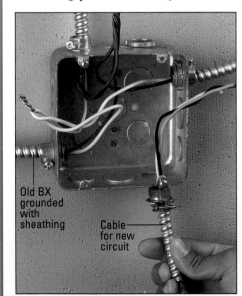

Old BX grounded with sheathing

Cable for new circuit

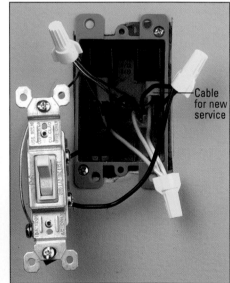

Cable for new service

To grab power from a junction box, **shut off power,** remove wire nuts, and splice the new wires. You may need to cover the resulting splice with larger wire nuts.

You can grab power from a switch box only if power enters the box (rather than going to the fixture) and two cables are present. Connect with pigtails as shown.

3 Pull out the box carefully—the cable may be stapled to a stud. Disconnect the cable(s) from the old box. Choose a remodel box to fit the hole *(pages 16–17)*. Clamp the old and new cables to the remodel box.

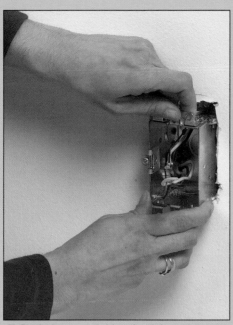

4 Push the remodel box back into place and clamp it to the wall.

5 If the new receptacle is at the end of the run (with only one cable entering the box), simply connect the new wires to the proper terminals and connect the grounds.

STANLEY PRO TIP

Wire into the old box

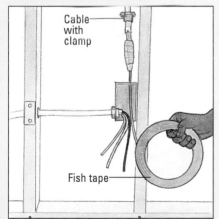

Cable with clamp

Fish tape

You may be able to avoid the step of removing the old box. Pry out a knockout slug and run a fish tape up through the hole. Attach the tape to cable that has been stripped and has a clamp attached (with the locknut removed). Pull the wires through, seat the clamp, and screw on the locknut.

WHAT IF...
You grab power from a mid-run receptacle?

If two cables enter the box, the receptacle is in the middle of a run. Splice the wires and connect to terminals with pigtails, as shown. The purpose of pigtails is to avoid multiple connections to one terminal screw where they could easily short or come loose. Make pigtails by removing the sheathing from about 8 inches of NM cable. Strip about ½ inch for each end of the black and white wires and attach them as shown.

Code issues: Cable must be clamped to the box or stapled to a stud within 8 inches of the box. NM cable is the easiest to run, but some localities require armored cable or conduit. Some localities require metal rather than plastic boxes.

INSTALLING BOXES IN FRAMING

Installing new wiring is much easier if the framing in a room is uncovered than if the walls and ceilings are covered with drywall or plaster *(pages 142–149)*.

Buy switch and receptacle boxes that meet local codes *(pages 118–119)* and that are large enough for the wires they will hold *(page 17)*. It's easy to underestimate, so buy extra supplies. At the same time you install boxes, attach fans, lights, or other fixtures that need to be hardwired.

Local codes specify where cable should run and at what height to place receptacle and switch boxes. Check codes before you begin.

PRESTART CHECKLIST

☐ **TIME**
About an hour to install eight wall or ceiling boxes

☐ **TOOLS**
Hammer, tape measure, drill, screwdriver

☐ **SKILLS**
Measuring; driving nails

☐ **PREP**
Expose framing; remove obstructions in the room; make and follow a written plan that plots the location of each box

☐ **MATERIALS**
New-work electrical boxes, 1¼-inch wood screws (not drywall screws)

1 Receptacle boxes are typically placed 12 inches up from the floor. Measure with a tape measure, or set your hammer upright on the floor, and rest the box on top of the handle.

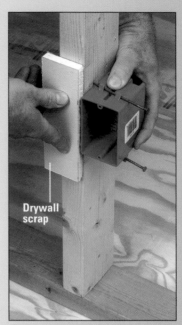

Drywall scrap

2 The front edge of the box must be flush with the finished wall surface, usually ½-inch-thick drywall. Some boxes have depth gauges. Or use a scrap of drywall to position the box.

3 Drive the box's nails into the stud or joist. If the box attaches with a flange, drive screws or nails to anchor the box (below).

Using a mud ring

Adapter rings, also called mud rings, are typically ½ inch or ⅝ inch thick. Choose a ring that matches the thickness of the drywall or paneling you will install. Attach the box flush with the front edge of the framing member, then add the ring.

STANLEY PRO TIP

Mounting a ceiling light fixture box

Decide where you want a ceiling light fixture to go (usually the center of a room). Attach a flanged box directly to a ceiling joist (left). For more precise placement, install a box attached to a hanger bar; the box slides along the bar. Note: A hanger bar cannot support a ceiling fan; you must use a fan-rated box *(page 16)*.

RUNNING CABLE IN FRAMING

Nonmetallic (NM) cable is acceptable under most building codes, but some localities require armored cable or conduit. Armored cable is run much like the NM cable shown, though you may need to drill larger holes and you'll have more difficulty turning corners. To run conduit through framing, use a level or a chalk line to make sure the holes are aligned for straight runs.

If a wayward nail pierces NM cable, the result could be disastrous. Place holes in the framing out of reach of drywall nails and attach protective plates at every hole.

PRESTART CHECKLIST

☐ **TIME**
About three hours to run cable and attach to seven or eight wall or ceiling boxes

☐ **TOOLS**
Drill, ¾-inch spade bits, screwdriver, strippers, lineman's pliers, hammer, tape measure, level

☐ **SKILLS**
Drilling; stripping cable sheathing and wire insulation; attaching staples

☐ **PREP**
Double-check that all the boxes are correctly positioned; clear the room of all obstructions

☐ **MATERIALS**
Correct cable (page 15), staples appropriate to cable type, nailing plates

1 Use a tape measure and level to mark holes that will line up in a straight line about 12 inches above the boxes. With a sharp spade bit, drill a ¾-inch hole through the center of each stud.

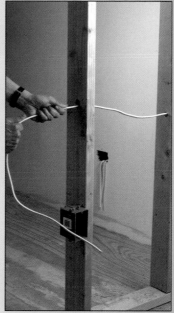

2 Uncoil cable carefully from the box to prevent kinks. Pull the cable through the holes. The cable should be fairly straight but should not be taut.

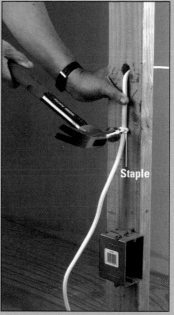

3 Within 8 inches of a plastic box or 12 inches of a metal box, anchor the cable in the middle of the stud with a staple. Drive staples every 2 feet where cable runs along a framing member.

INSTALLING NM CABLE

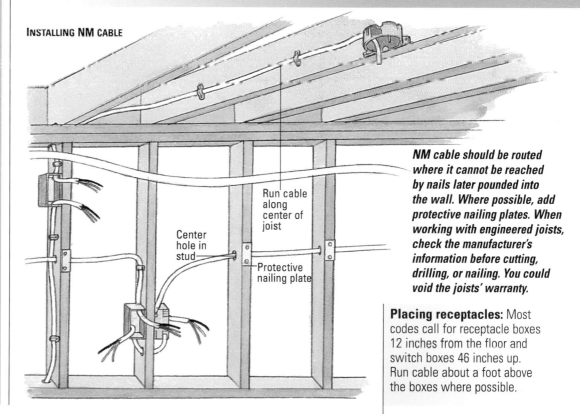

Run cable along center of joist
Center hole in stud
Protective nailing plate

NM cable should be routed where it cannot be reached by nails later pounded into the wall. Where possible, add protective nailing plates. When working with engineered joists, check the manufacturer's information before cutting, drilling, or nailing. You could void the joists' warranty.

Placing receptacles: Most codes call for receptacle boxes 12 inches from the floor and switch boxes 46 inches up. Run cable about a foot above the boxes where possible.

Running cable in framing (continued)

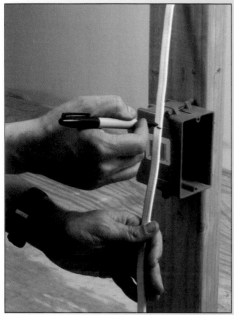

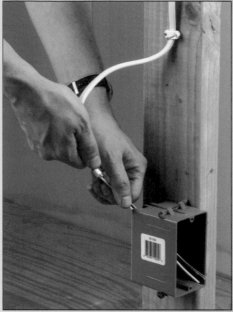

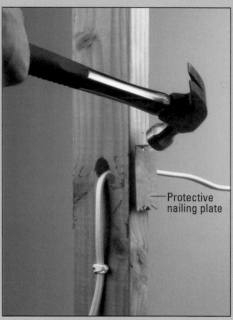

— Protective nailing plate

4 Mark where you will strip sheathing and cut the cable. About ½ inch of sheathing should enter the box, and the wires inside the box should be 8–12 inches long (you can always trim them later).

5 With a hammer and screwdriver, open the knockout. On some plastic boxes you remove the knockout entirely. For the one shown, crack open one end of the tab so it can grab the cable. A metal box may have a built-in clamp, or you may have to add a clamp before sliding in the cable.

6 Wherever a nail might accidentally pierce the cable, attach a protective nailing plate. Tap the plate in place and hammer it in. Attach a plate on both sides of the stud, if needed.

STANLEY PRO TIP: **Turning a corner**

Corner framing

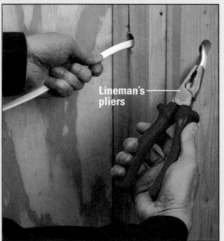

Lineman's pliers

1 When you reach a corner, drill a hole in each stud. Bend the cable into an L shape.

2 Poke the cable through the first hole and wiggle it into the next hole. When the cable starts to stick out the second hole, grab it with pliers and pull.

WHAT IF...
You have a lot of holes to drill?

A standard ⅜-inch drill may overheat after drilling four or five holes. If you have many holes to bore, rent a ½-inch, right-angle drill. When using it, hold on tightly and brace yourself; it has more power and can twist around, possibly causing an injury.

WORKING WITH METAL STUDS

Contractors have been using metal studs for decades. More and more homeowners are discovering that these save money and are easy to install.

Metal studs have precut holes designed to accommodate electrical and plumbing lines. When running NM cable through metal framing, inspect the holes to be sure that there are no rough or sharp edges that could damage insulation. Always use the special bushings (Step 2) designed to protect wiring.

PRESTART CHECKLIST

☐ **TIME**
About three hours to run cable and attach to seven or eight wall or ceiling boxes

☐ **TOOLS**
Screwdriver, tin snips, strippers, variable-speed drill, lineman's pliers, nonconducting ladder

☐ **SKILLS**
Installing metal framing; stripping cable sheathing and wire insulation; attaching bushings

☐ **PREP**
Assemble metal framing and clear the room of obstructions

☐ **MATERIALS**
Bushings, cable, boxes designed for metal studs

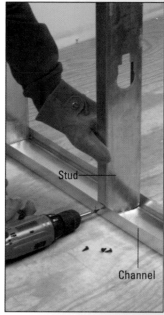

Stud

Channel

1 Cut metal studs and channels with tin snips. Slide the studs into channels at the bottom and top of the wall. Anchor each joint by driving a self-piercing screw.

Bushing

2 Where the cable will run through a stud, snap a protective bushing into place. These come in two pieces that press together.

3 Pull cable through as you would through holes in wood framing, sliding it through the protective bushings.

INSTALLING WIRING IN STEEL STUD FRAMING

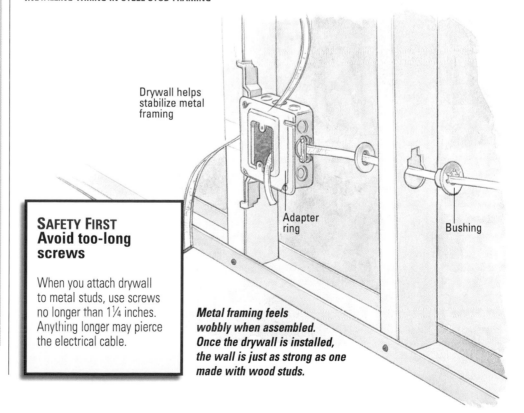

Drywall helps stabilize metal framing

Adapter ring

Bushing

SAFETY FIRST
Avoid too-long screws

When you attach drywall to metal studs, use screws no longer than 1¼ inches. Anything longer may pierce the electrical cable.

Metal framing feels wobbly when assembled. Once the drywall is installed, the wall is just as strong as one made with wood studs.

INSTALLING BOXES IN FINISHED WALLS

Running cable through walls that are covered with drywall or plaster is probably the most difficult wiring task you will encounter. Plan the job carefully before starting; see *page 144* for the order of work.

Special remodel boxes (also called "cut-in" or "old-work" boxes) clamp themselves to the drywall or plaster rather than attaching to a framing member, making the work easier. However they will be only as strong as the wall surface to which they are clamped. If the drywall or plaster is damaged, cut a larger hole and install a box that attaches directly to a stud or joist. Select boxes that meet local codes *(pages 16–17)*. For a ceiling fan or a heavy light fixture, buy a fixture box that attaches to a fan-rated brace.

Before cutting a hole, use a stud finder to make sure no joist or stud is in the way.

PRESTART CHECKLIST

☐ **TIME**
About 15 minutes to cut a hole and install a remodel box (not including cutting a pathway for the cable and patching walls)

☐ **TOOLS**
Stud finder, torpedo level, utility knife, screwdriver, hammer, drill, drywall saw (or rotary cutter or saber saw)

☐ **SKILLS**
Measuring and cutting drywall

☐ **PREP**
Carefully plan the routes for the cables and the locations for the boxes *(pages 144–147)*. Spread a drop cloth or large towel on the floor below them.

☐ **MATERIALS**
Remodel boxes acceptable under local code; cable clamps, if needed

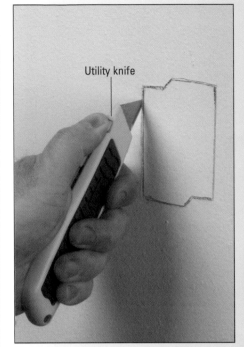

Utility knife

1 If the box does not come with a cardboard template, hold its face against the wall, use a torpedo level to make sure it is straight, and trace it. With a utility knife, cut the line deeply enough to cut through the drywall paper.

Drywall saw

2 Cut the hole with a drywall saw. Cut to the inside of the knife cut to prevent fraying the paper. Test to make sure the box will fit in the hole.

WHAT IF...
The wall is made of plaster and lath?

Take your time cutting a lath-and-plaster wall—it's easy to damage the surrounding area. Most plaster is attached to ⅜-inch-thick wood lath, which cuts fairly easily if it does not vibrate. If it does vibrate as you saw, sections of plaster can loosen from the lath. It is difficult to make a neat hole in plaster and lath, so have patching plaster on hand. If plaster is attached to metal lath, cut all the way through the plaster with a knife and then cut the metal lath with side cutters.

Make several passes with a sharp knife. Drill starter holes at each corner and then cut with a saber saw. Press the saw firmly against the wall to minimize lath vibration.

Or use a rotary cutter equipped with a plaster-cutting blade. Practice first because this tool is hard to control.

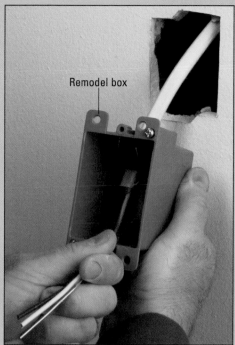

Remodel box

3 Run cable through the hole *(pages 144–147)*. Strip 12 inches of sheathing and run the cable into the box. Whichever clamping method the box uses, make sure ½ inch of sheathing shows inside the box. Tug to make sure the cable is clamped tight.

4 Push the box into the hole. If it fits tightly, do not force it or you may damage the drywall. If needed, use a utility knife to enlarge the hole.

5 This type of box has "wings" that extend outward when you start to drive the screw and then grasp the back of the drywall as the screw is tightened (see below). Tighten the screw until you feel resistance and the box is firmly attached.

STANLEY PRO TIP

The old-fashioned way

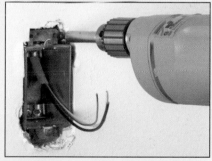

To install a box in a lath-and-plaster wall, cut the hole and then remove ¾ inch of plaster above and below the hole. Loosen the setscrews and adjust the depth of the box's plaster ears so the box will be flush with the wall surface. Insert the box, drill pilot holes (lath cracks easily), and drive screws through the ears into the lath.

Other remodel-box options

The round plastic ceiling box (left) has "wings" that rotate out and behind the wall surface. One metal box (center) has a flange that springs outward when the box is inserted; tightening a screw brings the flange forward. A variation on this has side clamps that move out and toward the front as screws are tightened. Yet another type (right) uses separate mounting brackets that slide in after the box is inserted and bend over the sides of the box to lock it in place.

RUNNING CABLE THROUGH FINISHED ROOMS

When running new electrical service through rooms that are finished with drywall or plaster, plan carefully to minimize damage to walls and ceilings. Sometimes you can go through a basement or attic to get at the finished wall or ceiling. Or you may choose to remove a large section of drywall, which often means less work than repairing many smaller holes.

Begin by making a drawing of the room that includes the locations of all studs and joists. Use a stud finder to locate them. Plan the easiest—not necessarily the shortest—routes for cables. Also determine where the boxes will go. Sometimes moving a box over a few inches makes the run easier.

Once you have a plan, cut the holes for the remodel boxes *(pages 142–143)*, run the cable, and install the boxes. Connect the cable to a power source *(pages 136–137)*.

PRESTART CHECKLIST

☐ **TIME**
About half a day to run cable through a wall and a ceiling

☐ **TOOLS**
Stud finder, fish tapes, strippers, screwdriver, hammer, drill, fishing drill bit, pry bar, drywall saw or saber saw

☐ **SKILLS**
Measuring; cutting through drywall or plaster; using fish tapes

☐ **PREP**
Spread a drop cloth on the floor of the room and cut holes for the remodel boxes *(pages 142–143)*

☐ **MATERIALS**
Electrical cable, protective nailing plates, electrician's tape

Behind base molding

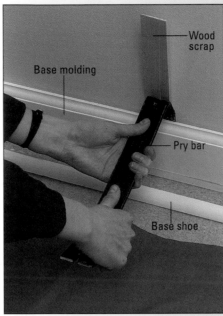

1 Pry away the base shoe (if any) and the base molding. Use a flat pry bar; place a scrap of wood under the bar to avoid damaging the wall.

2 Cut out a strip of drywall or plaster to reveal the bottom plate and studs. If possible, cut low enough so you can replace the base molding to cover your work. If the molding is less than 3 inches wide, see the tip on *page 145*.

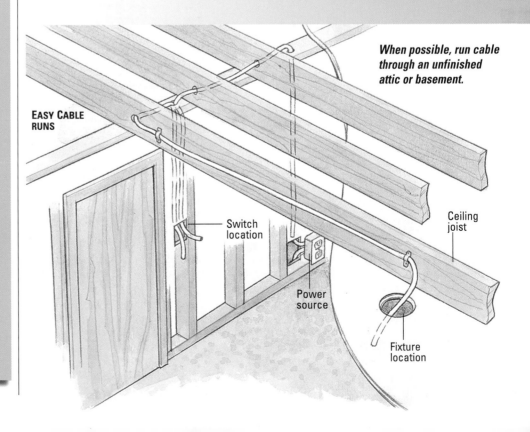

When possible, run cable through an unfinished attic or basement.

EASY CABLE RUNS

Switch location

Power source

Fixture location

Ceiling joist

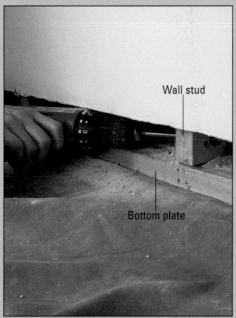

Wall stud

Bottom plate

3 Drill ¾-inch holes near the bottom of studs. You may hit a nail or two with the drill bit, so have extra drill bits on hand to replace broken or dull ones.

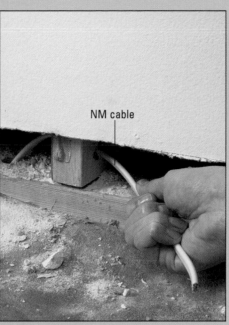

NM cable

4 Thread cable through the holes and pull it fairly tight. Once the cable is run, install a nail plate to protect each hole.

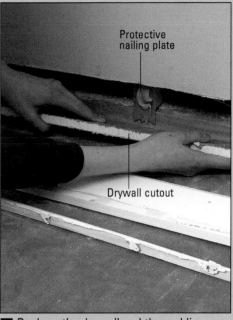

Protective nailing plate

Drywall cutout

5 Replace the drywall and the molding. (If the wall is plaster, shim out the bottom plate so the molding can sit flat.) You may need to attach the drywall with adhesive and reposition some nails to avoid hitting the protective plates.

Run cable behind a door casing

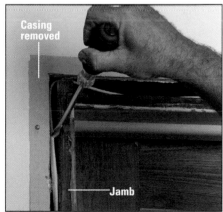

Casing removed

Jamb

1 Pry off the casing. Where there is a gap between the jamb and framing, thread the cable. Where the jamb is tight against a stud, drill a hole so you can run cable through the wall. Door frames are attached to a double stud so the hole will be 3 inches long.

Protective nailing plate

Jamb

2 Install a protective plate wherever cable is at risk of being pierced by a nail. Use a chisel to cut a notch for the plate in the jamb so the casing sits snug up against the jamb.

STANLEY PRO TIP

Base cap when the base is not wide enough

If you need to cut a hole too high for the base molding to cover, either replace the old molding with a wider base or install a base cap to add width to the base molding.

Through a basement

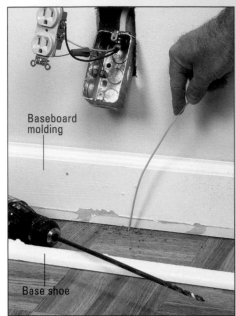

Baseboard molding

Base shoe

Locator wire

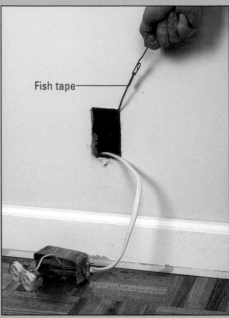

Fish tape

1 If the basement below is unfinished, remove the base shoe and drill a locator hole. Poke a wire down through the hole.

2 In the basement, find the locator wire. Drill a hole up through the middle of the bottom plate.

3 To run cable, remove the box. Thread one fish tape down through the knockout while a helper threads another fish tape up through the basement hole. Hook the tapes and pull up. If the box is difficult to remove, punch out a knockout slug and pull the cable through the hole in the box.

STANLEY PRO TIP: **Fishing into the attic**

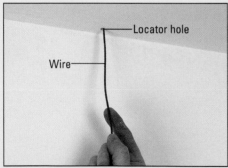

Locator hole

Wire

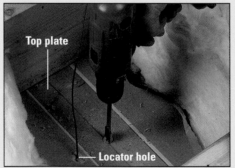

Top plate

Locator hole

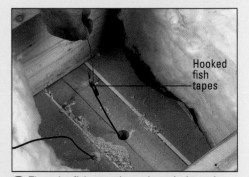

Hooked fish tapes

1 Drill a locator hole directly above the hole or box in the wall. Poke a wire through the hole. The wire may have to push through fiberglass or loose-fill insulation.

2 Near the locator hole, drill a ¾-inch hole through the center of the top plate. If your house has fire blocking *(page 147)*, cut a hole in the wall and drill a hole through the blocking.

3 Thread a fish tape down through the attic hole while a helper threads a fish tape up through a box or hole in the wall. Once the tapes hook together, pull up.

Code variations
Your building department may forbid running cable around a door frame or may require armored cable in finished walls and ceilings.

Through walls and ceilings

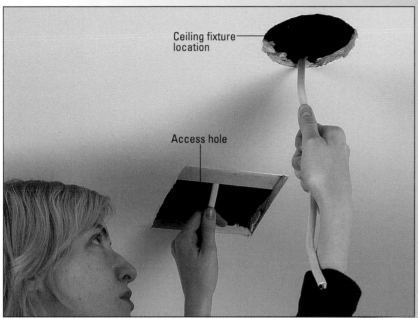

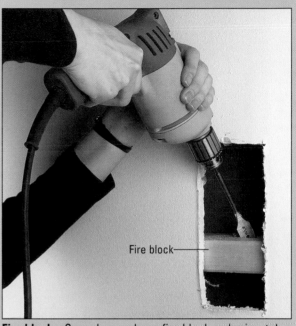

Middle of ceiling: If you need to run cable across the middle of a ceiling or wall, find the joists or studs and cut holes that are large enough for your hand to fit into. (Save drywall pieces and use them to patch the holes later.) Drill holes and thread the cable through. Once the cable is run, install protective nailing plates.

Fire blocks: Some homes have fire blocks—horizontal 2×4s between the studs, usually 4 or 5 feet above the floor. Use a stud finder to locate one. Cut a hole in the wall and drill a hole through the fire block.

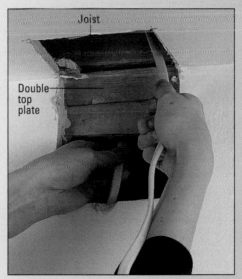

Behind a box: If the hole for a new box is behind an existing box, punch out a knockout slug in the existing box. Run fish tapes from both directions, hook them together, and pull through the box. Now you can pull cable through the box to the hole.

No attic access: To run cable up the wall and across the ceiling, cut holes in the wall and the ceiling. Drill a hole up through the top plate. If there is a joist in the way, drill a hole through it as well. Bend the cable and thread it through the holes.

Using a fishing drill bit

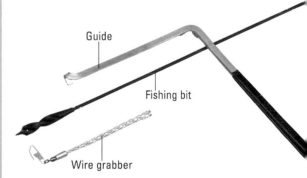

A fishing bit reduces the number of holes in walls and ceilings. Drill a hole through the next joist or stud, using the guide to aim the bit. Fasten a wire to the bit and pull it back through the hole.

PATCHING WALLS

However painstakingly you plan cable runs, chances are you will have to repair walls and ceilings after the wiring work is finished. Cut holes in drywall as neatly as possible and save the cutouts so you can use them as patches later.

Allow plenty of time for patching. After applying the first coat of joint compound, you must let it dry, scrape and/or sand it, then apply second, third, and maybe even fourth coats before achieving a smooth surface.

Dry-mix joint compound, which is strong but hard to sand, comes in bags labeled "90," "45," or "20." The numbers indicate roughly how many minutes before the product hardens. Ready-mix joint compound, which comes in buckets, is easier to apply and sand but is not as strong. A good plan is to apply dry-mix compound for the first coat and use ready-mix for subsequent coats.

PRESTART CHECKLIST

☐ **TIME**
About an hour to install a patch and apply the first coat of compound; several 15-minute sessions on following days, to sand and apply additional coats

☐ **TOOLS**
Drywall saw, utility knife, hammer, putty knife, drill, taping blades, corner trowel, drywall-sanding block with 80- and 100-grit sandpapers or screens

☐ **SKILLS**
Cutting drywall; applying joint compound; painting

☐ **PREP**
Make sure the wiring is correct and have it inspected, if required, before you cover it up. Spread a drop cloth on the floor below.

☐ **MATERIALS**
Drywall screws, drywall for patching, 1×4 scraps, mesh tape, joint compound

Drywall screw

1×4 scrap

Protective nailing plate

1 Where there is no framing member to attach the drywall to, slip a 1×4 or backer piece behind the hole so that half its width is behind the wall surface and half is visible.

2 Hold the backer piece tight against the back of the drywall and drive 1¼-inch drywall screws through the drywall and into the backer piece. Drive each screw until the backer piece is drawn tight to the drywall.

Patching plaster walls

1 Pry or chip away any loose plaster around the damaged area. If the whole wall has loose plaster, call in a professional plasterer.

2 Buy drywall that's no thicker than the plaster. Cut a piece to fit the hole and attach it to the lath with screws.

3 Fill the gaps between the patch and the wall with joint compound. Apply tape and joint compound as described above.

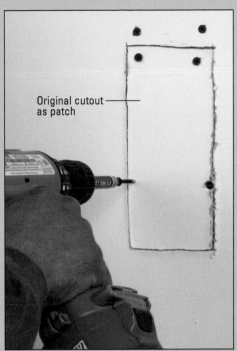

Original cutout as patch

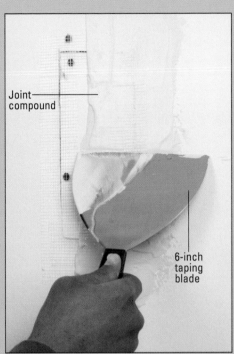

Joint compound

6-inch taping blade

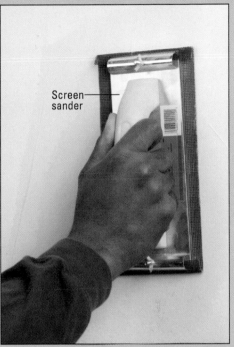

Screen sander

3 Use the original drywall cutout or cut a new piece to fit. Cut off any dangling scraps of paper. Attach the patch with drywall screws. Screw heads must sink below the surface of the drywall without tearing the paper.

4 Cut and apply pieces of self-sticking fiberglass mesh tape. With a taping blade, apply enough joint compound to cover the tape. Smooth the compound.

5 When the first coat dries, scrape away high spots and apply a second coat, feathering out the edges a bit farther. When it dries, sand it. Apply and sand as many coats as needed to achieve a surface that looks and feels smooth. Prime and paint.

Patching at a corner

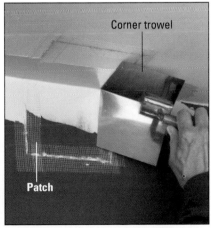

Corner trowel

Patch

A smooth surface in a corner is difficult to achieve. Use a corner trowel to form a perfect inside corner when applying the first coat. Use a straight trowel to smooth the wall and ceiling during subsequent coats.

STANLEY PRO TIP

Blending with textured surface

A textured wall surface may have been applied with a special tool. Patterns vary from one applicator to another. Try this trick: Make the cutout carefully, then replace it and caulk rather than tape the joints. To mimic a texture, practice on scraps of drywall, experimenting with various tools. (Sometimes it helps to add a handful of sand to a gallon of joint compound.) If a ceiling has a blown-on "popcorn" or "cottage cheese" surface, buy special patching compound, which can be sprayed on or applied with a trowel.

Need a small piece of drywall?
Most home centers sell broken pieces of drywall at a fraction of their original price.

Cover it beautifully

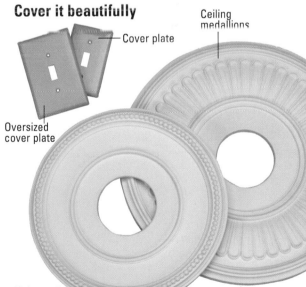

Ceiling medallions

Cover plate

Oversized cover plate

If the wall is damaged near a switch or receptacle, an oversized coverplate may hide the blemish and save patching work. To conceal a damaged ceiling near a light fixture, install a medallion, which can be painted to match the ceiling.

NEW RECEPTACLES & LIGHTS

Any wiring project should begin with a detailed plan. The chapter entitled "Planning New Electrical Service" will help you prepare a thorough, easy-to-read description. Make sure existing or new circuits can handle the new installation *(page 120).* Present your plans to the local building department and receive a permit before beginning work.

Getting ready
Your inspector may approve NM cable, or you might have to install conduit or armored cable. Metal boxes may be required; plastic may be allowed. Determine how ground wires should be connected *(page 118)* and how cable should be clamped to the boxes *(page 18).*

Most projects call for two-wire cable, but some require three-wire cable or even four wires running in conduit or Greenfield. Buy plenty of cable; it's easy to underestimate how much you'll need.

Unless you face special circumstances, use #12 wire for 20-amp circuits and #14 wire for 15-amp circuits. If your existing service uses armored cable or conduit, you can usually switch to NM cable if the cable runs into a box and the ground wire is connected according to code.

Test all new receptacles with a receptacle analyzer *(page 12).* It tells you instantly whether the receptacle is properly grounded and polarized.

Some building departments require that lights be on dedicated lighting circuits, rather than sharing a circuit with receptacles. Other departments allow circuits to combine the two.

Planning a remodeling project
If a wiring project is part of a larger job, plan the order of work so different tasks and contractors do not collide. The first order of business is removing wall surfaces and any framing. Then comes rough plumbing, then rough electrical—installing boxes and running cable. If you install receptacles and switches at this point, protect them with tape. Better yet wait until after the walls and ceilings are drywalled (with openings cut) and painted to install receptacles, switches, and fixtures.

Make your home more convenient and appealing by adding new receptacles and light fixtures.

CHAPTER PREVIEW

Adding a new receptacle
page 152

Adding a 240-volt receptacle
page 154

Two-circuit receptacles
page 156

Split receptacles
page 157

Switched receptacles
page 158

New light fixtures add style and illumination. Bathrooms are often prime candidates for new fixtures, especially when power can be grabbed from an overhead switched fixture.

Cable for wall-mounted fixtures can be run from below (through a basement or crawlspace) or from above (through an attic) to minimize damage to the ceiling and wall.

Installing a new switched fixture
page 160

Installing three-way switches
page 164

Undercabinet fluorescents
page 168

Recessed cans
page 170

Wall-mounted lighting
page 174

ADDING A NEW RECEPTACLE

The following steps show how to tap into an existing receptacle to grab power for a new receptacle. If doing this will cause the circuit to overload *(pages 120–121)* or if there is no conveniently located receptacle, consider grabbing power from a junction box in the basement or from a nearby light fixture or switch *(pages 136–137)*.

If one or more new receptacles will supply heavy power users, run cable all the way to the service panel and install a new circuit *(pages 230–231)*.

When connecting to a 15-amp circuit, install a standard receptacle and #14 wire. When connecting to a 20-amp circuit, use #12 wire and a special 20-amp receptacle.

PRESTART CHECKLIST

☐ **TIME**
About two hours to run cable and make connections (not including cutting a pathway for the cable and patching the walls)

☐ **TOOLS**
Voltage tester, drill, saw, hammer, fish tape, screwdriver, strippers, long-nose pliers, lineman's pliers, utility knife, stud finder, torpedo level, tape measure, pry bar, perhaps a drywall saw or saber saw

☐ **SKILLS**
Stripping and connecting wires to terminals; installing boxes; running cable through walls and ceilings

☐ **PREP**
Lay a drop cloth on the floor below

☐ **MATERIALS**
New receptacle, cable, remodel box and clamps, wire nuts, electrician's tape, protective nailing plates, cable staples

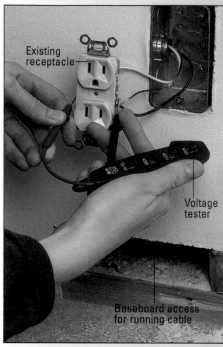

1 **Shut off power to the circuit.** Cut and drill a pathway for the cable *(pages 139–147)*. Pull out the receptacle from which you will be grabbing power and test to make sure power is not present *(page 46)*. Move the receptacle to the side or disconnect and remove it.

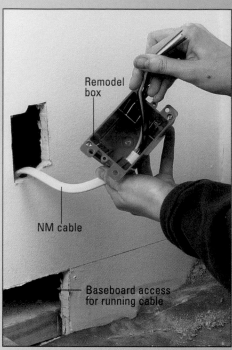

2 Cut a hole for a remodel box. Run cable from the area near the existing box to the hole, clamp the cable to the box, and install the new box *(pages 142–143)*.

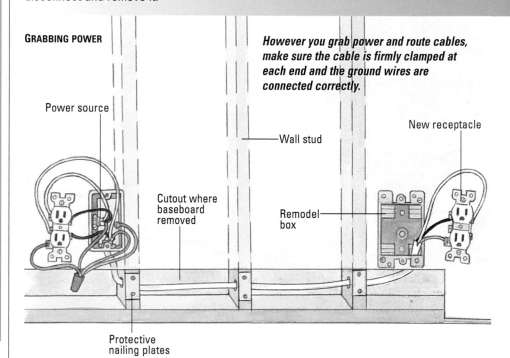

GRABBING POWER

However you grab power and route cables, make sure the cable is firmly clamped at each end and the ground wires are connected correctly.

Power source

Wall stud

New receptacle

Cutout where baseboard removed

Remodel box

Protective nailing plates

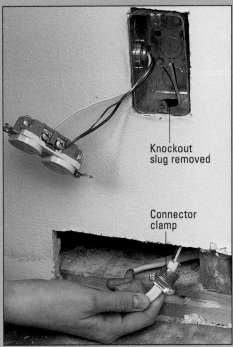

Knockout slug removed

Connector clamp

Wrap tape around receptacle before pushing into box

Locknut tightened

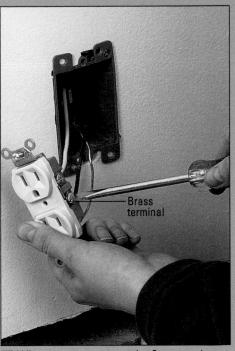

Brass terminal

3 Pry up a knockout slug in the old box and twist it out with pliers. (If you can't do this, remove the box and replace it with a remodel box.) Remove the sheathing from the cable, strip the wires, and attach a connector clamp to the cable. Push the cable into the box and fasten the clamp.

4 Strip and run cable into the existing box and tighten the clamp. Connect the new wires to existing wiring. Attach the ground wires using a pigtail. Connect the white wire to the available silver terminal and the black wire to the brass terminal.

5 Wire the new receptacle. Connect the ground wire to the ground screw, the white wire to the silver terminal, and the black wire to the brass terminal.

REFRESHER COURSE
Wiring a GFCI

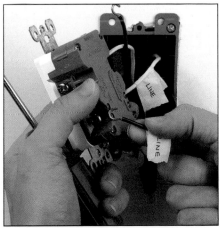

To wire a ground fault circuit interrupter (GFCI) at the end of the run, connect wires to the LINE terminals as marked on the back of the device.

To protect receptacles after the GFCI, connect wires supplying power to LINE terminals; wires leading to other receptacles are connected to LOAD terminals.

EXISTING WIRING
Wiring a middle-of-run receptacle

Pigtail

If the existing receptacle box has two cables and there are no available terminals on the receptacle, disconnect all the wires. Hook up pigtails and connect the pigtails to the terminals.

ADDING A 240-VOLT RECEPTACLE

Electric water heaters, dryers, ranges, and other major appliances use 240 volts—twice the voltage of most fixtures. Each appliance needs a separate double-pole breaker. (See *pages 230–231* for how to install a new breaker.)

Various 240-volt receptacles are made for specific amperages and types of appliance. Make sure your appliance will be able to plug in. Some receptacles deliver not only 240 volts, but also 120 volts to power lights and timers. In some cases, older receptacles use only three wires. But newer codes call for four wires—black and red hot wires, a white neutral wire, and a green or bare ground wire. Use #12 wire for 20-amp service, #10 wire for 30 amps, #8 wire for 40 amps, and #6 wire for 50 amps. Check local codes for what conduit, Greenfield, or cable to use.

Work with extreme caution: 240 volts can cause serious bodily harm.

PRESTART CHECKLIST

☐ **TIME**
About three hours to run cable (not including cutting and patching walls) and connect a breaker and receptacle

☐ **TOOLS**
Voltage tester, drill, saw, hammer, nonconductive ladder, flashlight, fish tape, screwdriver, strippers, long-nose pliers, lineman's pliers

☐ **SKILLS**
Stripping and connecting wires; installing boxes; running cable

☐ **PREP**
Lay a towel or drop cloth where you will cut into walls; cut a pathway for cable

☐ **MATERIALS**
240-volt (or 120/240-volt) receptacle, wire of correct size, Greenfield, conduit or NM cable (if allowed), wire nuts, clamps, double-pole circuit breaker

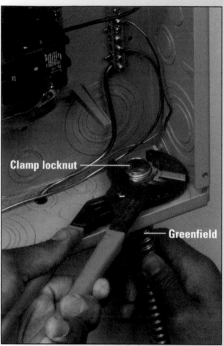

1 Choose conduit or Greenfield large enough so the wires can slide easily. Remove a knockout slug from the service panel (make sure it's the right size) and clamp the conduit or Greenfield to the panel.

2 Run the conduit or Greenfield from the service panel to the receptacle location *(pages 132–134, 144–147)* and attach a clamp. You may need to drill 1-inch holes. The receptacle may be mounted on the floor or in a wall box.

Air-conditioner receptacle

1 A large-capacity window air-conditioner calls for a 20-amp, 240-volt receptacle. Route 12/2 cable from the service panel to a receptacle box *(pages 136–147)*. Connect the grounds. Mark the white wire black. Connect the white and black wires to the terminals.

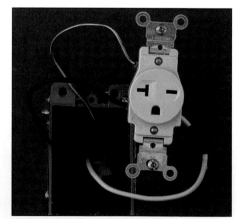

2 At the service panel, **shut off the main breaker.** Make room for a double-pole breaker. Connect the ground wire to the grounding bar and the black and white wires to the breaker. Snap in the breaker.

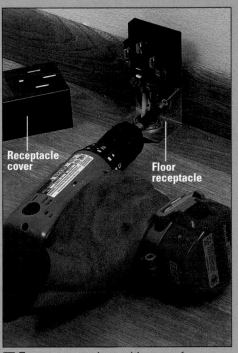

3 **Shut off the main breaker.** Fish wires *(page 135)* from the receptacle location to the panel. Attach the white wire to the neutral bus bar and the ground wire to the grounding bar.

4 Connect the red and black wires to the breaker terminals. Snap the breaker into place. (See *pages 230–231* for more detailed instructions.)

5 To connect a wire to this type of receptacle, strip the wire end, poke it into the terminal hole, and tighten the setscrew. Fasten the receptacle body to the floor or wall and install the cover.

Dryer receptacle

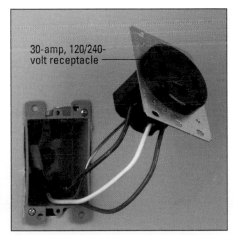

1 Install 10/3 NM cable or run four #10 wires through conduit or Greenfield cable from the service panel to a receptacle box *(pages 136–147)*. Connect the wires to the terminals of the receptacle.

2 At the service panel, **shut off the main breaker.** Connect the ground and white wires to the grounding and neutral bus bars. Connect the black and red wires to a double-pole breaker and snap in the breaker.

STANLEY PRO TIP

Use a whip

To connect to a cooktop or a wall-mounted oven, run cable from the service panel to a junction box. Connect an appliance whip— a short length of armored cable—to the junction box and to the appliance *(page 229)*. Some new appliances come with a whip already attached to the unit.

Keep it neat—and safe

If wires enter far from the breaker, route them around the perimeter of the panel. This eases future work in the panel, clarifies the circuitry, and avoids strain on connections.

TWO-CIRCUIT RECEPTACLES

Code may require that receptacles supplying several high-amperage appliances or tools be placed on alternating circuits. That way if an appliance causes a circuit to overload, you can simply plug it into a neighboring receptacle. Another option is to split the receptacles *(page 157)*.

Run three-wire cable from the service panel to the boxes *(pages 136–147)*. If codes call for 20-amp receptacles, use #12 wire. Codes may also call for connecting both circuits to the same double-pole breaker. That way if one circuit overloads, both circuits will shut off, ensuring that all wires in each box are dead.

PRESTART CHECKLIST

☐ **TIME**
About three hours to install several receptacles (not including cutting and patching walls)

☐ **TOOLS**
Voltage tester, drill, saw, hammer, fish tape, lineman's pliers, screwdriver, strippers, long-nose pliers

☐ **SKILLS**
Running cable; stripping, splicing, connecting wire

☐ **PREP**
Run three-wire cable from service panel to boxes; two-wire between last two boxes

☐ **MATERIALS**
Receptacles, three-wire cable, two-wire cable, boxes, double-pole breaker, wire nuts, tape

Blacks to brass terminals

Reds to brass terminals

1 **Shut off power to the circuits.** At the first receptacle, splice the red wires. Connect the grounds. Attach the white wires to the silver terminals. Connect the black wires to the brass terminals.

2 At the second receptacle, splice the black wires. Connect the grounds. Attach the white wires to the silver terminals. Connect the red wires to the brass terminals.

3 At the service panel, **shut off the main breaker.** Connect the white wire and the ground wire to the neutral and ground bus bars. Attach the red and black wires to a double-pole breaker.

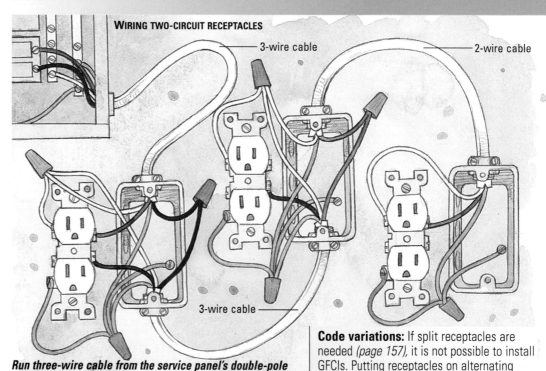

WIRING TWO-CIRCUIT RECEPTACLES

3-wire cable

2-wire cable

3-wire cable

Run three-wire cable from the service panel's double-pole breaker to the receptacles. Only two-wire cable is needed for the last receptacle.

Code variations: If split receptacles are needed *(page 157)*, it is not possible to install GFCIs. Putting receptacles on alternating circuits allows you to use GFCI receptacles.

SPLIT RECEPTACLES

If a receptacle is split, its two plugs are on separate circuits. If an appliance or tool causes a circuit to overload, just plug into the other outlet of the same receptacle. It's also possible to split a receptacle and have one outlet controlled by a switch *(pages 158–159)*.

Run three-wire cable from the service panel to the receptacle boxes *(pages 136–147)*. If codes call for 20-amp receptacles, use #12 wire. Codes may also call for connecting both circuits to the same double-pole breaker. That way if one circuit overloads, both circuits will shut off, ensuring that all the wires in each box are dead.

PRESTART CHECKLIST

☐ **TIME**
About three hours to install several receptacles (not including cutting and patching walls)

☐ **TOOLS**
Voltage tester, drill, saw, hammer, fish tape, screwdriver, strippers, longnose pliers, lineman's pliers

☐ **SKILLS**
Running cable; stripping, splicing, connecting wire

☐ **PREP**
Run three-wire cable from service panel to boxes

☐ **MATERIALS**
Receptacles, three-wire cable, boxes, double-pole breaker, wire nuts, electrician's tape

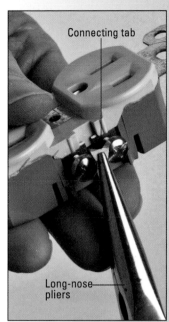

Connecting tab

Long-nose pliers

1 On each receptacle, twist off the tab that connects the two brass terminals. Now the two outlets are disconnected from each other.

2 **Make certain no power is present in the cable or boxes.** At each receptacle, pigtail the red, black, and white wires. Connect the red and black pigtails to separate brass terminals and connect the white pigtail to a silver terminal.

Double-pole breaker

3 At the service panel, **shut off the main breaker.** Connect the white wire and the ground wire to the neutral and ground bus bars. Connect the red and black wires to a double-pole breaker.

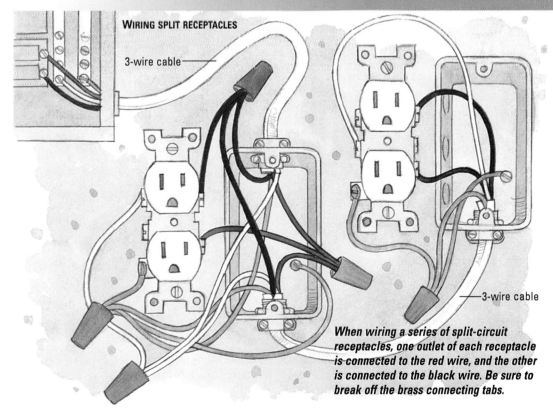

WIRING SPLIT RECEPTACLES

3-wire cable

3-wire cable

When wiring a series of split-circuit receptacles, one outlet of each receptacle is connected to the red wire, and the other is connected to the black wire. Be sure to break off the brass connecting tabs.

SWITCHED RECEPTACLES

A receptacle can be split and switched, so that one of its outlets is controlled by a wall switch while the other remains hot all the time. If a floor or table lamp is plugged into the switched plug, you can turn it on as you enter a room. Many codes allow a bedroom to have no ceiling light, as long as there is a switched receptacle.

The steps on these pages show how to split and switch an existing receptacle that is wired normally. If you need to install a new receptacle and switch, see the illustration on *page 159*.

If the wall is covered with drywall or plaster, most of the work will consist of running cable and perhaps patching the wall afterwards *(pages 142–149)*.

PRESTART CHECKLIST

☐ **TIME**
About three hours to run cable a short distance (not including cutting a pathway for the cable and patching walls), install a wall switch, and wire the receptacle

☐ **TOOLS**
Voltage tester, drill, saw, hammer, nonconductive ladder, fish tape, screwdriver, strippers, long-nose pliers, lineman's pliers

☐ **SKILLS**
Stripping, splicing, and connecting wires to terminals; installing boxes; running cable through walls

☐ **PREP**
Lay a drop cloth on the floor below

☐ **MATERIALS**
Single-pole switch, receptacle (if you want to replace the old one), two-wire cable, wire nuts, remodel box, cable clamps, electrician's tape

1 **Shut off power to the circuit.** Without touching the terminals, carefully pull out the existing receptacle and test for power.

Voltage tester

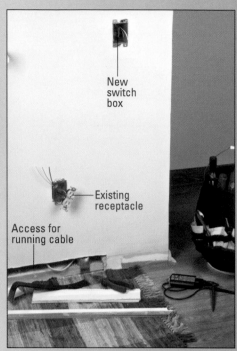

New switch box

Existing receptacle

Access for running cable

2 Cut a hole for a switch box, run cable from the hole to the existing receptacle box, and clamp the cable to the box *(pages 136–147)*.

IF POWER ENTERS THE RECEPTACLE BOX

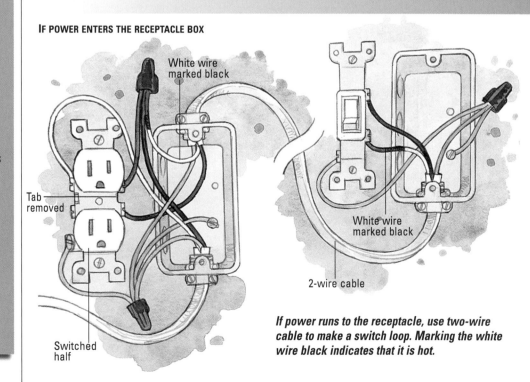

White wire marked black

Tab removed

Switched half

White wire marked black

2-wire cable

If power runs to the receptacle, use two-wire cable to make a switch loop. Marking the white wire black indicates that it is hot.

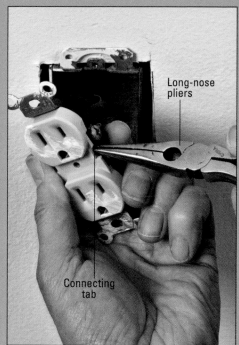

3 Either remove and replace the receptacle or continue to use the existing one. Remove the tab that connects the two brass terminals; now the two outlets are no longer connected to each other.

4 At the receptacle, mark the white switch wire with black tape and connect the grounds. Splice the feed wire with the black-marked wire and a pigtail. Connect the pigtail to a brass terminal, the remaining black wire to the other brass terminal, and the white wire to a silver terminal.

5 If only one cable originally entered the switch box, connect the ground and mark the white switch wire with black tape. Connect the wires to the switch terminals.

If power enters the switch box

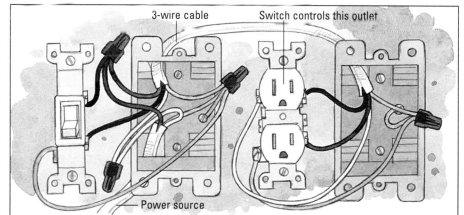

If you are installing a new receptacle and switch, this is the most common configuration. Bring power to the switch box via two-wire cable and run three-wire cable between the boxes. Connect the grounds. At the switch box, splice the white wires. Splice the black wires together with a pigtail and connect the pigtail to a terminal. Connect the red wire to a terminal. At the receptacle, connect the red and black wires to brass terminals and the white wire to a silver terminal.

WHAT IF...
A receptacle is middle-of-run?

If two cables originally entered the receptacle box, connect the grounds and mark the white switch wire black. Attach the black switch wire to one brass terminal. Splice the remaining black wires and the white switch wire together with a pigtail. Connect the pigtail to the other brass terminal. Connect the remaining white wires to silver terminals.

INSTALLING A NEW SWITCHED FIXTURE

A switched fixture can be hooked up in one of two ways: Through-switch or in-line wiring (shown in the steps at right) brings power first to the switch, then sends it on to the fixture; the switch interrupts the hot wire that leads to the fixture. End-line or switch-loop wiring (shown at the bottom of *page 161*) brings power first to the fixture; two-wire cable running from the fixture to the switch creates a loop that is interrupted by the switch.

Some inspectors prefer through-switch wiring, but both methods work equally well. Unless your inspector objects, choose the wiring method that makes for the easiest cable runs.

These two pages give instructions for installing a simple fixture with a switch. For various switch-receptacle-fixture combinations, see *pages 162–163*.

PRESTART CHECKLIST

☐ **TIME**
About two hours to run cable and install a switch and a receptacle (not including cutting a pathway for the cable and patching walls)

☐ **TOOLS**
Voltage tester, drill, saw, hammer, nonconductive ladder, fish tape, screwdriver, strippers, long-nose pliers, lineman's pliers

☐ **SKILLS**
Stripping, splicing, and connecting wires to terminals; installing boxes; running cable into boxes

☐ **PREP**
Lay a drop cloth on the floor below

☐ **MATERIALS**
Single-pole switch, light fixture or ceiling fan, two-wire cable, ceiling box, cable clamps, wall box, wire nuts, electrician's tape

1 Before tapping into a power source *(pages 136–137)*, list all the electrical users on the circuit and add up the wattages to see whether there is room on the circuit for a new light switch. See *pages 120–121*.

2 Cut a hole for the switch box, and run two-wire cable from the hole to a power source. In this example a receptacle directly below the switch makes for an easy cable run. *Pages 136–147* show how to install boxes and run cable.

THROUGH-SWITCH WIRING

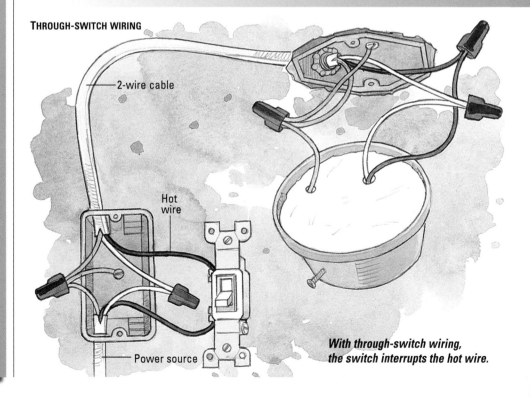

With through-switch wiring, the switch interrupts the hot wire.

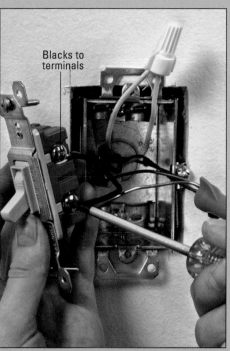

Blacks to terminals

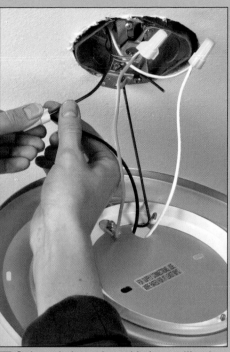

3 Cut a hole for the ceiling fixture box and run two-wire cable from that hole to the switch hole.

4 At the switch hole, strip and clamp the cables in a box and install the box. Connect the grounds. Splice the white wires and connect the black wires to the switch terminals.

5 Strip and clamp the cable in a ceiling box and install the box. Connect the grounds. Splice the white wire to the white fixture lead and the black wire to the black lead.

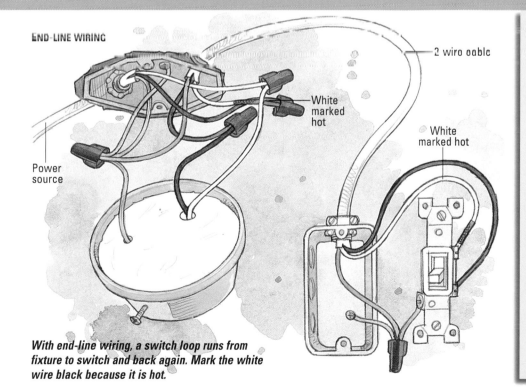

END-LINE WIRING

2 wire cable

White marked hot

White marked hot

Power source

With end-line wiring, a switch loop runs from fixture to switch and back again. Mark the white wire black because it is hot.

STANLEY PRO TIP

Switching a pull-chain fixture

To control a pull-chain fixture with a wall switch, run two-wire cable from the fixture to a switch box. Connect wires as for end-line wiring, left.

Switch, light, and receptacle

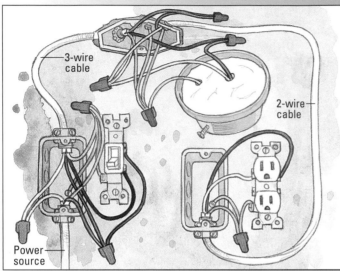

This setup has a switched fixture and an unswitched receptacle. Bring power into the switch box with two-wire cable; run three-wire cable to the fixture and run two-wire cable to the receptacle. Connect all the grounds. At the switch box, connect the black and red wires to the switch terminal and splice the white wires. At the fixture box, splice the black wires and splice the white wires together with the white fixture lead. Splice the red wire to the black fixture lead. Wire the receptacle.

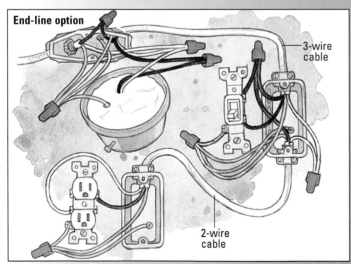

Bring power to the fixture via two-wire cable; run three-wire cable to the switch and run two-wire cable from the switch to the receptacle. Connect all the grounds. At the fixture box, splice the black wires and splice the white wires together with the white fixture lead. Splice the red wire to the black fixture lead. At the switch box, splice the white wires and splice the black wires together with a pigtail. Connect the black pigtail and the red wire to the switch terminals. Wire the receptacle.

Two fixtures on two switches

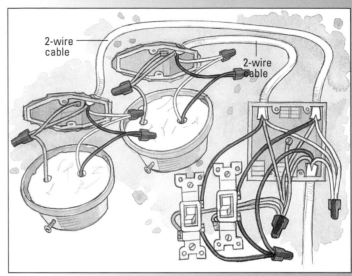

Here, two switches, each of which controls a separate light, share a double-gang box. Bring power into the switch box via two-wire cable and run two-wire cable to each of the fixtures. Connect all the grounds. At the switch box, connect the feed wire to the switches using pigtails. Connect each black fixture wire to a switch and splice the white wires. Wire the fixtures.

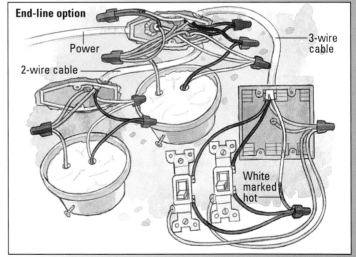

Bring power to the first fixture box with two-wire cable. Run two-wire cable between the fixtures; run three-wire cable from the first fixture to the switch box. Connect the grounds. At the first fixture box, mark the white switch wire black and splice it to the feed wire. Splice the other two black wires. Splice the remaining white wires with the white fixture lead. Splice the red wire with the black fixture lead. Wire the other fixture. At the switch box, connect the red wire to one switch and the black wire to the other. Mark the white wire black and connect it to the switches with pigtails.

Switch and two or more fixtures

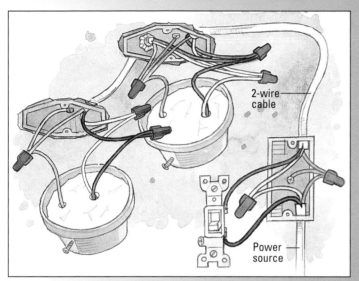

Here, a single switch controls two fixtures. Run two-wire cable into all the boxes. Connect all the grounds. At the switch box, splice the white wires and connect the black wires to the switch terminals. At the first fixture box, splice the two black wires with the fixture's black lead and splice the two white wires with the fixture's white lead. Wire the second fixture.

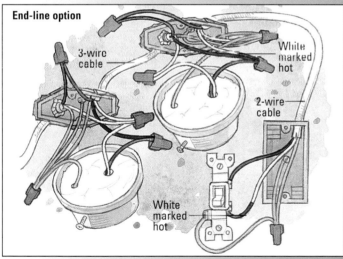

End-line option

Bring power into the first fixture box with two-wire cable; run three-wire cable between the fixture boxes and run two-wire cable from the second fixture box to the switch box. Connect all the grounds. At the first fixture box, splice the black wires. Splice the white wires together with the white fixture lead and splice the red wire with the black fixture lead. At the second fixture box, splice the black wires. Mark the white fixture wire with black tape and splice it together with the red wire and the black fixture lead. Splice the white wire to the white fixture lead. Wire the switch.

Switch and receptacle

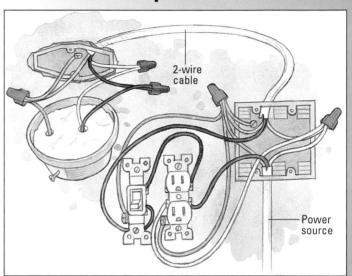

Here, a switch and an always-hot receptacle share a double-gang box. Run two-wire cable to both boxes. Connect all the grounds. At the switch box, connect the feed wire to a brass receptacle terminal. Run a short black wire from the other brass terminal to a switch terminal. Splice the white wires together with a pigtail and connect the pigtail to a silver receptacle terminal. Connect the black fixture wire to the remaining switch terminal. Wire the fixture.

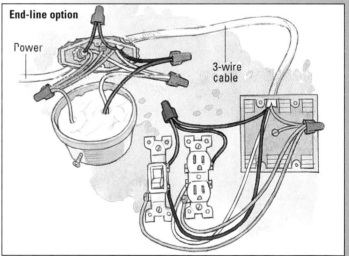

End-line option

Bring power to the fixture box with two-wire cable; run three-wire cable from the fixture box to the switch box. Connect all the grounds. At the fixture box, splice the black wires. Splice the white wires together with the white fixture lead and splice the red wire with the black lead. At the switch box, connect the black wire to a switch terminal and a brass receptacle terminal, using pigtails. Connect the red wire to a switch terminal and connect the white wire to a silver receptacle terminal.

INSTALLING THREE-WAY SWITCHES

Install a pair of three-way switches to control a fixture from two different locations. A three-way switch has three terminals: two traveler terminals and one common terminal, which is darker in color. The toggle is not marked ON and OFF, because flipping it down could turn a light on. Use three-ways to ensure that a person does not have to walk through the dark to get to the light switch. Install three-ways in hallways and stairways, in large rooms with two entrances, or to control a garage or basement light. These pages give instructions for one possible way to wire three-ways—with power entering a switch and traveling through the fixture to the other switch. *Pages 166–167* present three more possibilities and discuss four-way switches as well. Choose the setup that makes it easiest for you to run the cable.

PRESTART CHECKLIST

☐ TIME
About four hours to run cable and install a light and two switches (not including cutting a pathway and patching walls)

☐ TOOLS
Voltage tester, drill, saw, hammer, screwdriver, ladder, fish tape, strippers, long-nose pliers, lineman's pliers

☐ SKILLS
Stripping, splicing, and connecting wires to terminals; installing boxes; running cable through walls and ceilings

☐ PREP
Check that a new fixture won't overload the circuit and tap into a power source. Lay a drop cloth on the floor below.

☐ MATERIALS
Two-wire and three-wire cable, ceiling fixture, two three-way switches, switch and fixture boxes, cable clamps, wire nuts, tape

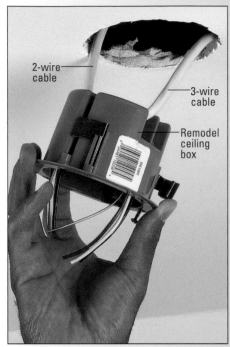

1 **Shut off power to the circuit.** Cut holes for two wall boxes and a ceiling box. Run two-wire cable from the power source to the first switch box, three-wire cable to the ceiling box, and three-wire cable to the second switch box *(pages 136–147.)*

2 Clamp cable to all three boxes. Install all the boxes and connect all the grounds. At the fixture box, splice the red wires. Mark the white wire from the second switch with black tape.

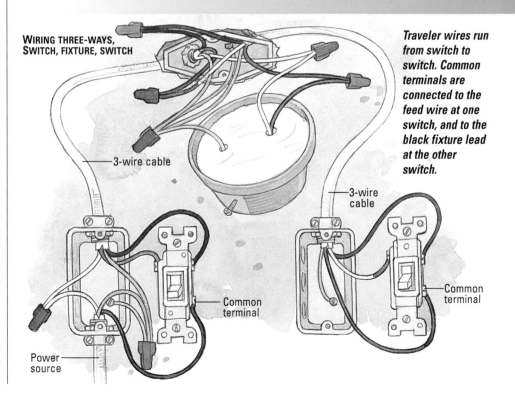

WIRING THREE-WAYS, SWITCH, FIXTURE, SWITCH

Traveler wires run from switch to switch. Common terminals are connected to the feed wire at one switch, and to the black fixture lead at the other switch.

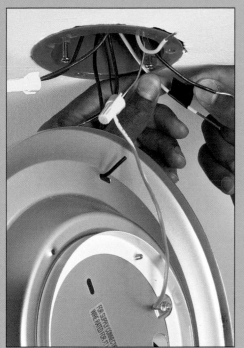

Incoming power

Feed to common

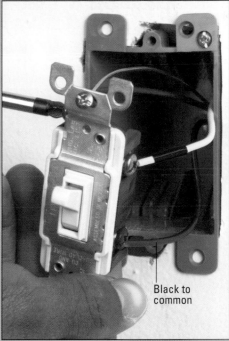

Black to common

3 Splice the black-marked white wire with the black wire from the first switch. Splice the remaining black and white wires with the fixture's black and white leads.

4 At the first switch (where power enters), splice the white wires. Connect the feed wire to the common terminal and the remaining red and black wires to the traveler terminals.

5 At the second switch, mark the white wire with black tape. Connect the black wire to the common terminal. Connect the red wire and the black-marked white wire to the traveler terminals.

How three-ways work

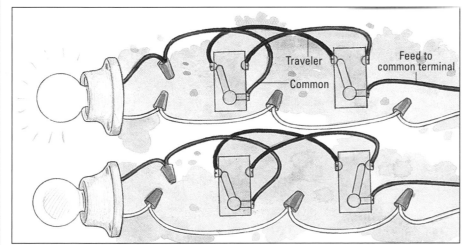

Traveler

Feed to common terminal

Common

In a three-way setup, the light is turned on when power can flow through both switches to the fixture. If the circuit is broken at either switch, the light is turned off. Traveler wires run from switch to switch and do not connect to the fixture. Common wires bring power to the fixture.

STANLEY PRO TIP

Three rules for three-ways

If a wiring diagram gets confusing, pause a minute and ponder these rules:
■ Route traveler wires so they run from traveler terminals to traveler terminals and never to the fixture.
■ Attach the feed wire to the common terminal of one switch.
■ At the other switch, the wire connecting to the common terminal should lead to the black fixture lead.

Where three-ways are required
Codes require all lights in hallways and stairways to be controlled with three-way switches.

Switch, switch, fixture

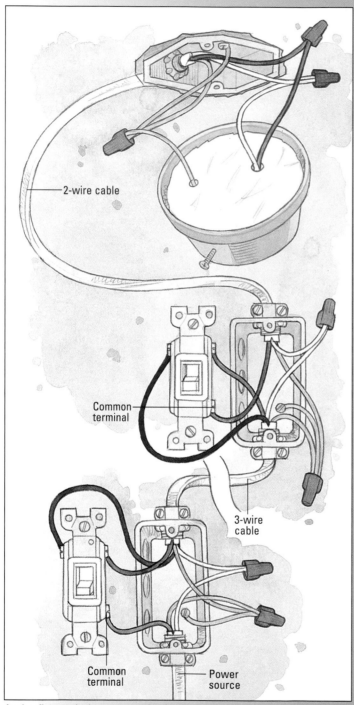

Fixture, radiating to switches

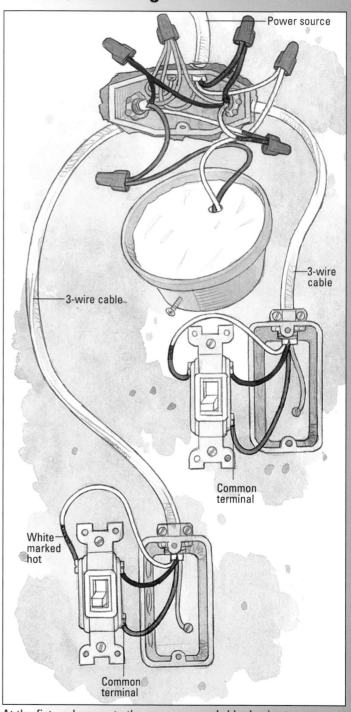

At the first switch, connect the feed wire to the common terminal, splice the white wires, and connect red and black wires to traveler terminals. At the second switch, connect the travelers to the traveler terminals and the black wire from the fixture to the common terminal. At the fixture, splice the white lead with the white wire, the black lead with the black wire from the switch's common terminal.

At the fixture box, route the power source's black wire to one switch's common terminal and the source's white wire to the fixture's white lead. Splice the fixture's black lead with the black wire coming from the other switch's common terminal. Red and black-marked white wires travel from switch to switch.

Fixture, switch, switch

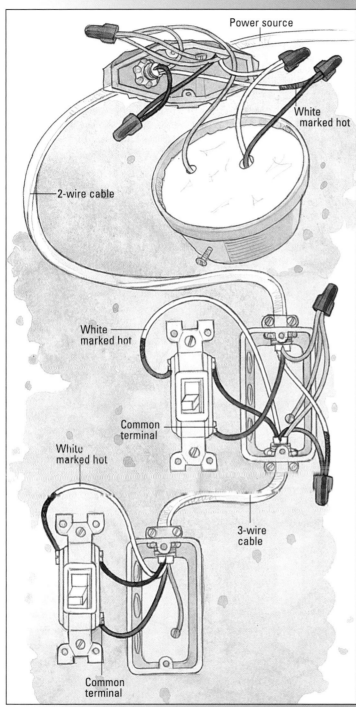

Route the feed wire to the first switch's common terminal. The black wire on the second switch's common terminal runs via a black-marked white wire to the fixture's black lead. A red wire and a black-marked white wire travel from switch to switch.

Four-way wiring

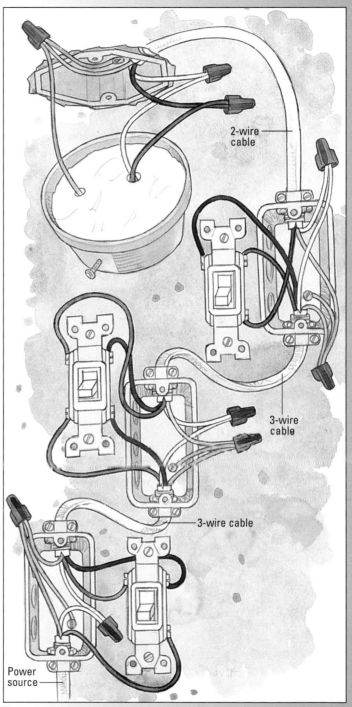

To control a fixture from three or more locations, install three-way switches at each end and one or more four-ways in between. A four-way switch has only traveler terminals and no common terminal. Connect wires from the first switch to the "input" terminals; wires connected to the "output" terminals lead to the third switch.

Undercabinet Fluorescents

Home centers carry a variety of lights designed to fit under cabinets to illuminate a countertop without shining in the food preparer's eyes. Plug-in lights (either fluorescent or low-voltage halogens) with their own switches are the simplest to install, but are not as convenient to use as a string of fluorescent lights controlled by a single wall switch.

When remodeling a kitchen, the wall cabinets are removed (shown). If wall cabinets are in place, see *page 169* for tips on snaking cable to minimize damage to walls.

Some undercabinet fluorescent lights have a single outlet, which comes in handy if the wall beneath is short on receptacles. Thin fixtures (1-inch thick) are more difficult to wire than standard (1½-inch thick) fixtures.

Prestart Checklist

☐ **Time**
About half a day to cut holes and run cable and another half-day to install the lights after the cabinets are up

☐ **Tools**
Voltage tester, drill, hammer, drywall saw, level, stud finder, fish tape, screwdriver, strippers, long-nose pliers, lineman's pliers

☐ **Skills**
Stripping, splicing, and connecting wires to terminals; installing boxes; running cable through walls and ceilings

☐ **Prep**
Find power source and check that the new lights will not overload the circuit *(pages 120–121)*. Clear the room of all debris and lay a drop cloth on the floor.

☐ **Materials**
Fluorescent undercabinet fixtures, cable, remodel box with clamps, single-pole switch, wire nuts, tape

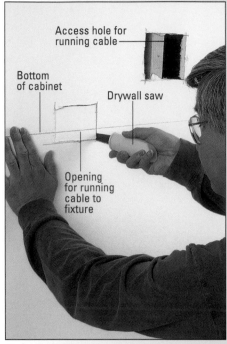

Access hole for running cable
Bottom of cabinet
Drywall saw
Opening for running cable to fixture

1 On the wall, use a level to draw the exact locations of the cabinets. Determine how the lights will fit onto the cabinets; you may need to cut a lip at the bottom of the cabinets. Cut access holes in the walls. Make sure all holes will be covered by the cabinets.

2 **Shut off power to the circuit.** Run cable from the switch hole to a power source *(pages 136–137)*. Run cables from the switch box to the fixture holes *(pages 142–147)*. Leave at least 16 inches of cable hanging out from each fixture hole.

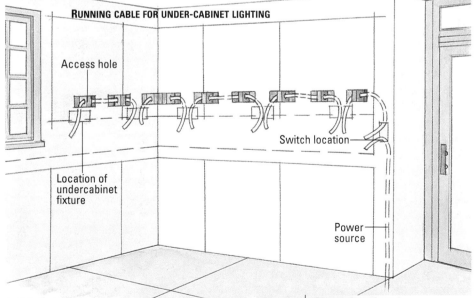

Running cable for under-cabinet lighting

Access hole
Switch location
Location of undercabinet fixture
Power source

In this installation the lights will mount against the wall and will cover the holes. Cable runs from the power source to the switch, then to each fixture. To make sure the gap between lights is never more than 6 inches, you may need to purchase lights of various lengths.

Check local code
Code may call for armored cable or require a box for each fixture.

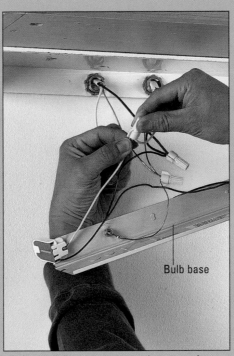

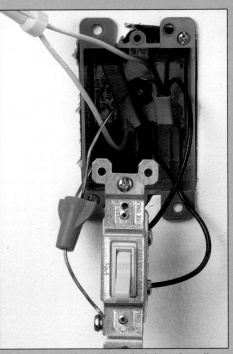

3 If the cabinet has a lip at the bottom, cut or drill a hole in it for the cable to pass through. After the cabinets are installed, strip sheathing and clamp the cables to the fixture body *(pages 128–131)*.

Fluorescent fixture body

4 At each fixture, connect the grounds. Splice black wires with the black fixture lead and white wires with the white fixture lead. Once connected, position and fold the wires carefully so they do not make contact with the ballast.

Bulb base

5 Pull cables into the switch box, install the box, and wire the switch. Connect the grounds and splice the white wires together. Connect the black wires to the switch terminals.

Two ways to run cable with cabinets in place

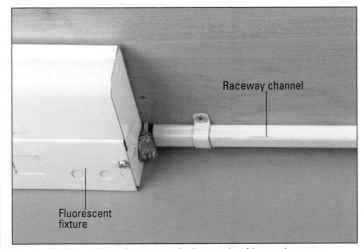

Raceway channel

Fluorescent fixture

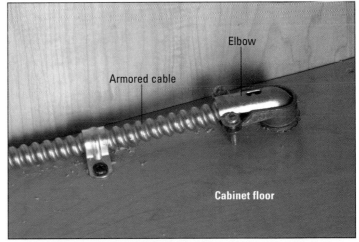

Elbow

Armored cable

Cabinet floor

If removing the cabinets is not practical, consult with your inspector for the best way to run wiring. One option is to run wires through metal or plastic raceway channels attached to the underside of the cabinets.

Or run armored cable through the inside of the cabinet. Use elbows to bring the wiring down to the light fixtures from the top, rather than the side. Both methods call for precise cutting of channels or cable sheathing.

RECESSED CANS

The most inconspicuous way to illuminate a large room is to install a series of recessed canister lights, also called "cans" or "pot lights." Install a grid of lights spaced 6–8 feet apart. Use eyeball-type can lights to highlight wall features, task lights to brighten a countertop or sink, and a watertight recessed fixture above a tub or shower.

Remodel can lights are easy to install in finished walls. Even running cable is not too difficult, because cans are usually spaced only two or three joists apart. Using a fishing drill bit *(page 147),* you may need to cut only a few holes in the ceiling.

See *page 172* for tips on buying recessed lights. Most inexpensive recessed cans are rated to use only 60-watt bulbs.

PRESTART CHECKLIST

☐ **TIME**
About a day to cut holes, run cable, and install six to eight lights with a switch

☐ **TOOLS**
Voltage tester, drill, spade bit or fishing drill bit, stud finder, ladder, drywall saw, level, hammer, fish tape, screwdriver, strippers, long-nose pliers, lineman's pliers

☐ **SKILLS**
Precision cutting of drywall or plaster; stripping, splicing, and connecting wires to terminals; installing boxes; running cable through walls and ceilings

☐ **PREP**
Find power source and make sure the new lights will not overload the circuit *(pages 120–121, 136–137).* Clear the room of all obstructions and lay a drop cloth on the floor.

☐ **MATERIALS**
Recessed canister lights, cable, switch box and clamps, wire nuts, electrician's tape

A. Rough-in the wiring

Mark center of fixture.

Template

1 Plan the locations for the lights and draw lines marking the center of each. Use a stud finder or a bent wire *(page 171)* to see if a joist is in the way. You can move the light several inches to avoid a joist—the inconsistency won't be noticeable.

2 Center the hole in the cardboard template over your location mark. Holding the template in place, mark your cut line.

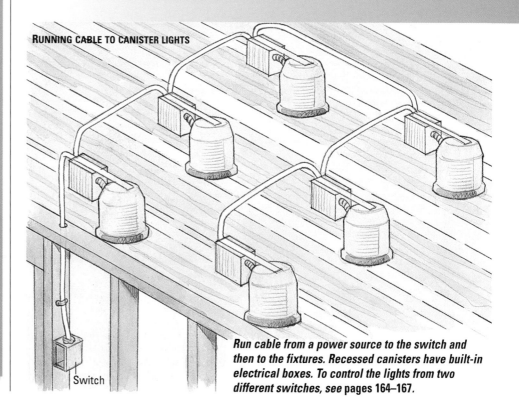

RUNNING CABLE TO CANISTER LIGHTS

Switch

Run cable from a power source to the switch and then to the fixtures. Recessed canisters have built-in electrical boxes. To control the lights from two different switches, see pages 164–167.

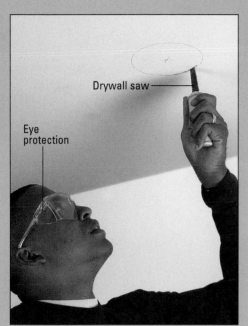

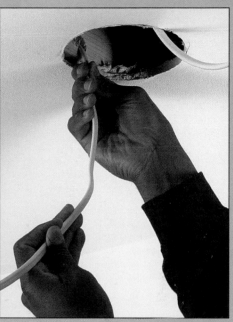

3 Cut the hole with a drywall saw. Wear safety glasses because drywall dust stings terribly if it gets in eyes. If the ceiling is plaster, see *page 142* for cutting tips. Cut precisely—the canister trim leaves little room for error.

4 Drill holes for the cable as far up the joist as possible so drywall nails cannot reach the cable. See *pages 142–147* for tips on running cable through walls and ceilings.

5 Run cable up from the power source to the switch box, then run cable to each fixture hole (see the illustration on *page 170*). Allow at least 16 inches of cable to hang down from each hole.

STANLEY PRO TIP

Bent wire test

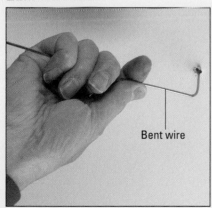

To make sure the fixture will not bump into a joist, use a stud finder. Or drill a ¼-inch hole, insert a bent wire, and spin the wire around to see whether you encounter an obstruction.

WHAT IF…
The ceiling framing is exposed?

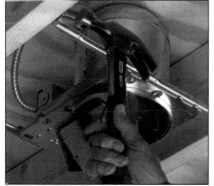

If the ceiling joists are not covered with drywall or plaster, install a new-work can light. Adjust the light to accommodate the thickness of the drywall that will be put up later. Slide the mounting bars out and hammer each tab into a joist. Slide the light to position it precisely.

Mapping can lights

With a standard flood bulb, a recessed light will illuminate an area about as wide as the ceiling is high. Make a scale drawing of your room and map a grid of lights that are at least fairly consistent in their spacing.

■ If your ceiling is 8 feet high, a typical recessed light will shine on a floor area with a diameter of 8 feet (a radius of 4 feet). To light the room, install a grid of lights spaced no more than 8 feet apart. The perimeter lights should be no more than 4 feet from the walls. Lights placed closer together—perhaps 6 or 7 feet apart and only 2–3 feet from the walls—will more fully light the room.

■ If you have a 10-foot ceiling, lights can be 7–10 feet apart and as much as 5 feet from the wall.

B. Install the lights

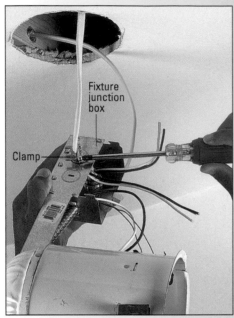

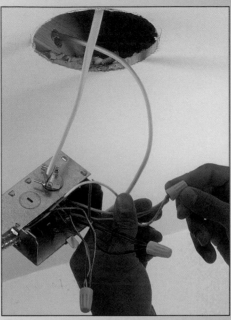

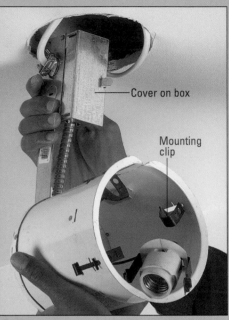

1 Strip about 6 inches of sheathing from the cable. Remove the cover from the fixture junction box and twist off a knockout for each cable. Slide the cable in and clamp the cable.

2 Connect the grounds. Splice white wires with white leads and black wires with black leads. Fold the wires into the junction box and replace the cover.

3 Pull the mounting clips inside the can so they will not be in the way when you push the canister into the hole. Without tangling the cables, guide the junction box through the hole and push in the canister.

STANLEY PRO TIP

"IC" light near insulation

If insulation will come within 3 inches of a recessed light, be sure to install a fixture rated "IC" (insulation compatible). A non-IC light will overheat dangerously.

WHAT IF...
Ceiling space is sloped or tight?

If the ceiling is sloped, buy special canisters that are adjustable so the light can point straight down.

If the vertical space above the ceiling is less than 8 inches, buy a low-clearance fixture. Some are small enough to fit into a space only 4 inches high.

Compact low-voltage halogen can lights are expensive, but they present new style options and produce an intense light.

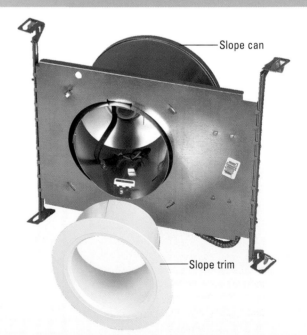

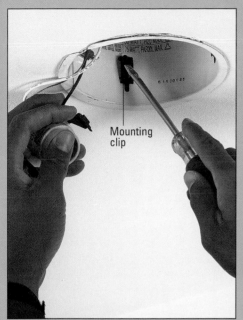

Mounting clip

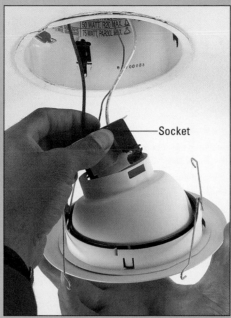

Socket

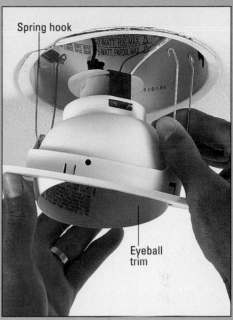

Spring hook

Eyeball trim

4 Push the canister so its flange is tight to the ceiling. With a slot screwdriver, push up each mounting clip until it clicks into place, clamping the canister to the drywall or plaster.

5 Many canisters have sockets that attach to the trim with two spring clips. Slip one clip into the notch provided and rock the socket so the clip engages.

6 If the trim has two spring hooks, squeeze and guide their ends into the slots provided, then push up the trim until it snaps into place. Twist an eyeball trim to face in the desired direction.

WHAT IF...
The canister has a spring-hook?

To mount trim that uses coil springs (shown), hold the trim in place up against the ceiling. Insert a pencil tip into the looped end of each spring and guide it up into the hole provided.

Trim options

Baffle trim (either white or black) diffuses the light, while reflector trim increases the brightness of a bulb. With open trim, the flood bulb protrudes slightly downward. For above a tub or shower, choose a watertight lens. An eyeball (or fish-eye) trim rotates to point where you want it; a wallwasher highlights the texture of a brick or stone wall.

Baffle trim

Reflector trim

Open trim

Flush watertight lens

Wallwasher trim

Eyeball trim

Extended watertight lens

WALL-MOUNTED LIGHTING

Wall sconces provide indirect lighting ideal for hallways or stairways, or on a large wall where a modest accent is needed. Place them just above eye level.

Use a standard ceiling box and wire just as you would a ceiling light. Most sconces mount with a center stud so you can adjust the fixture for level even if the box is not level. To control sconces from two locations, use three-way switches *(pages 164–167)*.

The two fixtures on both sides of a mirror *(page 151)* install just like sconces.

A strip of lights over a bathroom mirror or medicine chest calls for a similar installation method. Such fixtures use several low-wattage bulbs to reduce glare while providing plenty of light.

PRESTART CHECKLIST

☐ **TIME**
About three hours to run cable and install a switch and two sconces (not including cutting a pathway for the cable and patching walls)

☐ **TOOLS**
Voltage tester, drill, saw, hammer, fish tape, screwdriver, strippers, long-nose pliers, lineman's pliers

☐ **SKILLS**
Stripping, splicing, and connecting wires to terminals; installing boxes; running cable through walls and ceilings

☐ **PREP**
Find power source and make sure the new lights will not overload the circuit *(pages 120–121, 136–137)*. Spread a drop cloth on the floor below.

☐ **MATERIALS**
Sconce(s), ceiling boxes and a switch box with clamps, cable, switch, wire nuts, electrician's tape

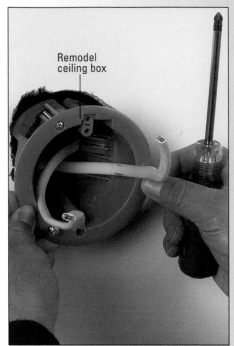

1 **Shut off power to the circuit.** Cut holes for the sconce boxes and the switch. Run cable from the power source to the switch then to the sconces *(pages 142–147)*.

2 Clamp cable to a wall box and install the box. Most sconces come with all the necessary hardware—usually a strap with a center stud. If the strap is provided, use it; it helps carry heat away from the fixture.

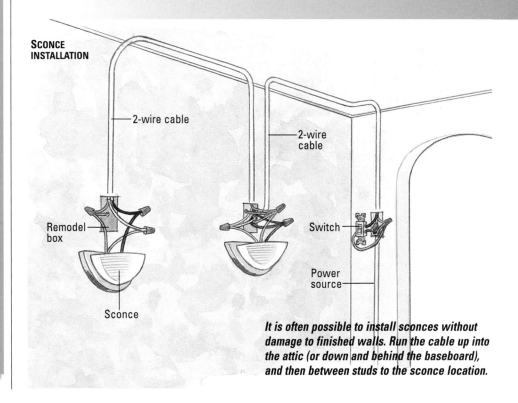

SCONCE INSTALLATION

It is often possible to install sconces without damage to finished walls. Run the cable up into the attic (or down and behind the baseboard), and then between studs to the sconce location.

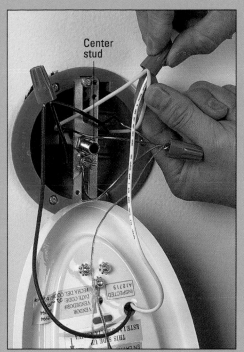

3 To wire a sconce, connect the grounds. Splice the white fixture lead to the white wire(s), and the black lead to the black wire(s).

4 Slip the sconce over the center stud, and start to tighten the nut. Stand back and check that the base is plumb, and then tighten the base.

5 Install the light bulb, making sure it does not exceed the manufacturer's recommended wattage. Clip the lens into place. Wire the switch *(pages 161–167)*.

Lights mounted on a mirror

To install a bathroom strip light, center the box over the mirror or medicine chest. Attach the fixture over the box, wire the fixture, and attach the cover.

To install a light fixture directly on a mirror, have a glass supplier cut three holes to match the fixture: a large hole for the electrical box and two smaller holes for mounting screws. Wire the fixture. Apply a thin bead of clear silicone caulk to its back to act as an adhesive. Attach with mounting screws, but don't overtighten them— you might break the mirror.

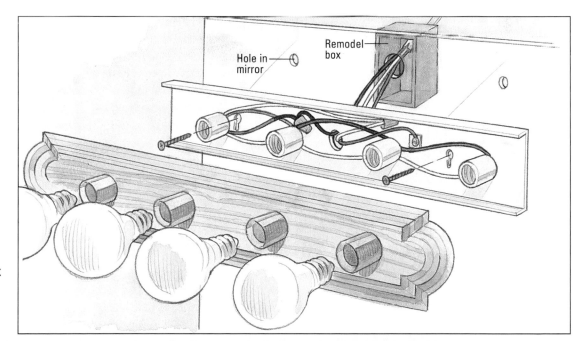

Installing Fans & Heaters

Fans that pull air through a room, an attic, or even the whole house contribute to making your home more comfortable, and they reduce energy costs. Small vent fans in the bathroom or kitchen expel unwanted fumes and moisture. Each requires relatively simple wiring; the installation of the fan and ducts or vents require the most time.

An attic must breathe

When the weather is hot and sunny, a stuffy attic can heat up like an oven, making it difficult to cool a house. In cold weather, an attic that is too warm collects moisture that can damage insulation. It can also cause snow on the roof to melt, leading to ice dams at the eaves, which can damage roofing, sheathing, and interior walls and ceilings. The solution to both problems is a well-ventilated attic.

Outside air must circulate freely through an attic. Modern building codes specify types and sizes of attic vents, but an older home may be inadequately vented. An attic should have vents below, at the eaves or the soffit, and above, on the roof, at the ridge, or in the gable. A gable fan or roof fan will pull hot air out of an attic, but only if the eaves or soffit vents are sufficient to allow the air easily to escape.

Choosing the right fan

Ask local builders or home center employees to find out which fan or combination of fans will work best in your house. If your attic is not adequately vented, a gable fan *(pages 182–183)* is usually the easiest way to get the air moving. Install a roof fan *(page 184)* if a gable fan is not feasible. To keep a house cool without turning on the air-conditioning, a whole-house fan *(pages 178–181)* can work wonders. Consult with a dealer to find out which size fan or fans will work most effectively.

If a bathroom stays steamy or a kitchen stays smoky even with a vent fan on, poorly designed or blocked ductwork may be the culprit *(pages 185 and 188)*. Or you may need a more powerful fan. Add warmth to a bathroom or other areas with radiant floor heating or an electric heater.

Built-in fans can reduce cooling costs, remove moisture, and vent unpleasant smoke and odors.

Chapter Preview

Whole-house ventilating fan
page 178

Gable fan
page 182

Roof fan
page 184

Range hood
page 185

If your home does not have adequate eaves, roof, or gable venting, install vents before adding an attic fan. An eaves vent is the easiest to install. Cut a rectangular hole in the soffit, then fasten the vent screen in place with corrosion-resistant screws.

Eaves vent screen

In a well-ventilated attic, air moves up through eaves vents and out through vents on the roof, at the ridge, or in the gable. As an alternative, two large gable vents may do the trick. Always check that vents are cleared of insulation and that items stored in the attic are not blocking air flow.

Bath vent fan
page 188

Installing electric heaters
page 192

Installing electric radiant heat
page 194

WHOLE-HOUSE VENTILATING FAN

On mild summer days the gentle air circulation provided by a whole-house fan may be all you need for cooling. The fan pulls fresh air through every room that has an open door or window and sends it out through the attic.

For the fan to work properly, the attic must be adequately vented, and doors or windows must be open in the rooms below. Locate the fan in the ceiling of a top-floor hallway. The one shown on these pages rests on top of an exposed joist. Other models require that you cut a joist and frame an opening—a more complicated project.

In winter make sure the fan's shutters close tightly and place insulation over the fan so the house won't lose heat.

PRESTART CHECKLIST

☐ **TIME**
About eight hours to run cable and install a fan with a wall switch (not including preparing a path for the cable)

☐ **TOOLS**
Voltage tester, stud finder, drywall saw, drill, circular saw, hammer, fish tape, nonconductive ladder, screwdriver, long-nose pliers, lineman's pliers, strippers

☐ **SKILLS**
Splicing and connecting wires to terminals; installing boxes; running cable through walls and ceilings; cutting and attaching boards

☐ **PREP**
Find a power source and make sure the fan will not overload the circuit (*pages 120–121, 136–137*). Spread a drop cloth on the floor below. Enlist a helper for lifting and placing the fan.

☐ **MATERIALS**
Whole-house fan, remodel box, switch, electrical boxes with clamps, three-wire cable, wire nuts, electrician's tape

A. Install the fan

3-wire cable for switch

Top plate of wall

1 Cut a hole for the switch box in a wall below the fan. Run three-wire cable down through the ceiling plate to the hole.

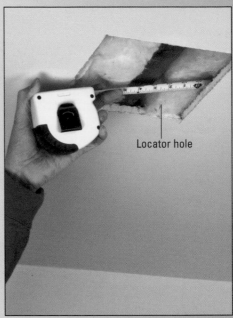

Locator hole

2 Plan to position the fan so it rests on joists at either side; one joist will run through the middle. Use a stud finder to find a center joist, then cut a locator hole and use a tape measure to find the exact location of the joists.

WHOLE-HOUSE FAN INSTALLATION

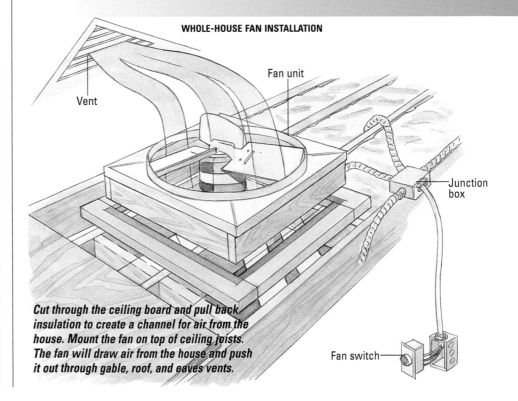

Vent

Fan unit

Junction box

Fan switch

Cut through the ceiling board and pull back insulation to create a channel for air from the house. Mount the fan on top of ceiling joists. The fan will draw air from the house and push it out through gable, roof, and eaves vents.

3 Cut the hole according to manufacturer's directions. Lay pieces of plywood on the attic joists to provide a safe work surface. Work with a helper in the attic to lift the fan up into place.

4 Remove any insulation that's in the way. If blocking is not provided with the fan, cut blocking pieces from lumber the same dimension as your joists. Use the pieces to fill gaps between the joists. Build a frame of 2×4s, lay it flat and square on the joists, and fasten it firmly.

5 Center the fan over the frame. Attach it by driving wood screws (not drywall screws) through the brackets provided and into the frame.

STANLEY PRO TIP

Locating the fan

The best location for a whole-house fan usually is in a top-floor hallway. If the fan is in a room, that room's door must be kept open while the fan is operating. To allow the fan to vent freely, there should be at least 30 inches of vertical space between the joists the fan rests on and the roof rafters. If the attic contains loose insulation, cover it with plastic sheeting.

Open up
Open windows to promote air flow, otherwise the fan will pull air down through the fireplace, water heater, or furnace chimney, which could include carbon monoxide. The back pressure could even shut off a furnace.

Select size and capacity

To cool properly, a whole-house fan should exchange the air in a house at least once every four minutes. The faster the air is exchanged, the cooler the house. Manufacturers offer several sizes of whole-house fans. Find out the total square footage of your home and consult with a salesperson or read the manufacturer's literature to choose the right size for your house. When in doubt buy the next size up; with a fan-rated multispeed switch, you can always adjust the power downward.

REFRESHER COURSE
Circuit analysis

Take care that your fan will not overload a circuit. Add up the wattages of all the electrical users on the circuit and then add in the fan's wattage. If the total is over 1,440 watts for a 15-amp circuit or 1,920 watts for a 20-amp circuit, the load exceeds "safe capacity." Look for another circuit to tap into (pages 120–121). If you cannot find a circuit with enough available wattage, you may need to run cable all the way back to the service panel and install a new circuit (pages 230–231).

B. Wire the fan

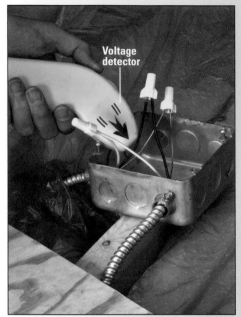

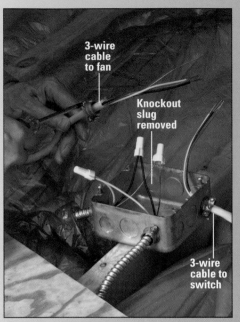

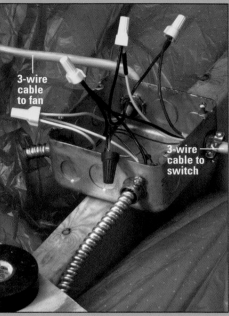

1 **Shut off power to the circuit** you will be using. If there is a junction box in the attic and its circuit can accommodate the fan, pull power from it. If several cables enter the box, **use a voltage detector to make sure all power is off.**

2 Remove knockout slugs and run two three-wire cables, one from the fan and one from the switch *(page 178)*. If the fan comes with a cable "whip" that does not reach the junction box, run it into an intermediate box and run cable from there to the junction box.

3 In the junction box, connect the grounds and splice all white wires in the box, except the one running to the switch. Mark it with black tape and splice it to the black wire running to the fan. Splice together the other black wires and splice the red wires.

SAFETY FIRST
Working safely in an attic

■ If an attic floor is unfinished with exposed insulation and joists, one misstep will put your foot through the ceiling below. Don't take chances; lay down sheets of plywood wherever you will be working.
■ Most insulation—whether fiberglass blankets or loose—is nasty stuff that causes eyes to smart and skin to itch. Wear protective goggles, a dust mask, and long sleeves when cutting or removing it.

Old attic wiring

If you find exposed wires running through porcelain knobs and tubes, the wiring is not necessarily unsafe. However, do not try to grab power from knob-and-tube wiring and take care not to disturb the wires.

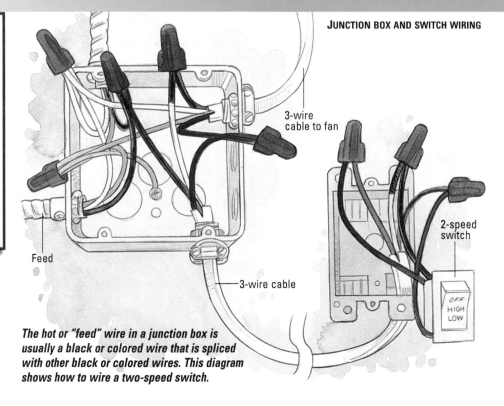

JUNCTION BOX AND SWITCH WIRING

The hot or "feed" wire in a junction box is usually a black or colored wire that is spliced with other black or colored wires. This diagram shows how to wire a two-speed switch.

4 At the switch hole, clamp cable to a remodel box and install the box. For the two-speed switch shown above (provided by the fan manufacturer), mark the white wire black with tape and connect it to the black switch lead. Splice the red wire to the red lead and the blue lead to the black wire.

5 Check the fan belt tension. When pressed, it should deflect about ½ inch. If necessary, follow the manufacturer's instructions for adjusting the tension. (Not all whole-house fans are belt-driven; some have blades powered directly by the motor.)

6 With a helper, position the shutter so it covers the ceiling hole. Drive screws into joists to attach it firmly to the ceiling. Restore power and test. Be sure the shutter freely opens and closes.

WHAT IF...
There is no power available in the attic?

If there is no usable power source in the attic, run power up through a wall switch and then on to the fan. Check that adding the fan to a nearby fixture or receptacle circuit will not create an overload *(pages 120–121).* **Shut off power to the circuit** and tap into the power source. Then run cable and install a switch box *(pages 136–137).* If using a fan-rated rheostat switch, wire it as shown.

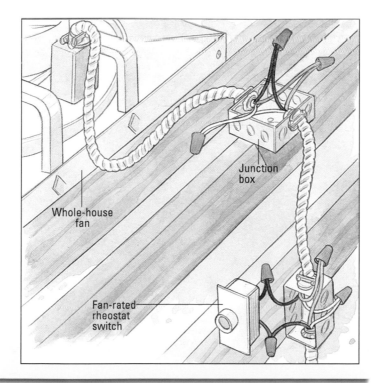

Switch options

In addition to the two-speed switch shown above, switch options include a sliding control with a toggle (which "remembers" the power level when turned on and off), a three-level toggle switch, a three-level sliding switch, a timer, and a pilot light toggle. Make sure any switch is fan-rated.

GABLE FAN

If an attic has a gable (a vertical end wall often pointed at the top), it is usually not difficult to install a fan there. A gable fan is easier to install than roof-mounted fans or vents, which are prone to leak if not sealed correctly.

If your gable does not already have a vent, install one. Plastic louvers are less attractive than fixed wooden units, but they seal out wind and rain more effectively.

Figure the square footage of your attic and total the square footage of your eaves vents. With these two figures in hand, you'll be equipped to shop for a gable fan of the correct size.

Gable fans come with thermostats to turn on automatically when the attic gets too hot and turn off when it cools off.

PRESTART CHECKLIST

☐ **TIME**
About four hours to run cable inside an attic and install a gable fan (not counting additional framing or cutting for gable vent)

☐ **TOOLS**
Voltage tester, drill, drywall saw, circular saw, hammer, screwdriver, strippers, long-nose pliers, lineman's pliers

☐ **SKILLS**
Stripping, splicing, connecting wires to terminals; installing rough wood framing

☐ **PREP**
Find power source and make sure the fan will not overload the circuit *(pages 120–121, 136–137).* Lay sheets of plywood on the attic floor if the joists are exposed. Wear long clothes, protective goggles, and a dust mask.

☐ **MATERIALS**
Gable fan, cable, wood screws, wire nuts, cable clamps, electrician's tape

1 If no gable vent exists, cut and install one *(page 183).* If the studs are too far apart, add some framing. Cut 2×4s to fit between the studs and attach them with 3-inch screws.

Junction box | Gable fan

Mounting flange | Thermostat

2 Mount the fan on the framing by driving screws through the mounting flanges and into framing members.

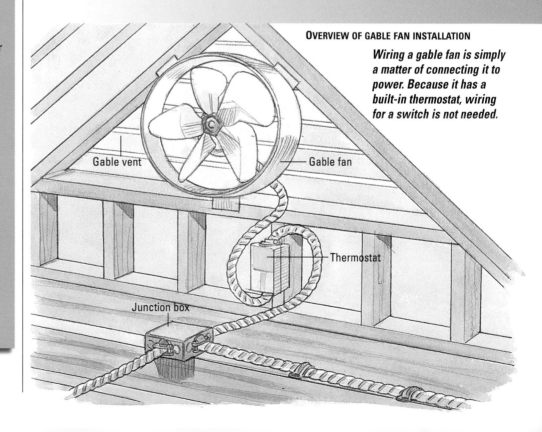

OVERVIEW OF GABLE FAN INSTALLATION

Wiring a gable fan is simply a matter of connecting it to power. Because it has a built-in thermostat, wiring for a switch is not needed.

Gable vent | Gable fan | Thermostat | Junction box

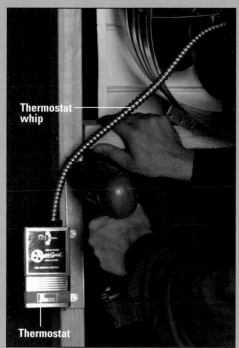

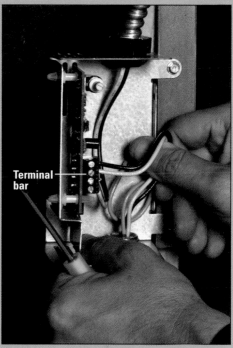

3 Fasten the fan's thermostat to a framing member. The fan's whip should be taut, so it won't wobble and bang against the framing when the fan is running.

4 Shut off power to the circuit. (To test a junction box for power, see *page 86.*) Run cable from the thermostat into a power source. If no junction box is available in the attic, bring power up from a circuit in the floor below *(pages 136–137)*. Make sure the circuit can handle the additional load.

5 Wire the thermostat following the manufacturer's directions. With the thermostat shown above, stripped wire ends are inserted in a terminal bar and screwed tight. Adjust the thermostat control and restore power.

WHAT IF...
No gable vent exists?

To install a vent shutter, you need not cut or modify framing. Use a saber saw or set a circular saw just deep enough to cut through the siding and sheathing. Cut a hole that will be covered up by the vent frame. Attach the louver by driving screws through its frame and into framing members.

Working with vinyl siding

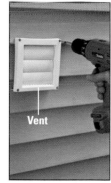

Cut vinyl with a fine-toothed handsaw, hole saw, or by repeated scoring with a utility knife. In some cases you may have to purchase a tool that "unzips" one course of siding from the next. For double protection, install the duct and carefully caulk around it. Then install the vent with galvanized screws and caulk around the duct and the vent housing.

ROOF FAN

If it is not possible to install a gable fan *(pages 182–183)*, a roof fan is the next best choice. Wiring is simple. The hard part is slipping it under shingles so the roof will not leak. Follow the manufacturer's instructions for exactly how to cut the hole and attach the fan. If the roof already has a turbine or other vent, you may be able to remove it and install a roof fan with little or no cutting.

Many roof fans have humidistats, which measure humidity, as well as thermostats. They rid the attic of excess moisture, which can damage insulation even if the attic is not hot.

PRESTART CHECKLIST

☐ **TIME**
About five hours to cut a hole in the roof, install the fan, and run cable inside an attic

☐ **TOOLS**
Voltage tester, drill, bit, reciprocating or saber saw, pry bar, utility and putty knives, screwdriver, strippers, long-nose pliers, lineman's pliers

☐ **SKILLS**
Cutting roofing; stripping, splicing, connecting wires

☐ **PREP**
Find power source and make sure the fan will not overload the circuit *(pages 120–121, 136–137)*

☐ **MATERIALS**
Roof fan, cable, roofing nails, roofing cement, screws, wire nuts, cable clamps, electrician's tape

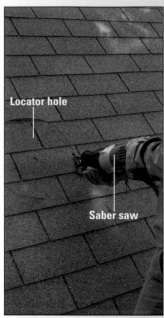

1 Drill a locator hole from the inside of the attic to ensure that you will not cut through a joist. Mark the roof with the manufacturer's template and cut the hole with a saber saw or reciprocating saw.

2 You may need to cut back some shingles. Slide the fan into place so that the top half of its flange is covered with shingles.

3 Drive roofing nails and cover them with roofing cement. Use roofing cement to seal down the roofing above and beside the vent. Wire the fan as you would a gable fan *(page 183)*.

THERMOSTAT SWITCH WIRING

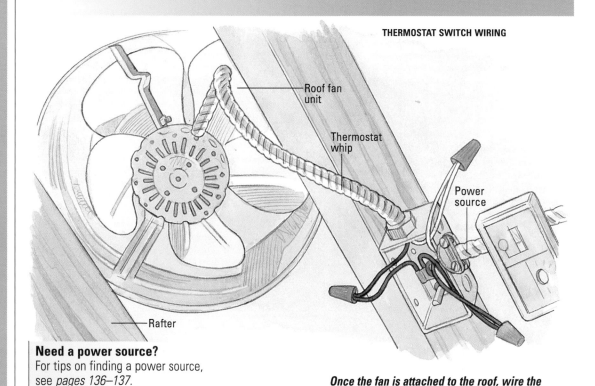

Need a power source?
For tips on finding a power source, see *pages 136–137*.

Once the fan is attached to the roof, wire the fan's thermostat directly to a power source.

RANGE HOOD

A range hood clears the air over a cooking surface. It may also provide illumination. Usually it is attached to the underside of a cabinet, about 30 inches above the range. The bottom of the hood should be about 24 inches above the range.

The larger a range hood's "cfm" rating (the cubic feet per minute of air it draws), the greater its capacity to expel smoke, heat, and odors.

If the ducts will have to travel more than a few feet or make several turns to reach the outside, a range hood will not be very effective. Consider purchasing a ductless unit, which runs air through a filter and sends it back into the kitchen.

To replace a range hood, **shut off power** and remove the existing hood. Take the hood with you when you buy a new one to make sure the duct work will line up.

PRESTART CHECKLIST

☐ **TIME**
About six hours to cut holes, run cable, and install ductwork and a range hood (not including cutting a pathway for the cable and patching walls)

☐ **TOOLS**
Voltage tester, drill, long bit, perhaps a masonry bit and cold chisel, saw, hammer, fish tape, long-nose pliers, screwdriver, strippers, lineman's pliers

☐ **SKILLS**
Stripping, splicing, and connecting wires to terminals; running cable through walls; cutting holes in walls

☐ **PREP**
Find power source and make sure the range hood will not overload the circuit *(pages 120–121, 136–137)*. Spread a drop cloth on the floor below.

☐ **MATERIALS**
Range hood, cable and clamps, ducts, duct tape, sheet metal screws, wall cap, caulk, wire nuts, electrician's tape

Drywall saw

1 Remove the range hood electrical cover and punch out the knockouts for the duct and for the electrical connection. Hold the hood in position and mark the wall for two holes. Cut a hole in the wall *(page 142)* for the duct.

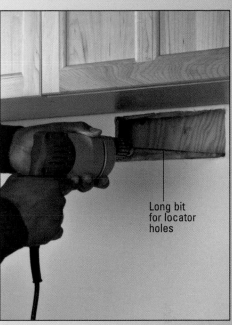

Long bit for locator holes

2 If necessary, drill a hole for the cable. Equip a drill with a long bit and drill locator holes through to the outside of the house.

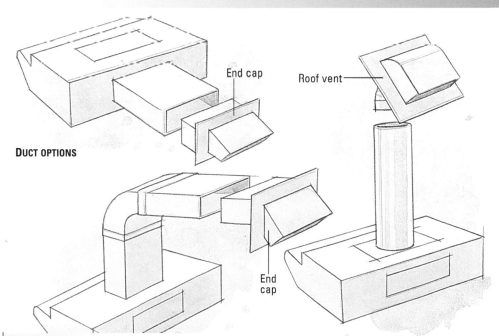

DUCT OPTIONS

End cap

Roof vent

End cap

A standard range hood pulls only about 3 amps (360 watts) so it is often possible to connect it to a kitchen's receptacle circuit.

Run ductwork in the most direct route possible. If you cannot go straight out the wall, route the ducts up through cabinets and then either out the roof or the wall.

Range hood *(continued)*

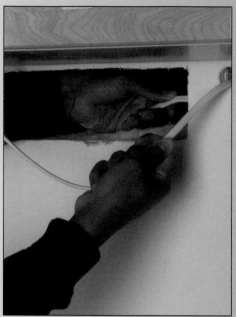

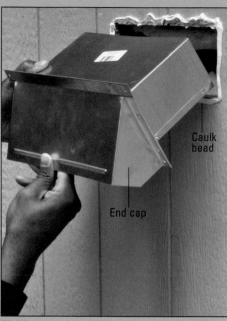

Locator holes · Saber saw

Caulk bead · End cap

3 Mark the cutout by connecting the locator holes. Check to see that the hole will be the right size for your duct. Cut through siding using a saber saw, reciprocating saw, or circular saw.

4 **Shut off power to the circuit.** Connect cable to a power source *(pages 136–137)* and run it up through the cable hole. You may use the cutout for the duct to help access and handle the cable, but make sure the cable will not be in the way of the duct.

5 Measure from the outside to the inside wall and cut a piece of duct to fit. Attach the duct to the end cap. Apply a bead of caulk around the hole on the outside and slide the duct and cap through the wall. Attach the cap with screws.

For vent hole in cabinet

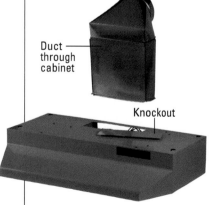

Duct through cabinet · Knockout

If the duct must run upward, remove the knockout on top of the hood and install the damper unit. Cut cabinets carefully to make room for the duct.

Bending sheet metal

To join a duct to a range hood (left) you may have to cut the duct to size and bend your own flange. For a straight, neat angle, score the bend with the end of a screwdriver, clamp on two 1×2s as shown above, and bend the flange.

Cutting and attaching to a masonry wall

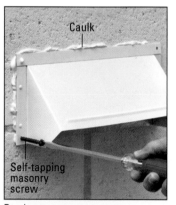

Caulk · Self-tapping masonry screw

Use a masonry bit to drill the locator holes (Step 2). To cut through brick, drill holes every inch or two, then chip away with a hammer and cold chisel. An older home may have two thicknesses of brick.

Purchase masonry screws along with a masonry bit of the appropriate size for the screws. Drill a pilot hole and drive the masonry screw into the block.

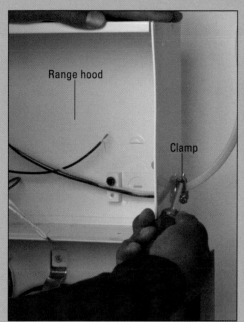

6 Stuff the cavity around the duct with insulation. Strip and clamp cable to the range hood.

7 Slip the range hood into place so the duct fits snugly over the hood's damper unit. Attach the hood with screws driven up into the cabinet above and/or into the wall studs.

8 Connect the grounds, including the pigtail, to the hood housing. Splice the hood's lead wires to the house wires. Reattach the electrical cover.

WHAT IF...
A stud is in the way?

If a stud is in the way of the most direct route for the duct, try working around it with flexible ductwork. Another option is to cut a wall opening large enough to install a header but small enough that it will be covered by the range hood and the cabinet above it. Cut the stud and install a header made of doubled 2×4s sandwiching ½-inch plywood.

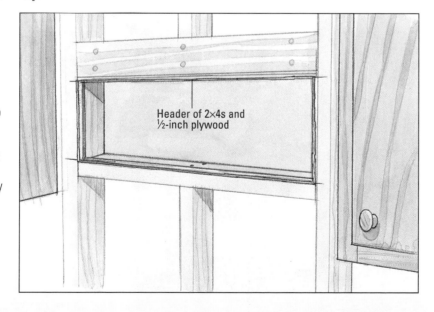

Header of 2×4s and ½-inch plywood

STANLEY PRO TIP

Range hood maintenance and use

■ Check that the damper flap moves freely so air can move out only when the fan is blowing.
■ Remove the filter every few months and clean or replace it.
■ Clean the underside of the hood regularly. Built-up grease poses a fire hazard.
■ When cooking with high heat, turn on the fan to cool the air and reduce the risk of a grease fire.

BATH VENT FAN

Many bathroom fans do little more than make noise, either because they are too weak or because their ductwork does not permit free movement of air. Usually venting is the culprit. Plan for a vent duct that is as short as possible and that makes as few turns as possible *(page 189)*.

In addition to a vent fan, a bathroom unit may have a light, night-light, and/or a heater unit. Because a heater uses much more power than a light and fan, it may need to be on its own circuit.

A fan-only unit or a light and fan that come on at the same time requires only two-cable wiring. The more features you want to control separately, the more complicated the wiring becomes. To replace an existing fan, check the wiring; you may need to replace two-wire cable with three-wire cable or even two cables.

PRESTART CHECKLIST

☐ **TIME**
About seven hours to install ducting, a fan, and a switch (not including cutting a pathway for the cable and patching walls)

☐ **TOOLS**
Voltage tester, pry bar, drill, drywall saw, saber saw, hammer, nonconductive ladder, fish tape, screwdriver, strippers, long-nose pliers, lineman's pliers

☐ **SKILLS**
Cutting through siding or roofing; stripping, splicing, and connecting wires; installing boxes; running cable

☐ **PREP**
Find the shortest path for the ductwork. Find power source and make sure the new lights will not overload the circuit *(pages 120–121, 136–137)*. Spread a drop cloth on the floor below.

☐ **MATERIALS**
Vent fan, switch, ductwork, duct tape, sheet metal screws, cable, clamps, switch box, wire nuts, electrician's tape

A. Install the vent fan housing

1 To replace an existing ceiling light with a fan/light, **shut off power to the circuit.** Remove the light and pry out the ceiling box. If you cannot work from above, cut carefully around the box before prying. You may need to cut through mounting nails.

2 Disassemble the new fixture and use the housing as a template to mark for the opening. The fan must be securely mounted; if there is no joist to attach it to, install blocking nailed to nearby joists.

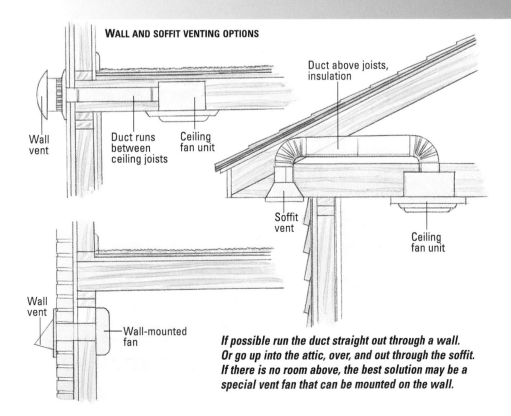

WALL AND SOFFIT VENTING OPTIONS

If possible run the duct straight out through a wall. Or go up into the attic, over, and out through the soffit. If there is no room above, the best solution may be a special vent fan that can be mounted on the wall.

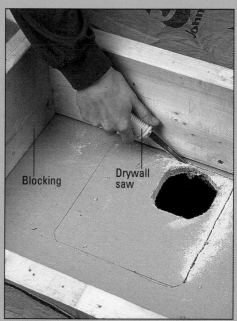

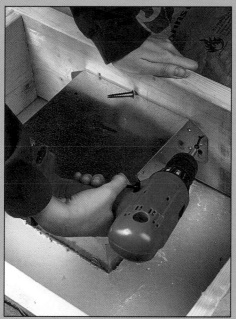

3 If necessary, install blocking to keep the insulation away from the fan. Cut the hole with a drywall saw or reciprocating saw. If the ceiling is plaster, drill locator holes at the four corners and cut the opening from below.

4 If necessary, run new cable from the switch to the box *(pages 144–147)*. (The fan pictured above has separate controls for fan and light and requires one three-wire cable.) Screw the fan to a framing member.

5 For the wall vent, drill a locator hole from the inside through the outside wall. Outside, cut a hole for the duct.

WHAT IF...
You must work from below?

If there is no access to an attic space above, cut the hole next to a joist. If the duct can run parallel to a joist and the outside wall is not too far away, use a long bit to drill the locator hole.

STANLEY PRO TIP

Ducts should be short, wide, and smooth

The shorter, smoother, and wider the ductwork, the more freely air can move through it. Most ductwork for bathroom fans is 4 inches in diameter; don't use anything smaller. Solid ducting is the smoothest and most efficient, but it may be difficult to install in tight places. All-metal flexible duct is bendable and fairly smooth. Plastic-and-wire ducting is the easiest to install but is the least efficient.

At every joint, use sheet metal screws or clamps to make tight connections; then cover the joint completely with professional-quality duct tape.

Venting through the roof

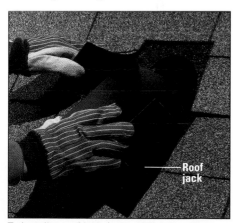

To install a roof jack *(page 190)*, follow the manufacturer's instructions exactly to ensure that the jack will not leak. First cut through the roof, then cut back shingles. Install the jack and cover its top half with shingles. Cover all nails with roofing cement *(page 184)*.

A. Install the vent fan housing *(continued)*

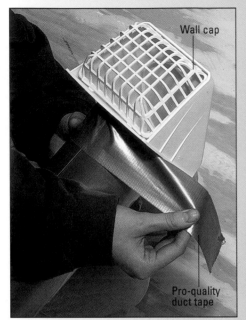

Wall cap

Pro-quality
duct tape

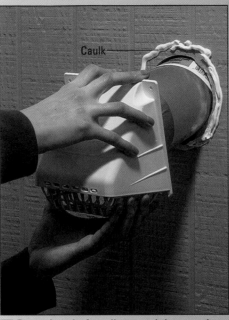

Caulk

Clamp

6 Measure from the outside to the fan. Attach a piece of solid duct to the wall cap so it is long enough to reach the fan or as close as possible. Fit the duct to the cap, drill pilot holes, and drive sheetmetal screws to hold it in place. Then cover the joint with professional-quality duct tape.

7 Run a bead of caulk around the exterior hole. Slide the duct through the hole and fasten the wall cap to the wall with screws.

8 Fill any gap between duct and fan with another piece of solid duct or with flexible metal ducting. At each joint attach clamps and wrap with duct tape.

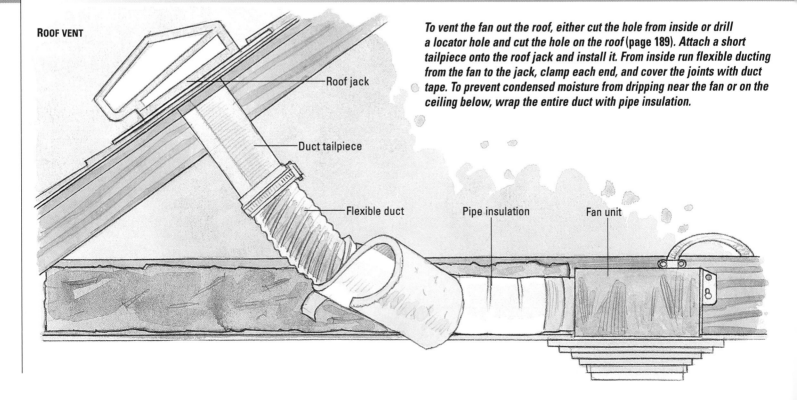

ROOF VENT

Roof jack

Duct tailpiece

Flexible duct

Pipe insulation

Fan unit

To vent the fan out the roof, either cut the hole from inside or drill a locator hole and cut the hole on the roof (page 189). *Attach a short tailpiece onto the roof jack and install it. From inside run flexible ducting from the fan to the jack, clamp each end, and cover the joints with duct tape. To prevent condensed moisture from dripping near the fan or on the ceiling below, wrap the entire duct with pipe insulation.*

B. Wire the fan

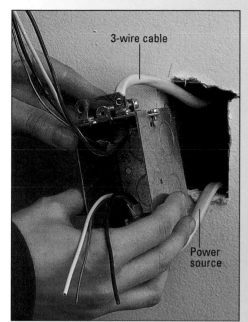

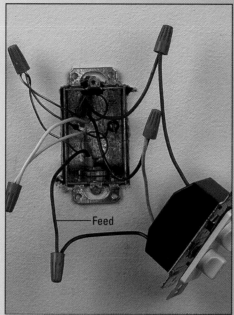

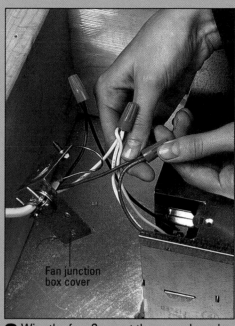

1 If necessary, run the correct cable or cables to the switch box. As shown above, power enters the switch box. If power enters the fan, consult the manufacturer's instructions.

2 To wire a fan/light switch, connect the grounds and splice the white wires. Connect the red and black wires from the fan to the fan and light terminals. Connect the feed wire to the remaining terminal.

3 Wire the fan. Connect the grounds and splice the white wires. Splice the black wire to the black fan lead and the red wire to the colored lead. Attach the junction box cover. In the bathroom install the light and the fixture canopy.

Timer switch for a fan with a heater

To avoid wasting energy and creating a hazardous situation by leaving on the fan heater, install a timer switch (above) along with a two-function switch for the fan and light. To do so, install a double-gang box.

WIRING A MULTIPURPOSE UNIT

The more functions a switch controls separately, the more complicated the wiring. For instance, to wire a fan/light/night-light with separate controls for each, run two cables— one two-wire and one three-wire— from the switch to the fan.

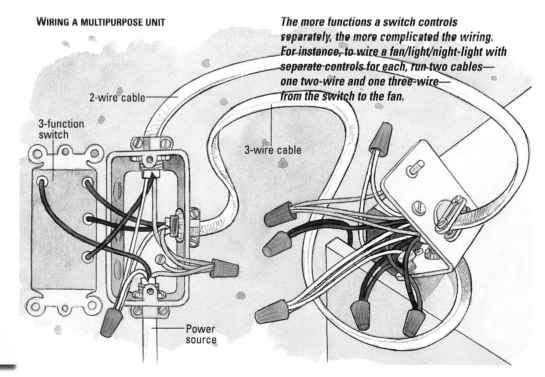

INSTALLING ELECTRIC HEATERS

Even if your home is not heated by electricity, adding an electric baseboard or wall heater can be a cost-effective way to bring heat to a cold spot in your home or an area that gets only occasional use.

When planning, assume 10 watts of heater capacity per square foot of room area. In other words a 10×10-foot mud room will need two 500-watt baseboard heaters. Check your local codes for circuit requirements; some municipalities require a dedicated circuit protected by a 20-amp double breaker. In some cases heaters can be added to existing 120-volt circuits— see *page 122* for how to calculate maximum permissible load. Confirm that the circuit voltage matches that of the unit—120-volt circuit for a 120-volt unit, 240-volt circuit for a 240-volt unit.

Place heaters on outside walls and below windows. Check manufacturer's specs for locating furniture and drapes. Never locate a heater beneath a receptacle. In general, baseboard units are best for enhancing whole-room heat; blower-heaters are best for intense heat of short duration.

PRESTART CHECKLIST

☐ **TIME**
About three hours to run cable, install a baseboard heater and thermostat; about two and one-half hours to run cable and install a blower-heater

☐ **TOOLS**
Voltage tester, drill, ½-inch bit, drywall saw, fish tape, screwdriver, stripper, long-nose pliers, lineman's pliers

☐ **SKILLS**
Cutting into walls; stripping, splicing, and connecting wires to terminals; installing boxes; running cable into boxes

☐ **MATERIALS**
Heater, box for thermostat, 12/2 cable, electrician's tape, wire nuts

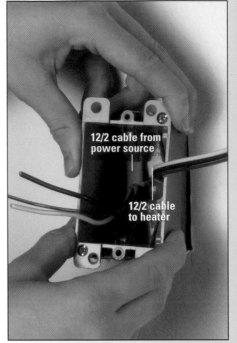

1 Cut an opening for a large-capacity remodel box. Run 12/2 cable to the location of the thermostat *(pages 144–147)*. **Do not connect the cable to its power source.** Run cable from the opening to the heater location. Strip cables and clamp in the box. Install the box *(pages 142–143)*.

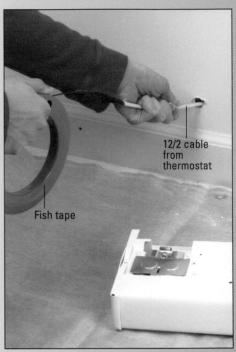

2 No junction box is required for the cable running to the heater—the box is built into the unit. Strip the incoming wires *(page 48)*. (You can also run the feeder line directly to the heater and then to the thermostat. Check the manufacturer's instructions.)

ASSEMBLING AND WIRING ELECTRIC HEATERS

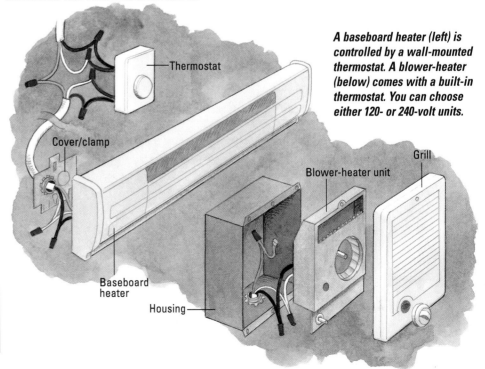

A baseboard heater (left) is controlled by a wall-mounted thermostat. A blower-heater (below) comes with a built-in thermostat. You can choose either 120- or 240-volt units.

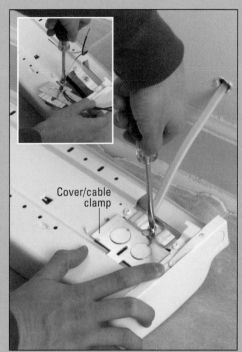

Cover/cable clamp

3 Place the heater face down on the floor and remove the cover/cable clamp. Attach the house ground line to the green screw on the heater (inset). Using wire nuts, connect incoming lines to the heater leads. Close and fasten the cover/clamp.

4 Locate and mark wall studs. Push the cable into the wall. Attach the unit with at least two 1½ inch drywall screws. Tighten, then back off a half turn to allow for the expansion and contraction of the metal housing when the unit is turned on and off.

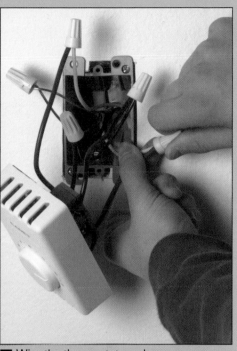

5 Wire the thermostat as shown (opposite), using wire nuts and electrician's tape. Install the thermostat and snap on its cover. Connect to the power source *(pages 136–137)* or new circuit *(pages 230–231)* and test the unit.

WHAT IF...
You're installing a blower-heater?

A blower-heater unit fits between wall studs and is somewhat simpler to wire because it has a self-contained thermostat. The unit shown runs on 240 volts. For how to hook up a new 240-volt circuit see *pages 230–231*. Check local codes for requirements.

A blower heater must be a safe distance from nearby walls and furnishings. When choosing a location for the heater, maintain 12 inches from any adjacent walls. For safe and effective operation, locate the box 12 inches above the floor and keep the area 3 feet in front of the box clear. Check the manufacturer's recommendations before locating the unit.

Before cutting an opening for the unit, drill a finder hole and use a wire to check that the wall cavity is clear of pipes and wires *(page 171)*. Use a drywall saw to cut the opening between studs. Run 12/2 cable to the opening.

1 Remove one of the knockouts in the housing. Insert a clamp and pull 10 inches of cable into the box. Clamp the cable and fasten the housing in place with 1-inch (longer if needed) drywall screws. Strip incoming wires *(page 48)*.

2 Attach the incoming wires to the heater leads (see opposite). Fasten the heater unit in the housing, being careful that the wires do not get caught between the motor and the housing. Attach the grill and thermostat knob. Connect to the power source.

INSTALLING ELECTRIC RADIANT HEAT

If you are planning to install an interior floor of ceramic or porcelain tile, brick, or stone, consider adding the warming influence of electric radiant heat. Installed directly over the substrate (cement board, plywood, a mortar bed, or a concrete slab), this system uses a plastic mat with interwoven heater cable. The mat is imbedded in thinset before the final flooring material is installed. Controlled by a wall-mounted thermostat or timer, the heater cable radiates warmth at a preset temperature.

The 120-volt circuit or power source for the radiant heat mats must be GFCI protected. Mats are available in a variety of lengths. Check the manufacturer's specifications for the wattage your situation will require. See *page 122* for how to check whether or not a circuit can manage additional demand.

PRESTART CHECKLIST

☐ **TIME**
About 8 hours to install mat, wire, and tile for an average bathroom

☐ **TOOLS**
Digital ohmmeter, drill, ½-inch bit, drywall saw, fish tape, chisel, hot glue gun, ⅜-inch trowel, screwdriver, stripper, long-nose pliers, lineman's pliers, tools for laying the flooring

☐ **SKILLS**
Stripping, splicing, and connecting wires to terminals; installing boxes; running cable into boxes; setting tile

☐ **PREP**
Rough in the plumbing; install the subfloor

☐ **MATERIALS**
12/2 cable, mat, box, armored power cable, thermostat and/or timer, thinset, flooring, mortar or grout

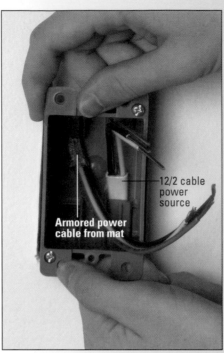

1 Install a large-capacity box 60 inches above the floor for the thermostat. Using 12/2 cable, add a new circuit *(pages 230-231)* or extend an existing circuit *(pages 136–137)*, but **do not connect the power source.** Pull to the box cable provided with the mat.

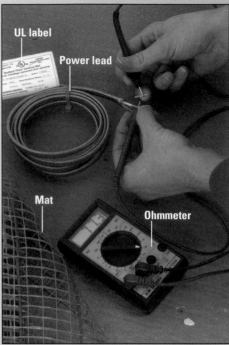

2 Unpack the mat. **Check the resistance using a digital ohmmeter.** The reading should be within 10 percent of the rating shown on the UL label. This will be your benchmark for confirming that the heat cable is not nicked during installation. Write the reading on a piece of paper.

INSTALLING UNDER-FLOOR ELECTRIC RADIANT HEATING

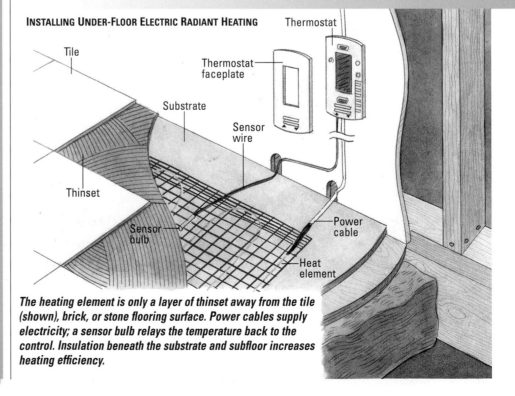

The heating element is only a layer of thinset away from the tile (shown), brick, or stone flooring surface. Power cables supply electricity; a sensor bulb relays the temperature back to the control. Insulation beneath the substrate and subfloor increases heating efficiency.

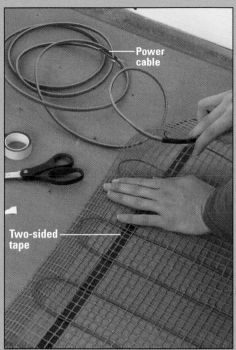

Power
cable

Two-sided
tape

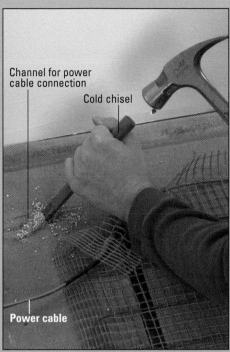

Channel for power
cable connection

Cold chisel

Power cable

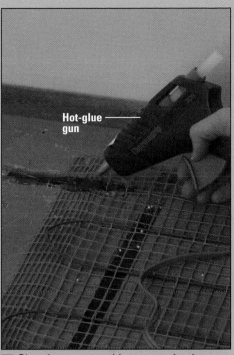

Hot-glue
gun

3 Clean the floor of debris and tighten any protruding screw or nail heads. Roll out the mat and position it. Check that it is no closer than 3–6 inches to walls and fixtures (see box, below right). Fasten the mat in place with double-sided tape located every 12–24 inches.

4 The armored power lead connection is thicker than the mat and must be sunk into the substrate (cement board is shown here). Trace around the connection; use a cold chisel to cut a channel for it.

5 Glue the power cable connection in the channel with hot glue. Mark along the power cable and slide it to one side. Working a few feet at a time, run a continuous bead of hot glue. Press the lead into the bead of hot glue.

REFRESHER COURSE
Strategies for running cable through walls

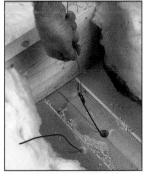

Go downstairs for power by drilling a finder hole directly in front of the wall through which you want to run the cable. Use a wire to mark the spot. Drill a ¾-inch hole and use a fish tape to pull the cable to where it is needed. See *page 146.*

By cutting away drywall (save the piece for replacing and taping later) you can run cable horizontally. This allows you to tap into a receptacle (check that the circuit can bear the additional load) in the same room. See *pages 144–145.*

If you have attic space above, drop power down to the room where you need it. Drill a finder hole to locate the wall plate. Drill an access hole, run fish tape, then pull cable to extend a circuit or create a new circuit. See *page 146.*

WHAT IF ...
You're working in tight quarters

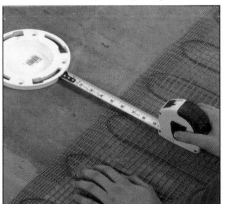

Mats can run under a toilet but must be 3 inches from the toilet ring. In addition, a mat can run beneath the kick plate of a vanity. Never overlap mats; never cut a mat to fit, and never attempt to repair a cut or nicked heating wire. If the wire is damaged the entire mat must be replaced.

Installing electric radiant heat *(continued)*

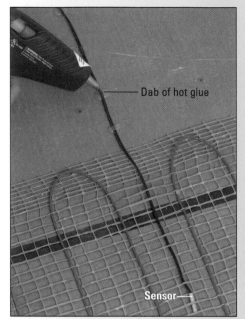

Dab of hot glue

Sensor

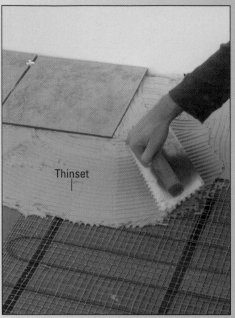

Thinset

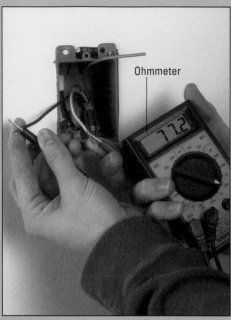

Ohmmeter

6 Press down on the tape to adhere it to the backerboard, then pull off the backing and firmly press the mat onto the tape. Weave the sensor bulb between two heating elements. Adhere the sensor bulb wire with dots of hot glue. **Check resistance with an ohmmeter. Record the reading.**

7 With the flat side of a ⅜-inch notched trowel, apply thinset over an area of the mat. Then turn the trowel over and rake the thinset to ¼-inch uniform depth. Be careful not to snag the mat. Do not clean the trowel by banging it on the mat. Tile the area of the floor covered with thinset.

8 **Check mat resistance once again**, using the ohmmeter. If the ohm reading drops to 0 or infinity, the heating element has been damaged. The tile must be removed and the mat replaced.

LAYOUT ALTERNATIVES

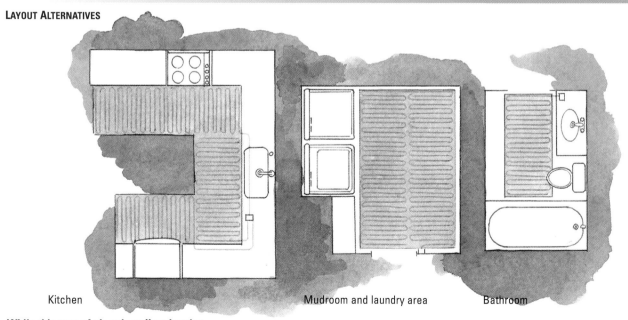

Kitchen

Mudroom and laundry area

Bathroom

While this type of electric radiant heating can only be used indoors, it can be installed wherever a tile, brick, or stone surface makes sense: bathroom, mud room, or kitchen.

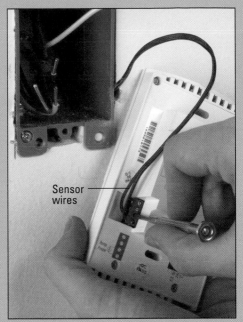

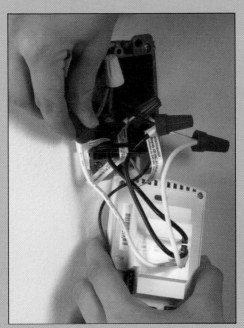

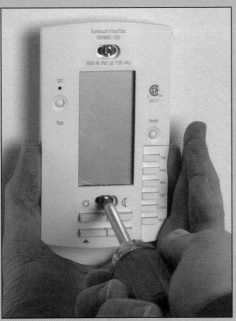

9 The control shown above has built-in GFCI protection. Using a jeweler's screwdriver, attach the two sensor wires to the screw terminals on one side of the control. Connect the ground from the mat power lead directly to the house ground.

10 Attach the black control lead marked LINE to the incoming black wire. Connect the white control lead LINE to the incoming white wire. Attach the black and white control leads marked LOAD to the black and white wires connecting to the mat. Fold the wires into the box.

11 Attach the face plate. Connect to the power source *(pages 136–137)* or connect the line to a new breaker *(pages 230–231)*. Turn on the power and follow the manufacturer's instructions for setting the temperature and timer.

ADDING A TIMER

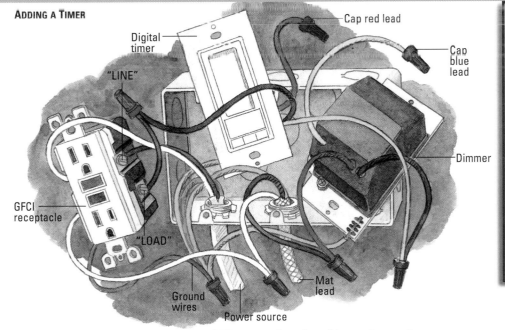

This configuration draws power from a GFCI receptacle and combines a timer and dimmer to control the heat level. The result: A warm bathroom floor greets morning bathers. A sensor bulb and line is not needed with this approach.

SAFETY FIRST
Don't overload circuit or components

Checking the amperage demanded by a new installation will tell you if an existing circuit can carry the load or if you'll have to install a new circuit. Each square foot of electric radiant heating mat draws 0.1 amp. That means adding radiant heating mats to the work area of an average-size kitchen will add only 5 or 6 amps to the circuit (50–60 square feet of mat). But each component included in the system also has to be up to that amperage. Check dimmers and timers to make sure they are rated to take the amperage.

HOUSEHOLD VOICE, DATA & SECURITY

Peek under any computer desk or behind the armoire that holds audio and video equipment, and you'll likely see a tangle of wires and cables. Stapled to the baseboard and popping out of holes drilled in the floor, such wires have been added over the years to meet the demands of new types of communication. These include speaker wire, phone lines, coaxial cable, and maybe the recent addition of high-speed, high-capacity Category 5 or 5e cable. These lines comprise the *other* wiring found in your home—low-voltage communication lines.

Household networking
Taming the tangle is made easier with newly available control panels and outlets designed specifically for household use. They help you wire your house for the present—and future—types of communication technology that you may choose to use. They help ensure that the quality of signal won't be compromised by bad runs or poor connections. In addition, they allow you to alter your communication network easily.

The heart of the system is a control panel installed in a central location. Incoming phone, cable, and satellite lines connect to it. Out of it run telephone, data, and video lines to various areas of the house. By using an attic, crawlspace, or basement, you can run Category 5 (and the higher-capacity Category 5e) and coaxial lines to outlets designed for phone, computer, fax, and video hookups.

This chapter shows you how to install just such a system in your home. If your needs are more modest, it also shows how to extend a phone line, run coaxial cable, or install a wall speaker.

Fire and break-in protection
A growing number of municipalities are requiring that smoke and carbon-monoxide detectors be wired in a series so that all units sound a warning. This chapter explains how to install such warning devices. In addition it explains how to plan and install a wide range of interior and exterior security fixtures and how to shop around for professionally installed and monitored security systems.

Low-voltage upgrades are safe to work with and can vastly improve household communication.

CHAPTER PREVIEW

Installing a media network
pages 200

Phone lines
page 204

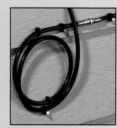

TV cable
page 207

Wall-mounted stereo speakers
page 209

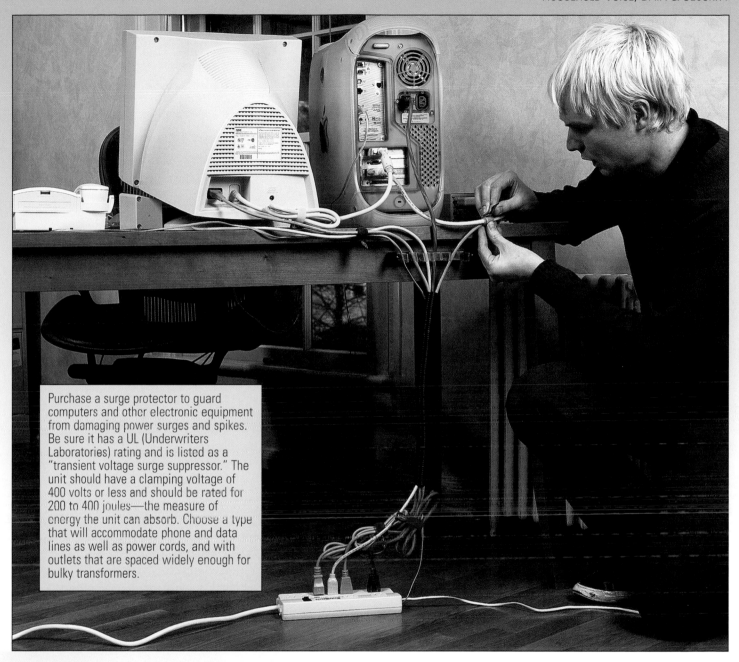

Purchase a surge protector to guard computers and other electronic equipment from damaging power surges and spikes. Be sure it has a UL (Underwriters Laboratories) rating and is listed as a "transient voltage surge suppressor." The unit should have a clamping voltage of 400 volts or less and should be rated for 200 to 400 joules—the measure of energy the unit can absorb. Choose a type that will accommodate phone and data lines as well as power cords, and with outlets that are spaced widely enough for bulky transformers.

Cords for monitors, computers, and add-on peripherals like modems, CD burners, and extra hard drives will be with us for some time to come. Organizers like the ones shown above diminish the tangle and lower the risk of cords being snagged and unplugged.

Planning security
page 210

Installing hard-wired smoke detectors
page 212

Motion-sensor outdoor light
page 213

INSTALLING A MEDIA NETWORK

If there is one word that describes the world of home entertainment and communication, it is *change*. Installing a media network panel with interchangeable modules for phone, data, and video lines will provide you not only with flexibility, but also the assurance that you have sound, organized connections.

Planning the network

Choose a central location for your network panel, away from any electrical load centers like a breaker panel or sub-panel. Avoid areas like attics or garages where there is a wide temperature variation. A closet, family room, or upstairs laundry area is ideal. Make sure no lines will have to reach more than 300 feet from the panel. Check with service providers for any special requirements. Choose the outlet locations—ideally several per room and no more than 12 feet from each other. Each should have at least a telephone and cable outlet. Draw a plan, noting the length of cable run and parts needed.

PRESTART CHECKLIST

☐ **TIME**
An hour or more to run each cable; about half a day to install the panel

☐ **TOOLS**
Drywall saw or reciprocating saw, cable connector crimpers, type-F connector crimpers, stripping tool, drill, fish tape, longnose and cutting pliers

☐ **SKILLS**
Planning; making electrical connections; running cable

☐ **PREP**
Plan the installation: clear space for installing the panel and outlets

☐ **MATERIALS**
Panel; cable and telephone distribution modules; power module, Cat. 5e and coaxial cable with connectors; outlets

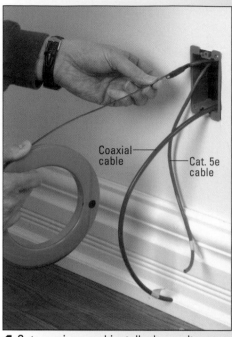

1 Cut openings and install a low-voltage box at each outlet location. Between two studs, cut an opening for the network panel. Run Category 5e cable for phone and data lines and coaxial cable for broadband or satellite lines. (See *pages 142–147* for how to run cable.) This is the hardest and most time-consuming part of the job.

Coaxial cable
Cat. 5e cable

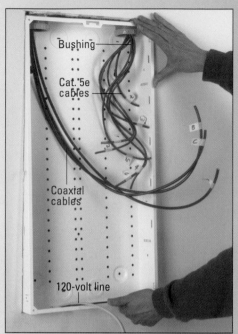

Bushing
Cat. 5e cables
Coaxial cables
120-volt line

2 Label each end of the cable as you pull it. Leave 12–18 inches of excess cable at each opening. Run a 14/2 electrical cable from the breaker panel to the network box opening. Remove knockouts and fit the box with bushings to protect the cables. Feed the cables into the box and fasten it to the studs.

PLANNING THE WIRED HOUSE

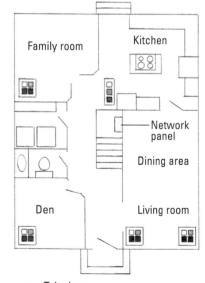

Family room
Kitchen
Network panel
Dining area
Den
Living room

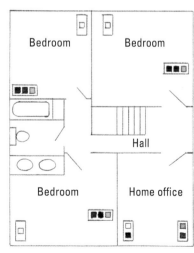

Bedroom
Bedroom
Hall
Bedroom
Home office

☐ Telephone
▨ Data
■ Video

A network panel should be centrally located to minimize the length of cable runs. The system shown reflects the services that might be provided to various rooms.

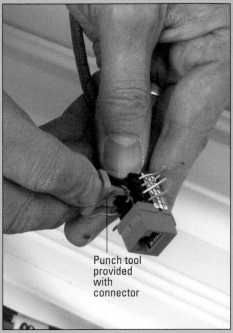

Punch tool
provided
with
connector

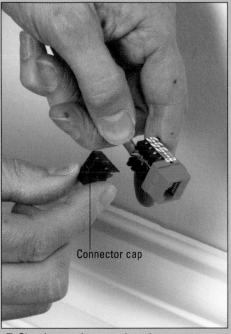

Connector cap

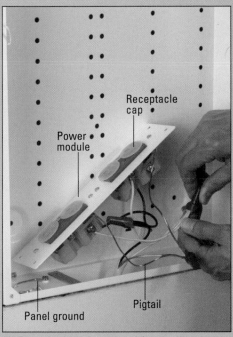

Receptacle
cap

Power
module

Pigtail

Panel ground

3 Purchase Cat. 5e connectors, selecting colors to indicate use (blue for data lines and white for phone lines, for example). Strip about 2½ inches of cable jacket and straighten the wires. Using the "A" color key on the 8-conductor connector, push the wires into their color-coded slots. Press them in place using the punch tool provided.

4 Check to make sure the wires are positioned correctly and then trim any excess wire with a diagonal cutter. Push the connector cap in place. Fit the coaxial cable with type-F connectors, following the steps shown on *page 207.*

5 Remove knockouts and fasten the surge protector and GFCI power module in the network box. Strip the 14/2 cable (see *page 128)* and make connections in the module, following the manufacturer's instructions. Fasten the module in place using screws provided. Leave caps in place to guard against debris falling into the receptacles.

Avoid kinks and bends

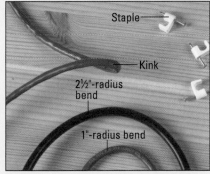

Staple

Kink

2½"-radius
bend

1"-radius bend

Category 5 and 5e cable can be safely bent to a 1-inch radius. Avoid kinks or strains—Cat. 5 and 5e cable cannot be spliced if damaged. Coaxial cable should be bent to no less than a 2½-inch radius. Secure wires with single-wire staples where accessible.

Attaching modular plugs on Cat. 5 and Cat. 5e cable

Modular
plug

Crimping
tool

1 Use stripping pliers to strip about 2 inches of jacket. Straighten each wire. Check packaging for recommended wire order.

2 Trim wires to ½ inch. Fan them in the order they will be inserted into the modular plug. Push the wires into the plug.

3 Use a crimping tool to fasten the wires in the plug. Give the plug a firm tug to make sure it is fixed on the wire.

Installing a media network (continued)

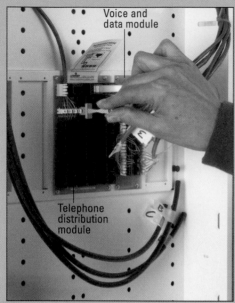

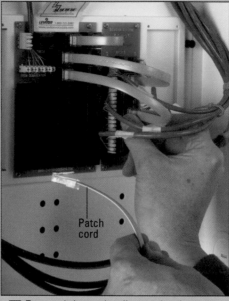

6 Snap in place a telephone distribution panel. It routes incoming telephone lines. Then attach a voice and data module (or more if you need them—each module serves six wall outlets). Wire each household extension line to this module. Connect patch cords between these modules and the appropriate plug-in.

7 For each incoming line, strip about 2½ inches of cable jacket from the Cat. 5e cable. Following the manufacturer's instructions, straighten and fan the wires, and place them in the color-coded bracket adjacent to the appropriate module. Press them into the bracket with a punch tool and snip off the excess.

8 Snap the internet gateway in place. Use Category 5e–rated patch cords to connect the incoming modem line to the "WAN" port. Patch computer lines to the gateway. Configure the gateway using the software provided on a CD packaged with the internet gateway.

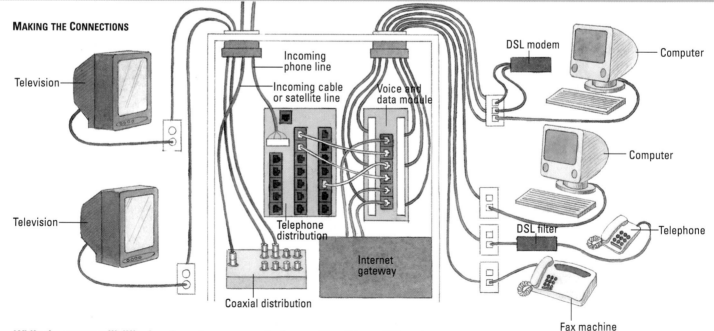

MAKING THE CONNECTIONS

While the system will differ from home to home, this is an example of a network including televisions, computer, telephones, *and a fax machine. It has a DSL modem installed separate from the panel. The panel can have its own built-in modem.*

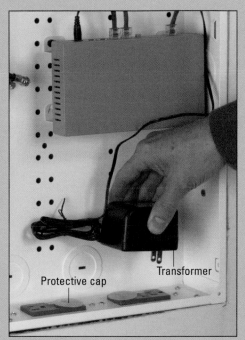

9 Install a new breaker (see *pages 230–231*) to power the dedicated 15-amp lines. Test for power (see *page 30*). Remove a protective cap from one of the GFCI receptacles and plug in the internet gateway transformer.

Protective cap

Transformer

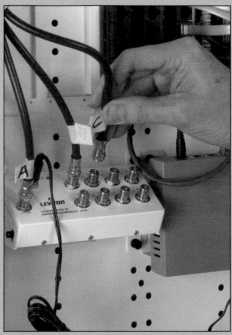

10 Attach Type-F coaxial connectors to each incoming coaxial line, using coaxial stripping and crimping tools (see *page 207*). Attach the incoming service cable to the "CATV/ANT" connection. Attach the other lines according to their label. Plug the module transformer into the power module.

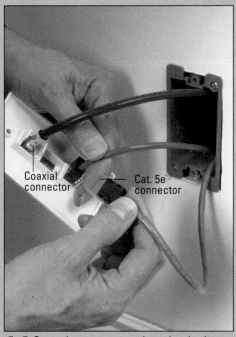

11 Snap the connectors into the duplex plate. (You can choose from plates that have from two to six openings.) Test each line (see box below). Gently feed the cables into the wall and attach the plate to the outlet box.

Coaxial connector

Cat. 5e connector

WHAT IF...
You want to revise service?

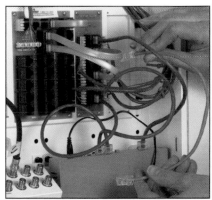

If a bedroom with only phone and video service is going to be transformed into a home office requiring a fax/modem line or a network connection, the change is easy. As long as you've already pulled an extra Category 5 or 5e cable to the room, you can simply add a patch cord to add the service.

Testing the system

1 With an inexpensive walkie-talkie, a willing assistant, and the testing device shown, you can quickly test each new line. This tester has plugs for coaxial, four-pair phone lines, and Cat. 5 and 5e lines. Have your helper check the plan to identify the line being tested and then announce the line number to you.

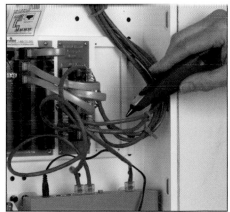

2 At the network panel, find the cable being tested and touch the tester to it. If the line is correct, the tester will emit a high-pitched sound. If there is no sound, use the tester to check other lines until the connected line is found. Adjust the connection at the panel to correct any mistakes.

PHONE LINES

Delivering phone service to the house is the telephone company's business. For a fee the phone company will also run lines and add jacks inside, but you'll save money—and get exactly what you want—doing it yourself.

Telephone wiring is straightforward, but running cable so it is hidden from view takes time and effort. Before running and stapling cable, plan the entire run. Extra effort may save trouble and eliminate an eyesore. For instance, running cable through a wall may mean that you do not have to run it around a door.

For easy and secure connections, buy telephone cable that has solid-core 24-gauge wire. Cheaper cables have stranded wires that are difficult to handle.

PRESTART CHECKLIST

☐ **TIME**
About three hours to tap into a junction box, run cable, and install a jack

☐ **TOOLS**
Screwdriver, drill, strippers, lineman's pliers, round-topped stapler, flat pry bar, stud finder, voltage detector, drywall saw

☐ **SKILLS**
Stripping and connecting wires to terminals

☐ **PREP**
Find the best route for the phone wires; if possible, avoid having to go around a doorway

☐ **MATERIALS**
Telephone cable or Cat. 5 cable, phone jacks, round-topped staples or plastic-coated staples

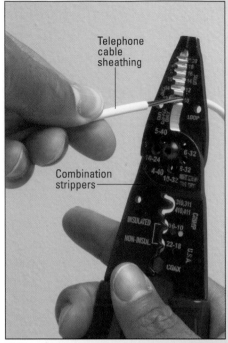

1 To add an extension line, first loosen the screw and remove the cover from a convenient existing phone jack. Using strippers remove about 2 inches of sheathing from the new cable using the 10 slot of the strippers.

2 Strip about ½ inch from each wire using the 22/20 slot on the strippers. Loosen each terminal screw, remove the wire attached to it, and twist it together with the new wire of the same color.

EXTENDING A TELEPHONE LINE

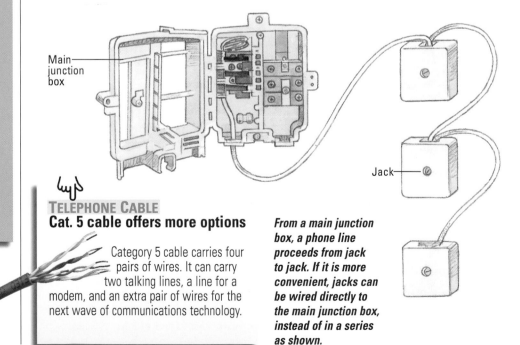

TELEPHONE CABLE
Cat. 5 cable offers more options

Category 5 cable carries four pairs of wires. It can carry two talking lines, a line for a modem, and an extra pair of wires for the next wave of communications technology.

From a main junction box, a phone line proceeds from jack to jack. If it is more convenient, jacks can be wired directly to the main junction box, instead of in a series as shown.

3 Loop each pair of wires clockwise around their terminal screws. Tighten the screws and push the cable into the hole provided. You may have to snap out a breakout tab.

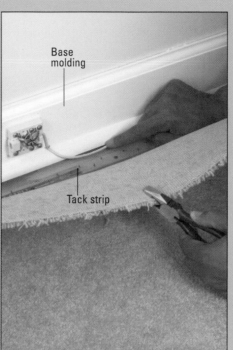

Base molding

Tack strip

4 Cable can be run under wall-to-wall carpeting. Use lineman's pliers to pull back a short section at a time and run the cable between the tack strip and the molding.

¼" bit

5 To run cable through a wall, drill a hole through both sides of the wall using an extended ¼-inch drill bit. Use a stud finder to avoid running into a framing member. Use a voltage detector to check walls for electrical cable before drilling.

Tapping into a junction box

It may be easier to run cable discretely by starting at a junction box rather than a phone jack. Many houses have a junction box, like the one above, attached to the exterior. One section of the box is accessible to the homeowner; attach wires as you would in a phone jack (Step 2).

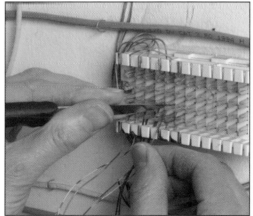

An indoor junction box or phone jack may have slide-on connectors. Do not strip the wire. Slide the wire end down onto the metal slit, using a thin slot screwdriver or a dull knife.

STANLEY PRO TIP

Running two or more lines using one cable

When installing a new line, it may be possible to piggyback on existing cable rather than running new cable. A phone line uses one pair of wires. With two-pair cable, the red and the green wires are used for the first line, and the yellow and black wires for the second. Three-pair cable, as well as four-pair Category 5 cable, is also available.

Phone lines (continued)

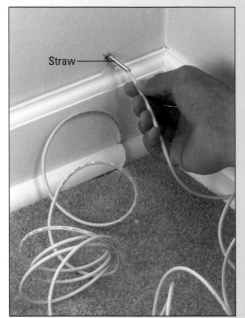

Straw

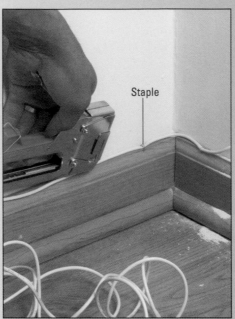

Staple

6 Poke a long soda straw through the hole and fish it around until it pushes through the hole in the wall behind. Feed the cable through the straw. Remove the straw from the other side of the wall.

7 If there is no carpeting to hide the line, staple it to the top of the base molding. Use round-topped staples or staples made specially for phone line.

8 Attach a new jack to the base molding by drilling pilot holes and driving screws. To attach to a drywall or plaster wall, drill holes, insert plastic anchors, and drive screws into the anchors. Connect wires and attach the cover.

WHAT IF...
A jack is needed for a wall-mounted phone?

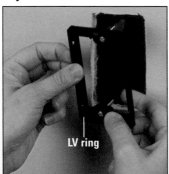

LV ring

Weight

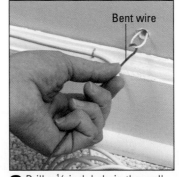

Bent wire

Wall jack

1 Use a stud finder to make sure the opening won't overlap a stud. Cut a hole in the drywall with a drywall saw. With plaster walls, cut with a utility knife first, then use a saber saw. Slip a low-voltage (LV) ring into the hole and tighten the screws to secure the ring to the drywall or plaster.

2 Attach a small weight, such as a nut, to a string, and guide it down the hole until it hits bottom.

3 Drill a ½-inch hole in the wall near the floor directly below the hole for the wall jack. Insert a bent piece of wire, snag the string (jiggle the string to help snag it), and pull it through. Attach the phone cable to the string with tape and pull it up through the hole above.

4 Strip and connect wires to the terminals of a wall jack. Mount the jack to the LV ring and install the cover plate.

TV CABLE

Coaxial cable used for cable TV installations uses special male/female connectors and splitters. Twist-on connectors are available but do not provide as solid a connection as a crimp-on connector. You'll need a special crimping tool to work with those connectors (see below). For outdoor locations use watertight connections—a standard connector or splitter will rust quickly. All are available at electronics or hardware stores.

Run cable into a low-voltage (LV) ring, which is like an electrical box without a back *(page 208)*.

Have the cable service provider do as much of the work of running the cable as possible. If service technicians run the cable in your house, provide specific instructions to route the cable, requesting that they adequately hide the cable. Or ask them to leave a coil of cable that you can install yourself.

PRESTART CHECKLIST

☐ **TIME**
About three hours to install a splitter or two, run about 40 feet of cable, and install a jack

☐ **TOOLS**
Drill, long ½-inch bit, screwdriver, strippers, utility knife, crimping tool, drywall saw

☐ **SKILLS**
Stripping cable; running cable through walls or behind moldings

☐ **PREP**
Spread a towel or drop cloth below where you will cut the wall

☐ **MATERIALS**
RG6 coaxial cable, cable staples, male connectors, splitters, LV ring, wall jack

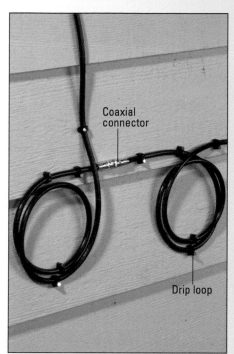

Coaxial connector

Drip loop

1 Where the cable enters the house, there is a watertight metal connector, or possibly a splitter, and a "drip loop" that carries water away from the connector. To split the line outside rather than inside, ask the cable company to provide the fitting and the cable.

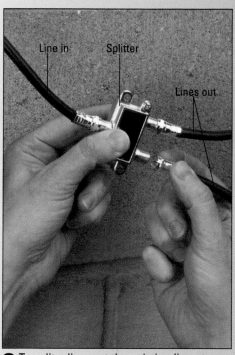

Line in   Splitter

Lines out

2 To split a line, cut the existing line at a convenient location. Make male ends on both cuts and on the new line (below). Screw the three male ends into a splitter and attach it to a wall or joist with screws. If you're attaching to masonry, drill holes and use plastic anchors with screws.

STANLEY PRO TIP: **Making the male end**

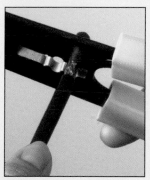

1 Strip ½ inch of outer sheathing. With strippers or a knife, cut just barely through the sheathing—don't cut through the wire mesh that lies inside. Pull the outer sheathing off with your fingers.

2 Push back the wire mesh. Strip ⅜ inch of plastic insulation from the center wire end. Slip a crimp-on connector on the cable end. Push until the wire protrudes beyond the front of the connector by about ¹⁄₁₆ inch.

3 With a special coaxial crimping tool (don't try to use pliers), squeeze the connector sleeve tightly onto the cable.

TV cable *(continued)*

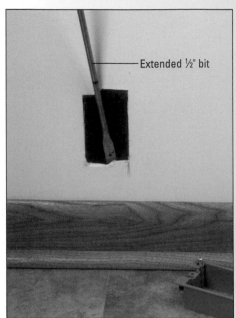

Extended ½" bit

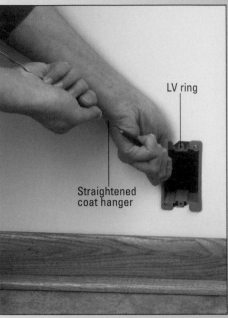

LV ring

Straightened coat hanger

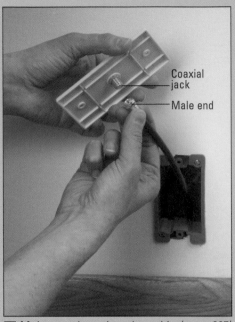

Coaxial jack

Male end

3 To run cable up from a basement or crawlspace, cut a hole in the wall to accommodate a low-voltage (LV) ring (Step 4). With an extended ½-inch bit, drill a hole down through the floor inside the wall.

4 Insert an LV ring into the hole and tighten the mounting screws. Poke a hanger wire down through the hole in the floor; from below, attach the end of the cable to the hanger wire with tape. Pull the cable up through the holes.

5 Make a male end on the cable *(page 207)* and screw it tightly to the back of a coaxial wall jack. Screw the jack to the LV ring.

Antenna alternatives

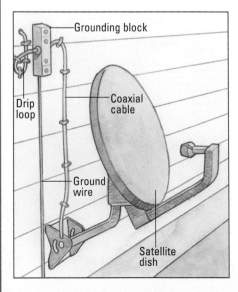

Grounding block

Drip loop

Coaxial cable

Ground wire

Satellite dish

Some satellite dishes are suitable for do-it-yourself installation. From a grounding block, run RG6 cable down an exterior wall, staple it in place with plastic staples, and connect it to the dish. Attach a grounded copper wire to the grounding block. Run the ground wire to a grounding stake *(page 27)*. Make a drip loop where the cable enters the house. Inside, run the cable to a wall jack and plug the dish receiver into the jack. Follow manufacturer's instructions for pointing the dish.

Even with a satellite dish, an old-fashioned TV antenna may be needed to receive local channels. Some antennas have a coaxial connection. Others have a twin-wire lead. Use an adapter, available from an electronics store or home center, to connect a twin-wire antenna lead to coaxial cable.

The right cable

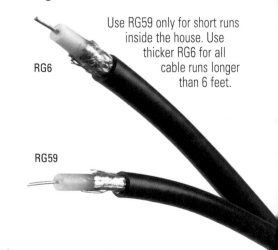

Use RG59 only for short runs inside the house. Use thicker RG6 for all cable runs longer than 6 feet.

RG6

RG59

Fuzzy reception?
If reception is fuzzy on one or more TVs, inspect all the splices and tighten, if needed. If the problem continues, ask the cable company about having a signal amplifier installed.

WALL-MOUNTED STEREO SPEAKERS

Speaker wires often lie exposed on the floor, where they are both a nuisance and an eyesore. But there are several ways to tuck the wires out of sight.

Thin speaker wire may degrade the sound quality of a speaker, especially if the wire extends longer than 8 feet. Take no chances; buy wire that is #12 or thicker.

Speaker cord has either two wires of different colors or one smooth and one ribbed wire. Be sure the connections are polarized. The wire attached to the receiver terminal labeled + or L should be connected to the + or L terminal on the speaker. The same goes for the - or R terminals.

PRESTART CHECKLIST

☐ **TIME**
About two hours to install a wall speaker or hide speaker wire for two speakers

☐ **TOOLS**
Flat pry bar, screwdriver, drill, strippers, round-topped stapler, drywall saw

☐ **SKILLS**
Cutting holes in walls; prying off moldings

☐ **MATERIALS**
Speakers, speaker wire, staples

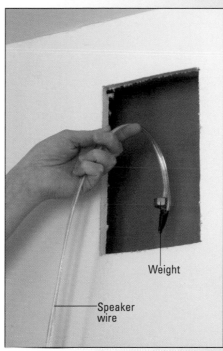

Weight

Speaker wire

1 Mark the wall using the measurements or template provided with the speakers. Cut the hole using a drywall saw. To run wire through a wall, attach a weight and drop it down. Cut or drill a small hole at the bottom of the wall, directly under the speaker hole. Fish the end of the wire out.

Speaker

2 Slip the speaker into the hole and drive the screws, which tighten the speaker's mounting flange to the wall. Snap the grill on and hook the speaker wire to the receiver.

STANLEY PRO TIP: **Hiding speaker wire**

Pry bar

Pry the base mold out just far enough to slip the wire behind it. You may need to use a block of wood while prying to avoid damaging the wall.

Tap the molding back into place with a hammer and wood block. If needed use a nail set to secure the nails.

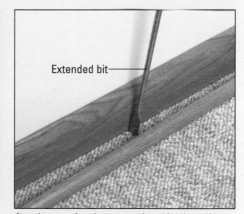

Extended bit

Another option is to run the wire into the basement or a crawlspace. Pry away the base shoe and drill a hole with a long ½-inch bit. Use a straightened coat hanger to guide the wire down through the hole. Cut or sand a small notch for the wire in the base shoe, then nail it back into place.

PLANNING SECURITY

Before you plan the electrical and electronic side of home security, make sure you've covered the purely physical aspects. Install solid-wood or metal-clad doors equipped with dead-bolt locks—not just the key-in-the-handle type of lock. Equip exterior doors with a peephole (don't bother with a door chain—it can easily be forced open.) If you have recently moved into your home, have the locks changed. Secure sliding doors with locks or a thick dowel set in the track to prevent opening. Install key locks or slip-in pins on double-hung windows. Cover basement windows with grilles.

Secure the perimeter
Illuminate the outside of your house and any areas near the house where intruders could hide. Use a combination of switched lights, lights on timers, and lights triggered by photocells or motion sensors to make a protective buffer of illumination. A motion-sensor floodlight fixture can be installed as a complete unit (see *page 213)*, or you can equip a standard floodlight fixture with a single or **dual retrofit motion sensor,** or a **screw-in** or **attachable photo cell**

switch or a **screw-in motion sensor.** (Be a good neighbor by checking that such lights don't shine into nearby homes and aren't a nuisance to innocent dog walkers.)

Uplight trees with low-voltage floods to eliminate a hiding place while providing an attractive effect. Trim bushes and small trees to eliminate remaining hiding places. Be sure to trim off any tree limbs that might help someone climb in an upper-story window. (Lock in place any ladders that are stored out of doors.) A **wireless motion sensor** can be placed outdoors to detect an intruder. A receiver, placed up to 400 feet from the sensor, chimes when motion is detected.

Provide illumination at each door so that your path is visible while walking in and, more importantly, so you can check out any visitors before opening the door. Have two single-bulb fixtures or one dual-bulb fixture in case a bulb burns out. For long pathways add mushroom fixtures or grazing lights to eliminate tripping hazards.

Check that your house numbers can be seen at night, to speed the arrival of emergency personnel if they should ever be needed.

While you're away
In addition to covering the essentials—stop your newspapers and mail or make sure a neighbor will gather them for you—do what you can to create a credible illusion that you are still home. Use **plug-in photocell light controls** so that lights switch on at dusk and off at dawn (such units must be exposed to natural light). Better yet, use a **plug-in timer** (two types are shown below) to switch lights off and on in different areas of the house. Lights left on through the night are better than leaving the house dark, but still signal that the house might not be occupied. Don't lower all the blinds and close all the curtains; make everything look occupied and as normal as possible.

Interior precautions
Window alarms can alert you to a break-in through a window. In the event of a power loss, battery-powered **emergency backup lights** in stairwells make an exit path less hazardous. Equip your home with adequate smoke and carbon-monoxide alarms. Or consider getting a professionally installed and maintained security system (see opposite page).

Emergency backup lighting

Wireless motion sensor

Wireless motion sensor receiver with warning chime

Plug-in timer

Plug-in photocell

Window alarm

Screw-in photocell switch

Screw-in motion sensor

Attachable photocell switch

Dual retrofit motion sensor for floodlight fixture

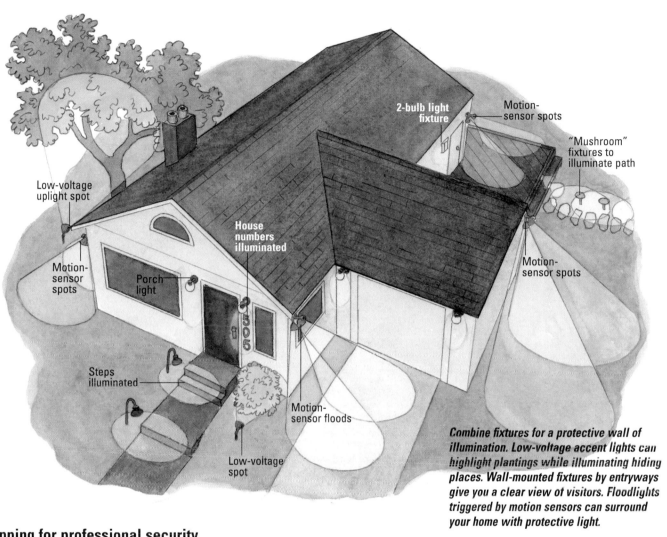

2-bulb light fixture

Motion-sensor spots

"Mushroom" fixtures to illuminate path

Low-voltage uplight spot

House numbers illuminated

Motion-sensor spots

Motion-sensor spots

Porch light

Steps illuminated

Motion-sensor floods

Low-voltage spot

Combine fixtures for a protective wall of illumination. Low-voltage accent lights can highlight plantings while illuminating hiding places. Wall-mounted fixtures by entryways give you a clear view of visitors. Floodlights triggered by motion sensors can surround your home with protective light.

Shopping for professional security

A professionally installed and monitored security system typically uses door and window contacts, motion detectors, and smoke detectors to protect your home. If you are considering such a system, here are questions to ask and features to look for:

■ Check that the company is licensed, but be aware that licensing requirements in some states are lax. Check how long the firm has been in business—look for 10 years or more. Officially, police or sheriff's departments won't make recommendations, but they will indicate if your candidates are sound ones. Contact two or three firms.

■ Will your alarm system be connected to police and fire dispatchers, or to the company's monitoring center? If the former, be aware that you'll need dedicated phone lines to police and fire departments. If the latter, ask about staffing and response time—30 to 60 seconds is acceptable. And ask who does the monitoring—smaller firms contract it out.

■ Does the company offer a range of services, such as break-in, fire, carbon monoxide, low temperature warning, and sump pump high water alarms? (You may not want all these features, but they indicate services beyond a "one-size-fits-all" approach.)

■ Can the company install alternate paths of communication (such as cellular or long-range radio) in case of an interruption of the primary line? Consider this if you live in a remote area.

■ Be wary of anyone willing to provide a quote over the phone. Require a detailed, written description of the services you are buying. Avoid leasing the installation—you won't have the option of transferring to another service.

■ Be wary of an over-elaborate plan prone to false alarms. Most municipalities charge for false alarms beyond a maximum limit.

■ Check that the system proposed will qualify your home for a lower homeowner's insurance premium. Expect a 10–20 percent reduction.

■ Glass-break detectors should be secondary, not primary, defense. They shouldn't be placed in kitchens or baths and shouldn't be activated during waking hours. Dropped objects—even a yipping dog—can set them off.

INSTALLING HARD-WIRED SMOKE DETECTORS

Unlike battery-powered smoke detectors, hard-wired smoke detectors (equipped with battery backup) run minimal risk of running out of power and, because they are wired in a series, have the advantage that when one alarm sounds, all sound. Now required by most municipalities, these detectors are a wise upgrade for your home.

Running the cable is the hardest part of the job—the time required can vary widely depending on the layout of your home. See *pages 144–149* for how to run cable through finished walls. In addition, you'll need to tie in to a single source of power (see *pages 136–137*).

1 For each detector, cut a hole for a standard 4-inch octagon or single gang box. Run 14/2 cable to the first detector in the series, 14/3 cable thereafter. Install the boxes *(pages 142–143)*.

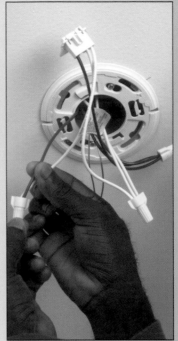

2 Align the slots of the mounting plate and attach the plate to the box. Gently pull the wires through the plate. After connecting the first box in the series (see below), connect wires as shown.

3 After securing the wire nuts with electrician's tape, gently push the wires into each box. Install the detectors, activate the backup batteries, and connect to the power source *(pages 136–137)*.

PRESTART CHECKLIST

☐ **TIME**
About 5 hours to run cable, install three detectors

☐ **TOOLS**
Voltage tester, drill, ½-inch bit, drywall saw, fish tape, screwdriver, stripper, long-nose pliers, lineman's pliers

☐ **SKILLS**
Installing boxes; running cable into boxes; stripping, splicing, and connecting wires to terminals

☐ **MATERIALS**
Smoke detectors, boxes, 14/2 and 14/3 cable, electrician's tape, wire nuts

WIRING SMOKE DETECTORS IN A SERIES

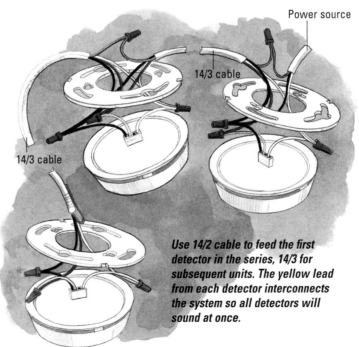

Power source

14/3 cable

14/3 cable

Use 14/2 cable to feed the first detector in the series, 14/3 for subsequent units. The yellow lead from each detector interconnects the system so all detectors will sound at once.

FOR EXTRA PROTECTION
Install a plug-in carbon-monoxide alarm

Carbon monoxide is an odorless, colorless, poisonous gas that results from combustion. Faulty venting for appliances, wood or charcoal burners, or the incursion of auto exhaust can put your household at risk. Plug-in units like this have battery backup.

MOTION-SENSOR OUTDOOR LIGHT

For little more than the cost of a standard porch light, you can buy a light that turns on automatically when it senses movement. It can be installed on a wall or under an eaves.

Most models allow you to adjust how sensitive the light will be to movement, how long it stays on, and even how bright the light will be. If your existing porch light is controlled by an indoor switch, the motion-sensor light you install in its place can be controlled either by the switch or by the sensor.

PRESTART CHECKLIST

☐ **TIME**
About two hours to remove the old light and install a motion-sensor light (wait until dark to adjust the light)

☐ **TOOLS**
Screwdriver, strippers, voltage tester, lineman's pliers, nonconducting ladder

☐ **SKILLS**
Stripping wire and splicing stranded wire to solid wire; mounting a fixture to a box

☐ **PREP**
Position a ladder so you can easily reach the existing light

☐ **MATERIALS**
Motion-sensor light, wire nuts, electrician's tape

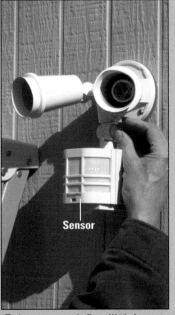

Mounting plate

Bracket

Sensor

1 **Shut off power to the circuit.** Remove the old fixture. Use the mounting bracket provided or install a swivel strap *(pages 94–95).* Some manufacturers provide a bracket to suspend the fixture temporarily while you splice the wires.

2 Mount the light using the screws provided. Position the rubber gasket to provide a watertight seal. Slip the mounting screws through their holes in the fixture and drive them into the holes in the bracket or strap.

3 Loosen each floodlight's locknut, swivel the light to the desired position, and tighten the locknut. Point the sensor toward where you expect motion. After dark, test the light and make adjustments.

EAVES-MOUNTED MOTION-SENSOR OUTDOOR LIGHT

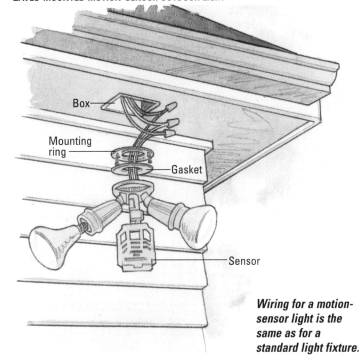

Box

Mounting ring

Gasket

Sensor

Wiring for a motion-sensor light is the same as for a standard light fixture.

MAKE ADJUSTMENTS
Range of motion

Adjustment control panel

Point the sensor and set sensitivity ("RANGE") to the middle position. Test to see that people approaching the house will turn on the light, but not neighbors walking by. Redirect the sensor or adjust the sensitivity, if necessary. Also adjust how long the light will stay on ("ON TIME").

Pickup:
3W p 97

OUTDOOR WIRING

Low-voltage outdoor lights are inexpensive and easy to install. Kits typically include five or more lights, cable, and a transformer/timer. Some lights are mounted on stakes poked into the ground; others can be attached to posts. The cable runs in a shallow trench or sits on top of the ground and is covered with mulch; the transformer/timer simply plugs into a standard receptacle.

Low-voltage lights are bright enough to light a path, accent foliage, or provide muted lighting for an outdoor dining area. For brighter illumination, or to install an outdoor receptacle, standard 120-volt wiring is needed.

Choosing lights and switches

The first step in an outdoor wiring project is to decide where to put lights and receptacles. *Pages 216–217* give some ideas. Gather more tips by consulting with neighbors and salespeople. For switches, there are four basic options: standard switches, timers, motion-sensor switches, and photocells, which turn lights on at dusk and off at dawn. Motion-sensors and photocells are often built into outdoor light fixtures such as floodlights, but they can also be installed as switches that control several lights.

If you already have an outdoor receptacle, and if its circuit will not be overloaded when you add new service *(pages 120–121),* grab power there. If this is not possible, see *pages 218–219* for moving power outdoors. *Pages 220–223* show how to run lines and install fixtures.

Meeting code

A permit is required for running standard-voltage cable outdoors. Local codes vary considerably, so have plans approved by your building department. Be clear on what sort of cable and/or conduit is required, how deep underground it must be buried, and what type of weathertight connections and fixtures are required. Always contact utilities for cable and pipe locations before digging.

Exterior lights and outlets add safety and enhance a home's appearance.

CHAPTER PREVIEW

Planning outdoor lighting
page 216

Extending power outdoors
page 218

Running outdoor cable
page 220

Outdoor fixtures
page 222

Low-voltage outdoor lights
page 224

Stripping UF cable: Underground feed (UF) cable is more difficult to strip than standard NM because the sheathing and insulation are molded together. Cut carefully with a knife to strip the sheathing and use standard strippers to strip insulation.

The wiring for typical outdoor installations is simple. Burying cable and protecting fixtures from damage is the difficult part. You'll need not only standard wiring tools, but also layout materials, a shovel for trenching, and possibly a clamshell digger for postholes.

PLANNING OUTDOOR LIGHTING

Outdoor lights not only provide a pleasant setting for outdoor activities, highlight interesting features of a yard or patio, and light a pathway, they can also make your home safer by deterring criminals. The most challenging stage of an outdoor lighting project is running cable from a power source inside your home and making sure the outdoor cable is protected. Otherwise the wiring is straightforward.

A system for all purposes

Aim for flexibility when choosing the type and number of outdoor lights and switches. For instance use low-voltage lights controlled by a timer or photocell to provide inexpensive lighting all night long.

For security and to light pathways when you come home at night, add bright standard-voltage lights that are controlled by motion sensors.

For a dramatic effect, point accent lights at trees or foliage and control them with a standard switch or a timer. To provide lighting for outdoor dining or parties, hang decorative standard-voltage lights overhead and control them with a dimmer switch.

Choosing lights

Make scale drawings of your property, including foliage, sidewalks, and paths. Pencil in the type of lighting you want in various areas.

Bring the drawing to a home center or lighting store and think through the possibilities. You'll find a wide selection of lights that poke into the ground, mount on posts, attach to siding, or hang overhead. Mix and match fixtures, choosing from the many available options *(page 222)*.

Floodlights provide plenty of illumination for a small cost, so you may be tempted to light up your entire yard with them. However, while floods are excellent for security purposes, most people find them too glaring for dining and entertaining.

Cable and conduit

Outdoor rooms are casual, so exposed conduit may not be considered unsightly. Plastic (PVC) conduit is pretty rugged, but metal conduit is more resistant to hard knocks. Consider installing metal wherever it might get bumped—for example, by a lawn mower. See *pages 132–134* for instructions on running plastic and metal conduit. Codes prohibit exposed cable outdoors, because it can be easily damaged.

Always use approved UF cable for outside wiring. *Pages 220–221* show how to hide it underground. Though resistant to moisture, UF cable is vulnerable to damage from a shovel or hammer, so protect it well. When installing an eaves or porch light, run standard cable through the attic or through a wall *(pages 142–147)*. When installing a post light on top of a 4×4, one option is to

run the cable through a groove in the post, then cover the groove with a 1×2.

Easy lights

In addition to permanent lights, you can also put up decorative lanterns or even a string of holiday lights, which can be quickly added and easily moved. Miniature lights strung from trees render a magical feeling all year long. Exterior-rated rope lights can be hung under railings or stair treads, or over doorways. If stretched taut they have a high-tech look; draped in casual loops, they make for a party atmosphere.

Holiday lighting

If you're one of those people who love outdoor holiday decorations, don't assume that you can just plug all those colored lights and illuminated reindeer into any old receptacle. Typically these setups use lots of low-wattage bulbs. They can quickly add up to a circuit overload, especially if the circuit runs to a living or family room where a home entertainment system is plugged in.

Plan for holiday lights as you would any electrical installation. Add up the wattages of all the bulbs and check to see that you won't overload a circuit. You may need to plug half the lights into a receptacle on one circuit and the other half into a receptacle that's on another circuit. Elaborate displays may call for a new circuit.

Shedding light on home security

Even the most brazen thief prefers the cover of darkness. By adding a combination of these security features you can add an inexpensive layer of defense against home invasion.
■ The brighter the light, the greater the deterrent. Bright lights triggered by motion detectors can have a startling effect. However, set your detector so it is not tripped by innocent dog walkers.
■ Surprise potential intruders with motion-sensor lights that turn on when they approach.

■ Make sure all pathways—both front and back—are illuminated.
■ Have at least two lights pointed at each area of your lot, in case a bulb burns out.
■ Place some lights out of easy reach; some thieves like to unscrew or break bulbs. High-placed porch lights or eaves lights fit the bill.
■ An indoor light controlled by a motion sensor provides the greatest surprise, making it look like someone is home.

SAFETY FIRST
Check before you dig

Hidden under your lawn may be several utility lines—the main water supply, the gas or propane line, or even an underground electrical line. Find out where all four lines—water, gas, electricity, and telephone—run, as well as how deep they are buried, before you start digging trenches or postholes in the yard. Utility companies often provide one number to call for locating all lines.

Pole lamp

Bulkhead
lamp

Floodlight with
photocell

GFCI
receptacle

Riser light

Low-voltage
up lights

Low-voltage
pathway lighting

*When lighting a yard, first make sure all pathways are lit and take care
of security concerns (page 216). Then turn your attention to lights that
enhance your yard's appearance at night. Upward-shining lights
dramatically highlight bushes and trees. Smaller lights can spotlight
lower plantings or shine from inside a hedge or flower bed. Lights that
swivel can be adjusted as foliage grows and seasons change. With its
mixture of low-voltage and standard-voltage lights, this outdoor space
can brighten an evening get-together and provide enough light for safety.*

EXTENDING POWER OUTDOORS

Position an outdoor receptacle where it will stay dry—at least 16 inches above the ground—and out of harm's way. An in-use cover (Step 5) increases protection from the weather. A simple wooden box built around it shields it from bumps by the lawn mower or kids at play. Outdoor receptacles must be GFCI-protected. Check local codes for the types of cable, conduit, and boxes approved for your home.

The quickest way to extend power outdoors is to install a receptacle back-to-back with one inside the house *(page 219)*. Another simple solution is to drill through the wall from a basement or crawlspace and attach a receptacle on the side of a house using an extension ring (Steps 1 and 2).

PRESTART CHECKLIST

☐ **TIME**
About two hours to install a new outdoor receptacle with extension ring and in-use cover (not including cutting a pathway for the cable, patching walls)

☐ **TOOLS**
Voltage tester, screwdriver, hammer, drill, saw, lineman's pliers, long-nose pliers, strippers

☐ **SKILLS**
Stripping, splicing, and connecting wires to terminals; installing boxes; running cable through walls and ceilings

☐ **PREP**
Make sure the new service will not overload the circuit *(pages 120–121)*

☐ **MATERIALS**
GFCI receptacle, outdoor box with extension ring and in-use cover, remodel box, cable, conduit and fittings, wire nuts, electrician's tape

Rim joist

1 Find the easiest path for cable to reach an outside wall, perhaps through a basement or crawlspace. Use a long drill bit to drill a locator hole. If the location is inconvenient or does not satisfy codes, install an LB fitting *(page 219)* rather than a receptacle to run power elsewhere.

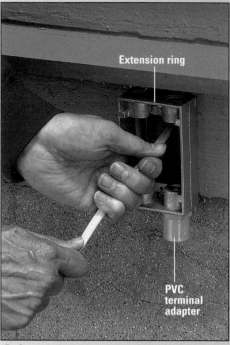

Extension ring

PVC terminal adapter

2 Cut a hole for a remodel box using a reciprocating saw or keyhole saw. If the exterior is masonry, see *page 186*. Run cable through the hole and into a remodel box. Install the box and add an extension ring and a terminal adapter if using PVC (shown).

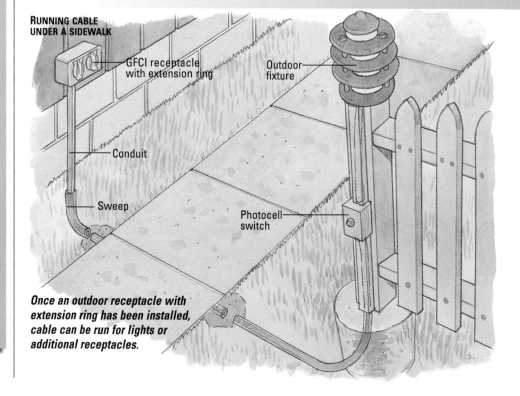

RUNNING CABLE UNDER A SIDEWALK

GFCI receptacle with extension ring

Outdoor fixture

Conduit

Sweep

Photocell switch

Once an outdoor receptacle with extension ring has been installed, cable can be run for lights or additional receptacles.

3 Beneath the box, dig a trench deep enough to satisfy local codes *(page 220)*. **Call before you dig**. Using PVC or rigid metal conduit, attach a length of pipe to a sweep. Cut the pipe to fit, attach it, and anchor the conduit with straps.

4 **Shut off power to the circuit**. Connect the black and white wires to the LINE terminals of a GFCI receptacle. After you run cable for the new service *(pages 220–221)*, connect those wires to the LOAD terminals. This way all the new service will be GFCI-protected. Connect to the power source.

5 Install an in-use cover, which protects the receptacle from moisture even when a cord is plugged in.

Metal conduit

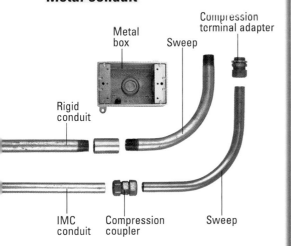

Metal conduit must be installed so it is watertight. Use rigid conduit with threaded fittings or IMC conduit with compression fittings.

Back-to-back wiring

One way to bring power outdoors is with back-to-back receptacles. **Shut off power,** pull out an indoor receptacle, and drill a locator hole through the wall to the outside.

WHAT IF...
You don't need a receptacle?

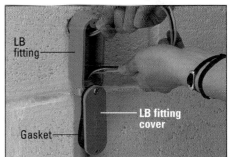

To make the transition from indoor to outdoor wiring, use an LB fitting. Essentially a watertight pulling elbow, it is ideal for connecting to conduit.

Ground fault circuit interrupter (GFCI)
A GFCI receptacle isn't necessary if the circuit is protected with a GFCI breaker or if the new line taps into a GFCI receptacle.

RUNNING OUTDOOR CABLE

While some building departments require underground wiring to run through metal or plastic conduit, most codes call for conduit only where the wiring is exposed or buried in a shallow trench. (Even when conduit is watertight, condensation can moisten underground wiring. UF cable offers the only real protection against water damage.)

Before you start to dig, ask your utility companies to mark the locations of water, gas, electric, or phone lines. Most have a toll-free number available.

A square-bladed spade will handle short runs. If you need to dig more than 50 feet of trenches, consider renting a powered trench digger.

Consult local building codes carefully. For instance some codes allow for a shallower trench if the cable or conduit is covered with a 2×6 pressure-treated plank.

PRESTART CHECKLIST

☐ **TIME**
Once power is brought outside *(pages 218–219),* about a day to dig trenches, run 60 feet of cable, and install several lights *(pages 222–223)*

☐ **TOOLS**
Shovel, posthole digger, hammer, drill, fish tape, pliers, garden hose or sledge hammer

☐ **SKILLS**
Laying out and digging trenches; fishing cable through conduit

☐ **PREP**
Install a receptacle or LB fitting bringing power to the outside and check that the new service will not overload the circuit *(pages 120–121).* Call the utility company to mark lines.

☐ **MATERIALS**
Conduit and fittings, conduit clamps, stakes, string line

1 **After the utility companies have marked the location of any underground lines,** plan a route that stays several feet away from them. Use string lines and stakes to indicate the path for the underground cable.

2 Cut the sod carefully with a square-bladed shovel so you can replace it later. Dig a trench deep enough to satisfy local codes. If you encounter a large root or rock, consider running the cable under it.

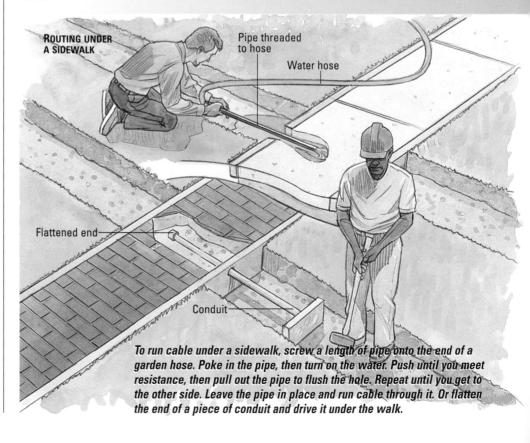

To run cable under a sidewalk, screw a length of pipe onto the end of a garden hose. Poke in the pipe, then turn on the water. Push until you meet resistance, then pull out the pipe to flush the hole. Repeat until you get to the other side. Leave the pipe in place and run cable through it. Or flatten the end of a piece of conduit and drive it under the walk.

3 Run metal conduit under the sidewalk (use one of the methods shown on *page 220)* and attach a protective bushing to each end. Push the UF cable through the conduit.

4 Unroll the cable carefully to avoid kinks. Have a helper feed it through the conduit as you thread it through the trenches and conduit all the way to the power source.

5 When running cable to a lamp post, be sure to set the post so its access hole faces the trench (see *page 222* for more on setting fixtures). Carefully push the cable into the access hole and up the body of the post.

STANLEY PRO TIP

Bushing at end of conduit

Codes typically require a bushing at the end of the conduit to protect the cable sheathing. This is especially important when using metal conduit, which can easily slice through plastic sheathing.

Sink that cable

Local codes specify how deep cable or conduit must be buried. Encase it in conduit wherever it is less than the required depth.

Running wires through metal conduit

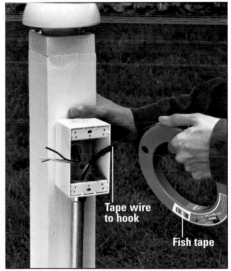

If codes call for a continuous run of metal conduit, purchase watertight boxes and fittings. Take care to tighten each fitting; one bad connection will result in wet wires.

Run wire through the conduit using a fish tape, as shown on *page 135.*

OUTDOOR FIXTURES

Home centers carry a variety of lights designed for outdoor use. Fixtures that use standard incandescent bulbs provide plenty of light for most residential purposes. Outdoor fluorescent fixtures may save energy costs but are usually more effective in an enclosed space like a garage (some may not work in cold weather). For the brightest illumination, use mercury vapor or halide fixtures.

Whatever fixture you install, pay special attention to its gasket. When you attach the cover, the gasket should be sandwiched tightly to seal out all moisture.

These two pages show how to set posts in concrete. In many areas, filling the hole around the post with well-tamped soil is considered just as strong.

Some lights come with cylindrical metal posts. Install these in much the same way as the post light shown here.

PRESTART CHECKLIST

☐ **TIME**
Once cable is run, about four hours to install a post and light; less time for other types of lights

☐ **TOOLS**
A posthole digger, post level, screwdriver, hammer, drill, chisel, strippers, long-nose pliers, lineman's pliers

☐ **SKILLS**
Running cable outdoors; stripping, splicing, connecting wires to terminals

☐ **PREP**
Run cable and connect it to a circuit that will not be overloaded by the new service

☐ **MATERIALS**
An outdoor fixture, conduit, post, wire nuts, electrician's tape, concrete mix

1 **Don't start digging until the utility company has marked lines.** Plan locations of fixtures and trenches to avoid utility lines. Dig a trench to the fixture location *(pages 220–221)*. Use a clamshell digger to bore a hole at least 36 inches deep (including the depth of the trench).

2 Set the post in the hole. Plumb it with a level and brace it firmly with 1×4s. Fill the hole with concrete, leave the braces in place, and allow a day or so for the concrete to cure.

Gentle lighting options

Outdoor lights run the gamut from familiar low-voltage tier lights and undereaves floodlights to light-equipped, outdoor-rated ceiling fans. For a subtle effect, consider the following options: Low-voltage **post lights** mount to the top of a 4×4 post, linking into a low-voltage run for their power.

Some **rope lights** are designed for outdoor use. Staple them to the underside of railings or decking overhangs or drape them from above.

For deck lighting without glare use low-profile **edge lights** or **surface lights** to illumine traffic areas and stairways or simply to add an accent.

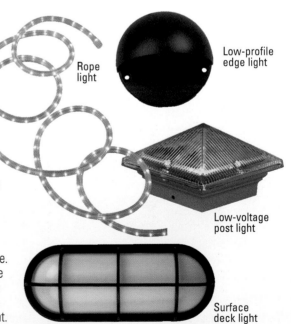

Rope light

Low-profile edge light

Low-voltage post light

Surface deck light

3 After the concrete has cured, attach the conduit and sweep to the box and fasten the box to the post. Attach a bushing to the sweep *(page 221)*.

4 Strip about 8 inches of sheathing from the UF cable and push the wires up through the conduit to the box. Run the cable to the power source, removing any kinks and laying the cable flat in the trench. Connect a GFCI receptacle *(page 153)* to the cable wires.

5 Fold in the wires and fasten the receptacle to the box. Place the gasket around the receptacle and fasten the outdoor receptacle cover.

Receptacle and post light

Bore a channel down from the top of the post to the level of the box using a ¾-inch bit. Drill from the side to connect the hole. Run cable through the channel and through a punch-out hole in the back of the box.

Undereaves light

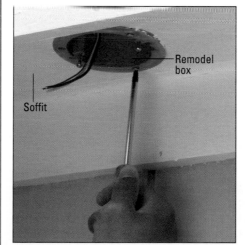

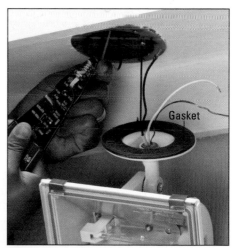

1 To install a light that hangs under the eaves, cut a hole for a round remodel box in the soffit. Run cable to the hole and clamp it to the box. Install the box.

2 Strip and splice the wires to the fixture's leads and attach the fixture. Check the gasket to make sure it is seated evenly and securely around the box to seal out water.

LOW-VOLTAGE OUTDOOR LIGHTS

Low-voltage outdoor lights simply poke into the ground with stakes. The cable can be hidden under ground cover, buried in a shallow trench, or covered lightly with soil or mulch. If there is an outdoor receptacle, attach the transformer nearby and plug it in. To connect cable to a light, snap together components.

Plan carefully before installing outdoor lights. Make a drawing of your property, including plants and structures. Choose from a variety of light fixtures: tiered or flower-shaped lights to mark a pathway, floodlights to accentuate foliage or provide security, and deck lights to illuminate vertical surfaces such as step risers.

Add up the wattage of the lights you want to use and choose a transformer/timer that will supply enough power. For instance, eight 18-watt lights and five 20-watt lights add up to 244 watts. A 250-watt transformer will handle the load, but you will not have the option of adding lights in the future—so you may want to buy a larger transformer.

PRESTART CHECKLIST

☐ **TIME**
About four hours to install 10–15 lights and cover the cable

☐ **TOOLS**
Screwdriver, lineman's pliers, hammer, gardening trowel, perhaps a drill

☐ **SKILLS**
Stripping and splicing wires

☐ **PREP**
If there is no outdoor receptacle, have one installed. Or plug the transformer into an indoor receptacle and drill a small hole for the cable to run through to the outside.

☐ **MATERIALS**
Low-voltage outdoor light kit, including lights, transformer/timer and cable (you may buy additional lights and cable)

1 Insert the tip of each lamp stake into the ground and push it in. If the soil is hard, first cut a slit with a gardening trowel, then push in the stake.

2 Run the cord from the house receptacle to each of the lamps. Hide the cord under ground cover, dig a shallow trench for the cord, or cover it with mulch. On a deck or porch, staple the cord where it will be out of sight.

INSTALLING LOW-VOLTAGE OUTDOOR LIGHTS

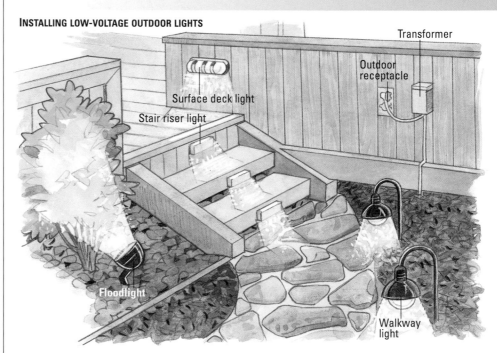

This system combines several types of lights. The cable is run in a shallow trench in the ground or stapled to the house or deck.

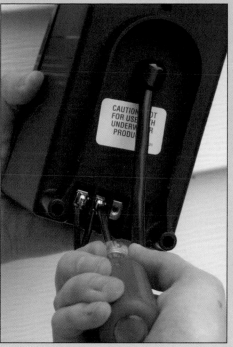

3 To connect a light to power, slip the two parts of its connector around the cord and snap them together. They'll pierce and pinch the cord to make the connection.

Snap-on connector

4 Mount the transformer near a receptacle, where it will stay dry and won't be damaged. Strip the cord's wire ends and connect them to the transformer terminals, following the manufacturer's instructions.

5 Plug in the transformer. Most models turn lights on automatically when it gets dark and give you the option of setting the lights on a timer. Follow the manufacturer's instructions for programming.

WHAT IF...
There is a HI/LO switch?

A HI/LO switch allows you to boost the power to the lights. First try running the lights with the switch set to LO.
If some lights do not come on, or if they are too dim, flip the switch to HI.

REFRESHER COURSE
Use a GFCI outdoors

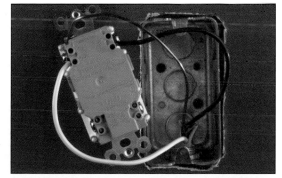

Any receptacle that is exposed to moisture should be a GFCI. To replace a standard receptacle with a GFCI, **shut off power** to the circuit, remove the old receptacle, and restrip the wire ends. If only one cable enters the box, connect the wires to the LINE terminals. If two cables enter the box, connect the wires that bring power into the box to the LINE terminals, and connect the other wires to the LOAD terminals. See *page 86* for more instructions.

Solar light

Solar-powered lights are easy to install. Just push them into the ground; no wiring is required. Solar lights are handy for spots far away from a power source. The location must receive at least three or four hours of sunlight a day to provide light at night. It generally takes a few days for the battery to build up power. A solar light may not work well during prolonged periods of cloudy weather.

APPLIANCES & NEW CIRCUITS

Wiring an electrical appliance such as a dishwasher, disposer, or electric water heater is often the easiest part of a job—moving the unit in and connecting the plumbing will take most of your time. This chapter shows how to install many of the most common types of major household appliances. It also walks you through how to run a new circuit if the appliance requires it.

Whenever you add a new appliance or upgrade an old one, check the wattage ratings to make sure you will not overload a circuit *(pages 120–121)*. With an upgrade, you may be surprised to find that your new appliance actually *reduces* the load. The reason is that many new appliances—refrigerators, toasters, microwaves, dishwashers, and water heaters, for instance—use less power than the older models they replace.

Installing a new circuit
Some new appliances—spas, baseboard heaters, or window air-conditioners—may need a new circuit. As long as your service panel has room for a new circuit, the wiring is not difficult. Running the cable will consume most of your time. *Pages 230–231* show how.

Before adding a new circuit, consult *pages 122–123* to make sure your basic electrical service can handle the extra load. If not, have an electrician install a new service panel.

Adding a subpanel
If the service panel does not have enough room for a new circuit, but your basic service can handle a new circuit, install a subpanel with room for a number of new circuits *(pages 232–233)*.

Some of these projects involve 240-volt circuits. The wiring is no more complicated than wiring for a 120-volt circuit, but the danger is much greater. A 240-volt shock can be very serious, even fatal. Work closely with a building inspector. **Double-check to see that power is shut off** before beginning any work. Call in a professional electrician to advise you, or have a pro do the work if you are at all unsure of yourself.

Here's how to add new circuits to a panel and connect permanently installed appliances.

CHAPTER PREVIEW

Hardwiring appliances
page 228

Hooking up a new circuit
page 230

Installing a subpanel
page 232

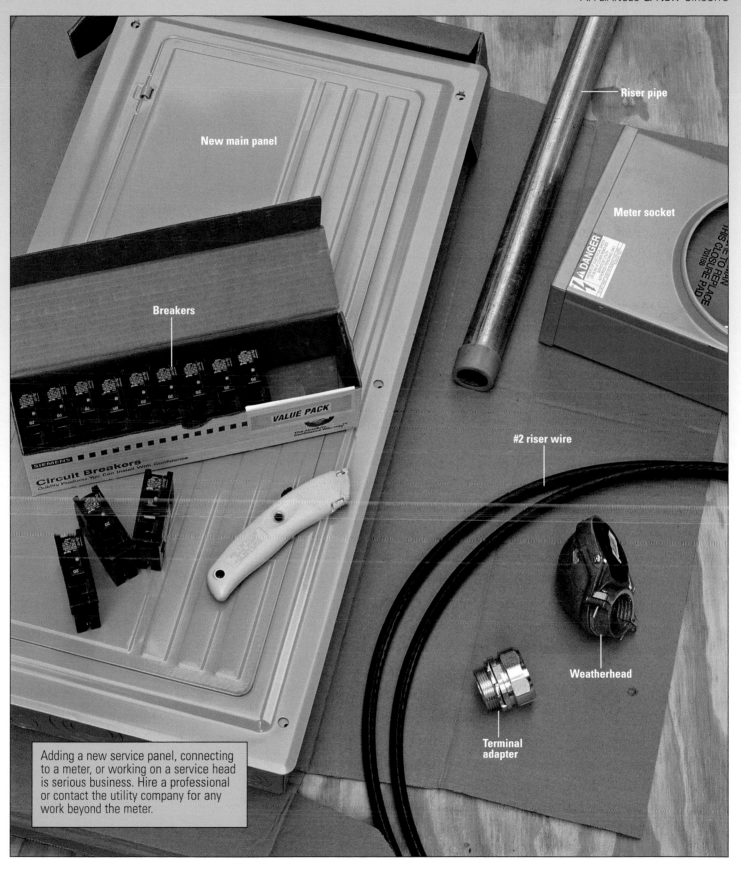

New main panel

Breakers

Riser pipe

Meter socket

#2 riser wire

Weatherhead

Terminal adapter

Adding a new service panel, connecting to a meter, or working on a service head is serious business. Hire a professional or contact the utility company for any work beyond the meter.

HARDWIRING APPLIANCES

Most 120-volt appliances simply plug into a standard receptacle. Some 240-volt appliances plug into special 240-volt receptacles *(pages 154–155)*. Other appliances—those that use 240 volts and are stationary—are "hardwired," meaning that cable is attached directly. Garbage disposers and dishwashers may be either plugged in or hardwired.

Shut off power to the circuit before installing any appliance. These pages give general directions for some typical installations. Consult the manufacturer's instructions before wiring—wire colors and cable connections may vary.

Appliance disconnects

If you shut off a circuit breaker to work on a 240-volt appliance, another person may mistakenly flip the breaker on while you are doing the wiring, creating a very dangerous situation. That is why building codes may require a hardwired appliance to have a "disconnect"—basically, an on/off switch. The disconnect must be positioned within sight of the appliance. An alternative is to install a circuit breaker with a lockout feature, which allows you to lock the breaker shut to prevent an accident.

PRESTART CHECKLIST

☐ **TIME**
About an hour to make most connections once cable has been run

☐ **TOOLS**
Screwdriver, flashlight, strippers, lineman's pliers, long-nose pliers

☐ **SKILLS**
Stripping, splicing, and connecting wires to terminals

☐ **PREP**
See that the new appliance will not overload the circuit *(pages 120–121)*. Remove the old appliance or run cable for a new appliance.

☐ **MATERIALS**
Appliance, wire nuts, electrician's tape

WIRING A DISPOSER

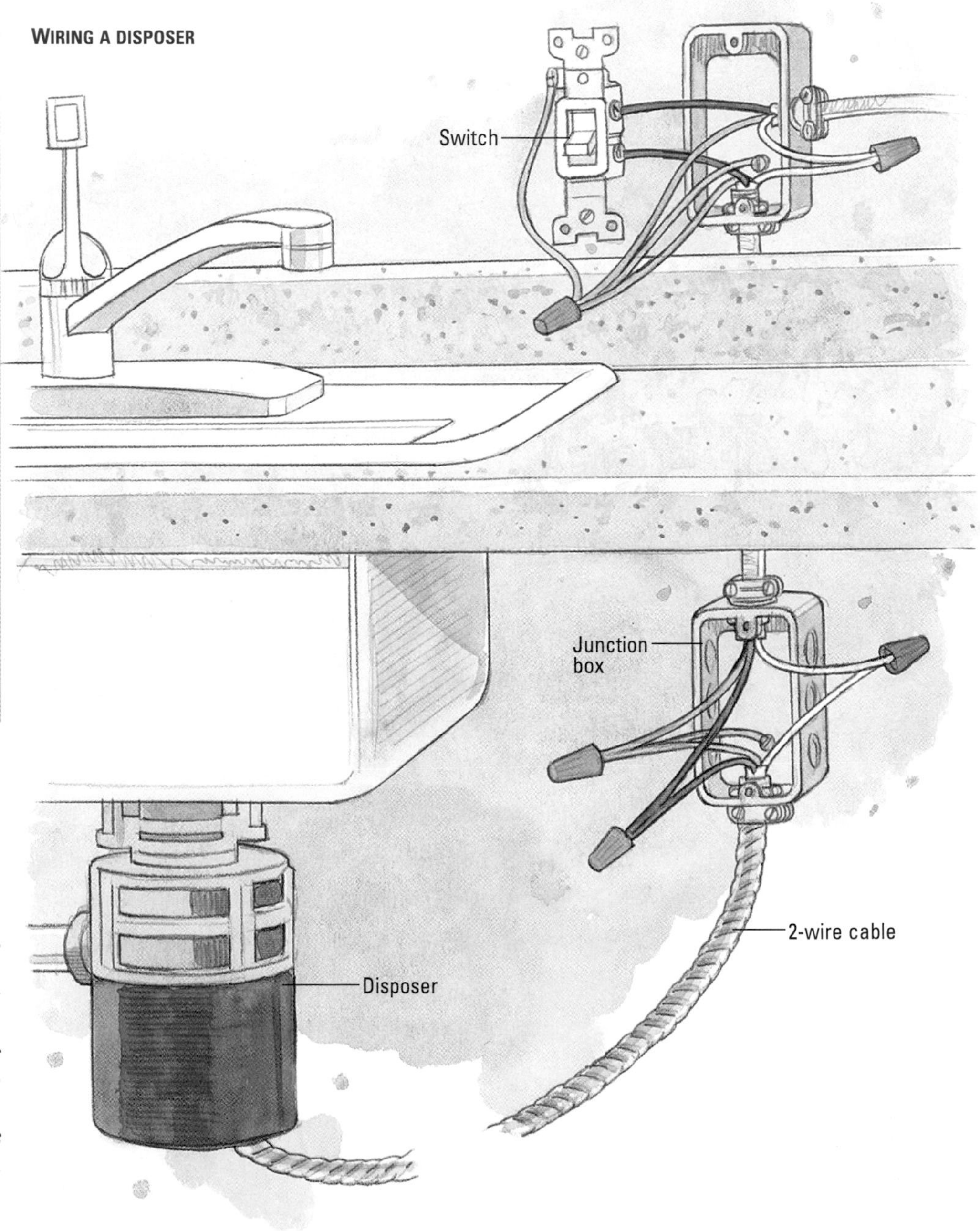

Switch

Junction box

2-wire cable

Disposer

Under the sink, a split and switched receptacle (pages 158–159) can provide an always-hot plug for a hot-water dispenser and a switched plug for the garbage disposer. Some codes may require the disposer to be hardwired, in which case a separate, switched junction box is needed (shown above).

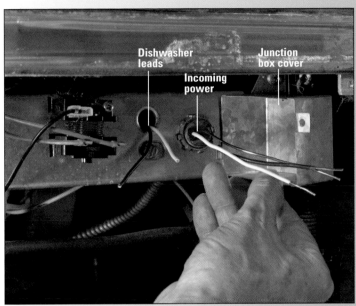

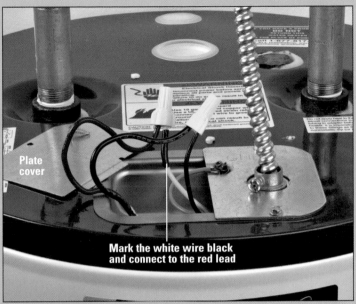

Dishwasher: Codes may require a dishwasher to be on a dedicated circuit. Some models plug into receptacles, but most are hardwired. Provide a cable that can reach to the front of the dishwasher. Slide the dishwasher into the space and make the plumbing connections. Open the dishwasher's junction box and splice wires to the dishwasher's leads. Replace the junction box cover.

Electric water heater: A water heater needs a dedicated 240-volt circuit. Check the unit's amperage rating and make sure the circuit can handle at least 120 percent of the rating. For most homes, a 30-amp circuit with 10/2 cable is sufficient. Because of the heat generated by the unit, use Greenfield or armored cable rather than NM cable. Remove the coverplate, splice the wires (note that a neutral is not required), and replace the coverplate.

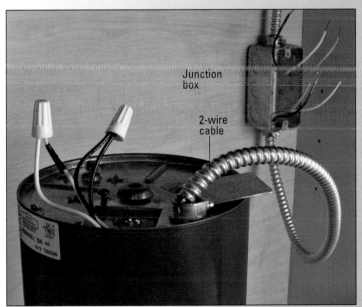

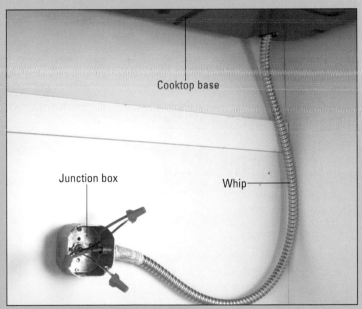

Garbage disposer: Garbage disposers are sold without cords, so they can be wired directly to cable (hardwiring) or to an appliance cord with a plug. Install armored cable (shown above) or buy a thick cord that can handle the disposer's amperage rating. Splice the wires to the disposer first. Install it in the sink. Then hardwire or plug it into a switched receptacle. A disposer should not be on a light circuit, or lights will dim when it starts.

Electric cooktop: An electric cooktop or wall-mounted oven requires a 120/240-volt circuit—120 volts to power lights and timer, 240 volts for the heating elements. A cooktop and an oven can be wired to the same circuit. Run cable to a nearby junction box. An electric oven or cooktop usually has a short length of armored cable, called a "whip." Clamp the whip to the junction box; make the splices. Make sure the wire and breaker are big enough for both.

HOOKING UP A NEW CIRCUIT

Though it may sound complicated, connecting a new circuit is no more difficult than the other projects in this book. You'll spend most of your time running cable from the new service to the service panel *(pages 138–147)*.

Make sure that adding a new circuit will not overload your electrical system. Review *pages 122–123* and talk with an inspector or an electrician about your plans. If the service panel cannot accept another circuit, install a subpanel *(pages 232–233)*. If your system cannot accommodate a new circuit, have an electrician install a new service panel.

If there is an available slot for a new circuit breaker in your service panel, you can add a breaker there. If not, you may be able to replace a regular circuit breaker with a tandem breaker (below right).

PRESTART CHECKLIST

☐ **TIME**
About two hours to make connections for a new circuit once cable has been run

☐ **TOOLS**
Flashlight, hammer, screwdriver, strippers, lineman's pliers, long-nose pliers, voltage tester

☐ **SKILLS**
Figuring loads on circuits; stripping sheathing and wire insulation; connecting wires to terminals

☐ **PREP**
Install boxes for the new service and run cable from the boxes to the service panel

☐ **MATERIALS**
New circuit breaker and cable

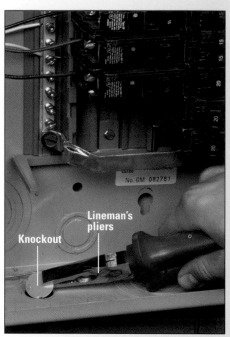

1 **Shut off the main breaker** and remove the panel's cover. Remove a knockout slug from the side of the cover.

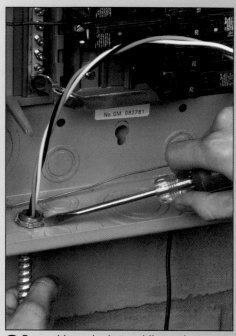

2 Run cable to the box, adding at least 2 feet extra for wiring work within the service panel. Strip enough sheathing from the cable to allow wires to travel most of the way around the panel. Slide the wires through the knockout hole and clamp the cable in place.

REFRESHER COURSE
When do you need a new circuit?

If new electrical service—lights, receptacles, or appliances—use so much wattage that they cannot be added to an existing circuit without overloading it, then a new circuit is called for. See *pages 120–121* for the calculations.

Extra protection
Install an Arc Fault Circuit Interrupter (AFCI) instead of a standard circuit breaker. It provides extra protection against fire due to frayed or overheated cords. They are now required for bedroom wiring.

Two for one with a tandem breaker

A tandem circuit breaker makes it possible to install two circuits in the space of one. Unlike double-pole breakers *(page 231)*, tandem breakers can be switched off and on individually. Some panels do not allow for tandem breakers. Others allow only a certain number of tandems. Get an inspector's OK before you install a tandem.

3 Route the wires so they skirt the perimeter of the panel and stay far away from hot bus bars. Strip ½ inch of insulation from the neutral wire and connect it to the neutral bus bar. Connect the ground wire to the ground bus bar.

4 Bend the hot wire into position along the side of the panel, cut it to length, and strip ½ inch of insulation. Poke it into the breaker and tighten the setscrew.

5 Slide one end of the breaker under the hot bus bar and push the breaker until it snaps in place and aligns with the surrounding breakers. Twist out a knockout slot in the service panel's cover and replace the cover.

WHAT IF...
There is only one neutral/ground bar?

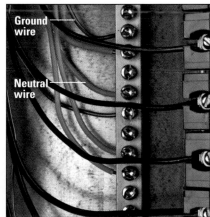

Some service panels have separate bus bars for neutral and ground wires. Others have only one bar that serves both. Connect neutral and ground wires in any order.

STANLEY PRO TIP

Double-pole breakers

A double-pole breaker takes up twice the space of a single-pole breaker. You'll need it for 240-volt circuits and with two-circuit and split receptacles *(pages 156–157)*. Connect the ground and neutral wires to bus bars and connect the hot wires to the breaker.

GFCI breaker

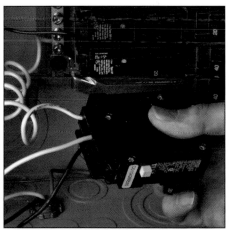

A GFCI circuit breaker protects all the receptacles, lights, and appliances on its circuit. Connect both the hot and neutral wires to the breaker. Connect the breaker's white lead to the neutral bus bar.

INSTALLING A SUBPANEL

If the service panel does not have room for new circuit breakers and you cannot use tandem breakers *(page 230)*, a subpanel may be the answer. Before installing one consult with an inspector to make sure you will not overload your overall system.

A subpanel has separate bus bars for neutral and ground wires and typically has no main breaker. It may not be labeled "subpanel," but instead be labeled "lugs only." It may be a different brand than the main panel.

Have the inspector approve the subpanel, the feeder cable, and the feeder breaker (see *page 233*).

Shut off the main breaker in the service panel before you begin.

PRESTART CHECKLIST

☐ **TIME**
About four hours to install a subpanel with several new circuits, not including running cable for the new circuits

☐ **TOOLS**
Screwdriver, hammer, voltage tester, strippers, drill, lineman's pliers, long-nose pliers

☐ **SKILLS**
Stripping sheathing and wires; connecting wires to terminals

☐ **PREP**
Run cables for the new circuits to the subpanel location. In the main service panel, make room for the double-pole feeder breaker.

☐ **MATERIALS**
Subpanel, mounting screws, approved feeder cable, staples or cable clamps, approved feeder breaker, breakers for the new circuits

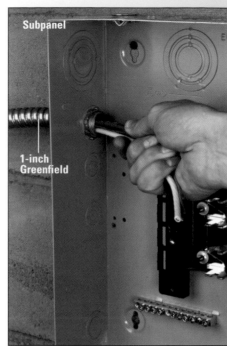

1 Mount the subpanel about a foot away from the main service panel. Determine how far the wires will have to travel in the subpanel and pull wires (shown above) or add cable and strip sheathing accordingly. Remove a knockout slug, slide the wires through, and clamp the cable.

2 At the main service panel, plan the routes for the four wires: ground, neutral, and two hot wires (black and red). Strip the sheathing, remove a knockout slug, and clamp the cable. Route the neutral and ground wires carefully and connect them to the bus bar(s).

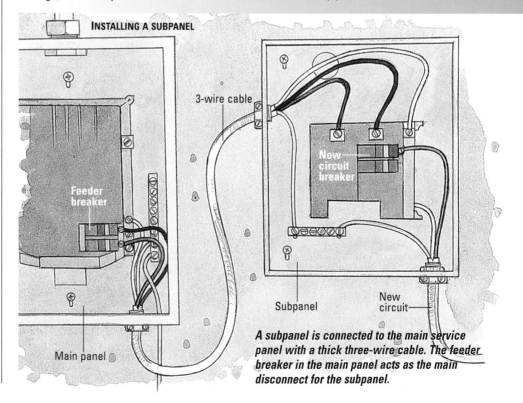

INSTALLING A SUBPANEL

A subpanel is connected to the main service panel with a thick three-wire cable. The feeder breaker in the main panel acts as the main disconnect for the subpanel.

MAIN PANEL

Feeder breaker

3 Route, cut, and strip the red and black wires. Connect them to the feeder breaker. Snap the breaker into place.

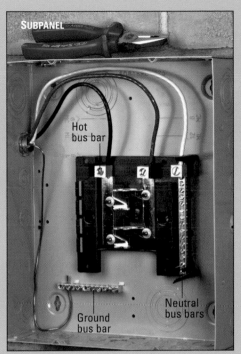

SUBPANEL

Hot bus bar

Neutral bus bars

Ground bus bar

4 In the subpanel, route the feeder wires, cut and strip them, and connect to terminals. Connect the black and red wires to the hot bus bars, the neutral wire to the main neutral terminal, and the ground wire to the ground bar.

SUBPANEL

New circuit

New circuit

5 Run cable for new circuits into the subpanel and clamp the cable. For each circuit, route wires around the perimeter, connect the ground wire to the ground bar, the white wire to the neutral bar, and the hot wire to a circuit breaker.

Choosing a feeder breaker and cable

Buy a subpanel larger than you currently need so you'll be ready for future electrical improvements. The three parts—subpanel, feeder breaker, and cable—should be compatible in capacity.

To figure sizes, add up the wattages of all the new electrical users (see *pages 120–121*) and add 20 percent to take into account safe capacity. Then divide by 230 to get the amperage you will need.

For instance if the new service will total 4,000 watts, add 20 percent (multiply by 1.2) to get 4,800; then divide 4,800 by 230 to get 20.8 amps. A subpanel supplying 30 amps of service will suffice.

As a general rule, to supply up to 5,700 watts of new power, install a 30-amp subpanel, a 30-amp feeder breaker, and 10/3 feeder cable. To supply up to 7,500 watts, install a 40-amp subpanel, a 40-amp feeder breaker, and 8/3 cable.

Cable with wires this thick may be difficult to find. If a home center does not carry it, call an electrical supply source.

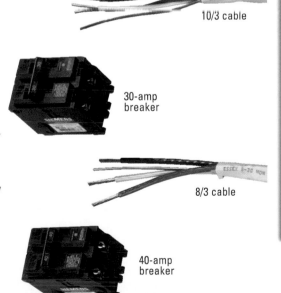

10/3 cable

30-amp breaker

8/3 cable

40-amp breaker

SAFETY FIRST
Keeping cable out of harm's way

Professional electricians take pride in the way they run wires in a service panel or subpanel. In a well-wired panel, wires are routed in neat paths around the perimeter, making it easy to tell which wire goes to which breaker. More importantly, orderly wires are less likely to brush against hot bus bars, which, if it happened, would create a serious fire hazard.

GLOSSARY

For terms not included here, or for more about those that are, refer to the index on pages 118–120.

Amp: Short for ampere, this is a measurement of the strength of electrical current flowing through a wire or appliance. An amperage rating tells the greatest amount of current a wire, device, or appliance can carry.

Antioxidant: A paste applied to aluminum wires to inhibit corrosion and maintain safe connections.

Armored cable: Flexible cable, containing two or more wires, with a protective metal sheathing. See BX cable and MC cable.

Box: A metal or plastic container with openings for cable. All electrical connections must be made inside a code-approved electrical box.

Bus bar: A long terminal inside a service panel. Circuit breakers or fuses connect to hot bus bars; neutral and ground wires connect to neutral and grounding bus bars. Some service panels have separate bus bars for neutral and ground wires (required in Canada), while others have only one neutral/ground bus bar.

BX cable: Armored cable containing insulated wires and no ground wire; the sheathing acts as the grounding path.

Cable: Two or more insulated wires wrapped in metal or plastic sheathing.

Circuit: Two or more wires carrying power from the service panel to devices, fixtures, and appliances and then back to the panel. Each circuit is protected by a circuit breaker or fuse in the service panel. Also called a branch circuit.

Circuit breaker: A protective device in a service panel that automatically shuts off power to its circuit when it senses a short circuit or overload.

Codes: Local regulations governing safe wiring practices. See National Electrical Code (NEC).

Common terminal: On a three-way switch, the darker-colored terminal (often marked COM) to which the wire supplying power is connected.

Common wire: In a three-way switch setup, the wire that brings power to the switch or to the fixture.

Conductor: A carrier of electricity—usually, a wire.

Conduit: Plastic or metal pipe through which wires run.

Continuity tester: A device that tells whether a circuit is capable of carrying electricity.

Cord: Two or more insulated stranded wires encased in a flexible plastic or cloth sheathing.

Current: The flow of electrons through a conductor.

Device: Usually an electrical receptacle or switch.

Duplex receptacle: The most common type of receptacle with two outlets.

Electrical Metallic Tubing (EMT): Thin rigid metal conduit suitable for residential use. Also called Thinwall.

End-line wiring: Also called switch-loop wiring. A method of wiring a switch, in which power runs to the fixture box. Compare through-switch wiring.

End-of-run: A receptacle at the end of a circuit.

Feed wire: The hot wire that brings power into a box.

Fixture: A light or fan that is permanently attached rather than being plugged into a receptacle.

Four-way switch: A switch used when a light is controlled by three or more switches.

Fuse: A safety device, located in a fuse box, which shuts off power when a circuit overloads.

Greenfield: Flexible metal conduit.

Ground: Wire or metal sheathing that provides an alternate path for current back to the service panel (and from there to a grounding rod sunk in the earth, or to a cold-water pipe). Grounding protects against shock in case of an electrical malfunction.

Ground fault circuit interrupter (GFCI): A receptacle with a built-in safety feature, which shuts off when there is a risk of shock.

Hardwired: An appliance that is wired via cable directly into a box rather than having a cord that plugs into a receptacle.

Hot wire: The wire that carries power; it is either black or colored.

Junction box: An electrical box with no fixture or device attached; it is used to split a circuit into different branches.

Kilowatt (kW): One thousand watts.

Knockout: A round slug or a tab that can be punched out to allow room for a cable or circuit breaker.

LB fitting: A pulling elbow made for outdoor use.

Lead: A wire (usually stranded) connected to a fixture.

MC cable: Armored cable with a ground wire in addition to at least two insulated wires.

Middle-of-run: A receptacle located between the service panel and another receptacle. Wires continue from its box to one or more other receptacle boxes.

Multitester: A tool that measures voltage of various levels, tests for continuity, and performs other tests.

National Electrical Code (NEC): The standard set of electrical codes for the United States, updated every few years. Local codes sometimes vary from the NEC.

Neon tester: See Voltage tester.

Neutral wire: A wire, usually covered with white insulation, that carries power from the box back to the service panel. See also Hot wire and Ground.

Nonmetallic (NM) cable: Usually two or more insulated wires, plus a bare ground wire, enclosed in plastic sheathing. Older NM cable may have no ground wire and cloth rather than plastic sheathing. See also Romex.

Old-work box: See Remodel box.

Outlet: Any point in an electrical system where electricity may be used. Receptacles, fixtures, switches, and hardwired appliances are all outlets.

Overload: A dangerous condition caused when a circuit carries more amperage than it is designed to handle. Overloaded wires overheat. A circuit breaker or fuse protects wires from overheating.

Pigtail: A short length of wire spliced with two or more wires in a box and connected to a terminal so that two or more wires will not be attached to a terminal.

Plug: A male connection at the end of a cord designed to be inserted into a receptacle outlet.

Polarized plug: A plug with its neutral prong wider than the hot prong. It can be inserted into a receptacle outlet in only one way, thereby ensuring against reversing the hot and neutral sides of a circuit.

Raceway: Surface-mounted channels made of plastic or metal through which wires can be run to extend a circuit.

Receptacle: An electrical outlet into which a plug can be inserted.

Recessed can light: A light fixture that contains its own electrical box designed to be installed inside a ceiling so that its trim and perhaps lens is flush with the ceiling surface.

Remodel box: A metal or plastic electrical box that clamps to a wall surface (either plaster or drywall) rather than being fastened to framing. A remodel box must have an internal clamp to hold the cable.

Rigid conduit: Metal conduit that can be bent only with a special tool.

Romex: A common name for nonmetallic cable.

Service entrance: The point where power from the utility enters the house. A service entrance may be underground, or it may be at or near the roof.

Service panel: A large electrical box containing either fuses or circuit breakers. Power from the utility enters the service panel where it is divided up into branch circuits. Also called a panel box or main panel.

Short circuit: A dangerous condition that occurs when a hot wire touches a neutral wire, a ground wire, a metal box that is part of the ground system, or another hot wire.

Splice: To connect together the stripped ends of two or more wires usually by twisting them together and adding a wire nut.

Stripping: Removing insulation from wire or sheathing from cable.

Subpanel: A subsidiary service panel, containing circuit breakers or fuses and supplying a number of branch circuits. A subpanel is itself controlled by the main service panel.

System ground: The method by which an entire electrical system is grounded. Usually a thick wire leading either to one or more rods sunk deep in the earth or to a cold-water pipe.

Three-way switch: A switch used when a light is controlled by two switches.

Through-switch wiring: A method of wiring a switch, in which power runs to the switch box. Also called in-line wiring.

Transformer: A device that reduces voltage usually from 120 volts to between 4 and 24 volts. Doorbells, thermostats, and low-voltage lights all use transformers.

Traveler wires: In a three-way switch setup, the two wires that run from switch to switch. See Common wire.

Underwriters knot: A special knot used to tie the wires in a lamp socket.

Volt (V): A measure of electrical pressure.

Voltage detector: A tool that senses electrical current even through insulation and sheathing.

Voltage tester: A tool that senses the presence of electrical current when its probes touch bare wire ends. Some voltage testers (often called voltmeters) also tell how many volts are present.

Watt (W): A measure of the amount of power that an electrical device, fixture, or appliance uses. Volts × amps = watts.

Wire nut: A plastic protective cap that screws onto two twisted-together wires to complete a splice.

INDEX

METRIC CONVERSIONS

U.S. Units to Metric Equivalents			Metric Units to U.S. Equivalents		
To convert from	Multiply by	To get	To convert from	Multiply by	To get
Inches	25.4	Millimeters	Millimeters	0.0394	Inches
Inches	2.54	Centimeters	Centimeters	0.3937	Inches
Feet	30.48	Centimeters	Centimeters	0.0328	Feet
Feet	0.3048	Meters	Meters	3.2808	Feet
Yards	0.9144	Meters	Meters	1.0936	Yards
Square inches	6.4516	Square centimeters	Square centimeters	0.1550	Square inches
Square feet	0.0929	Square meters	Square meters	10.764	Square feet
Square yards	0.8361	Square meters	Square meters	1.1960	Square yards
Acres	0.4047	Hectares	Hectares	2.4711	Acres
Cubic inches	16.387	Cubic centimeters	Cubic centimeters	0.0610	Cubic inches
Cubic feet	0.0283	Cubic meters	Cubic meters	35.315	Cubic feet
Cubic feet	28.316	Liters	Liters	0.0353	Cubic feet
Cubic yards	0.7646	Cubic meters	Cubic meters	1.308	Cubic yards
Cubic yards	764.55	Liters	Liters	0.0013	Cubic yards

To convert from degrees Fahrenheit (F) to degrees Celsius (C), first subtract 32, then multiply by ⁵⁄₉.

To convert from degrees Celsius to degrees Fahrenheit, multiply by ⁹⁄₅, then add 32.